The Jaguar XK

CHRIS HARVEY

St Martin's Press, Inc.
New York

First published in the US 1979
St Martin's Press, Inc., 175 Fifth Avenue,
New York, NY 10010

Set in Monotype Ehrhardt and originated by
Oliver Burridge and Co. Ltd
Printed and bound in the UK by Butler and Tanner Ltd

ISBN 0 312 43947 4
Library of Congress Catalog Number 78 64813

Contents

Acknowledgements

THIS is a book which I approached with wild enthusiasm; I thought I knew quite a bit about the Jaguar XK already. After all, I seemed to have grown up with the car: I still remember blasting through pre-motorway Britain in my father's 120 roadster; and gobbling up the miles in my 150 fixed-head twenty years later. Then I met Joss Davenport and realized how little I knew. With Paul Skilleter, he pointed me in the right directions and provided his fine 120 roadster for the cover picture. Those directions led to people such as Bill Lawrence, who with the ever-present Skilleter, told me so much about rebuilding an XK today; my own experiences were those of an enthusiast trying to stop his car falling apart years ago. Things are different now, I am happy to report. Phil Porter and Dave Cottingham helped in this sphere too, and on the competition and modifications chapters with John Harper, Ron Beaty, Warren and Lawrence Pearce. Much valuable information was also supplied by Rick Reading and Roger Ludgate.

The response to my pleas for help from abroad were truly gratifying: Bob Smiley, Bruce Carnachan, Art Kinnear, Norma Dana, Fred Horner, Jack Stamp and John Graves were of tremendous help in America, not only with words but with pictures, too; Les Hughes, Ian Cummins and Maurice Vickerman provided similar help in Australia; Heinz Schendzielorz produced one of the biggest sets of pictures I have ever seen for which I am truly grateful and another Australian, Ian Fraser, managing editor of the British *Car* magazine, dismantled his family photo album to produce yet more historic pictures; Grant McMillan, Harvey Hingston and Sybil Lupp were also of great help in New Zealand. In South Africa, Trevor Woodiwiss devoted much time when hard-pressed to helping me, as did Jens Roder in Denmark, Aldo Vinzio in Switzerland, Dr Phillipe Renault in France, Arthur Winship in Rhodesia, and Paul Ashton in Singapore. Nearer home, Ernie Foster in Belfast and Ian Russell-Hill in Dublin helped with both pictures and words; Barry Eccleston and Ian Dawson (of *Car* magazine) provided wonderful pictures; and Bryan Corser helped not only with pictures, but actually produced the cars!

I am deeply indebted to them all, and especially to Jaguar Cars, who, through Andrew Whyte, provided the bulk of the pictures for this book with Warren Allport of *Autocar* and Jim Lee of *Motor*, and the indefatigable Paul Skilleter. I must also thank my illustrator, Tim Holder, for maintaining a sense of humour in the difficult times associated with producing such a book and Oxford Illustrated Press for their unfailing support and encouragement. I owe them and my family so much, and must also thank Gloria Callaway for saving me from a fate worse than death by doing the index.

Colour Plates

I

Tribute to the XK

SINCE EMILE LEVASSOR produced the first recognizable car in 1891, others of varying significance have followed. But there have been few that have meant as much as the Jaguar XK 120. It was the sports car that had everything: a beautiful body, the like of which has yet to be surpassed; a sound, dependable chassis that had taken years to develop, and a wonderful engine that made history in itself. It was so far ahead of its time that there's been hardly anything to touch it in the thirty odd years that have passed since its first howl was heard. The vital statistics of 3442 cc, 83 mm bore by 106 mm stroke, and six cylinders in a line are legendary. Jaguar's famous XK engine was unique: it was the first production unit to harness the sophistication of twin overhead camshafts in a cylinder head with hemispherical combustion chambers.

That's where the power came from, a piece of alloy as beautiful as the car it was to power, designed during midnight fire watching sessions in a grim wartime factory! The four fire-watchers, William Lyons, Bill Heynes, Claude Baily and Walter Hassan, drew up the XK engine in a tiny office in Coventry before creeping off to their camp beds. And when the Second World War was over, they set about building a car fit to take their wonderful new engine. First it was to be a magnificent saloon like the pre-war designs being produced as a matter of contingency straight after the war. But that saloon car was too long in coming and William Lyons, the stylist with a touch of the showman, decided to build a few sports cars to emphasize how good the engine was. This sports car featured most of the good things the famous four had dreamed up: the lines of Lyons, the engine of Baily and Heynes, Heynes's super new suspension (he was involved in everything), the dedicated development of Hassan and the chassis work of a fifth man, Bob Knight. It is only fair to point out that there was also a sixth man, the freelance gas flow expert, Harry Weslake. He perfected the cylinder head and extracted more and more power as time went on.

The brave new machine was christened the XK 120 at its unveiling in October 1948. The 120 stood for 120 mph, and although it certainly looked as though it could reach that magic speed, some people were sceptical. How could such a car be produced for only £998? You can't kid us, they said. If this new Jaguar can do 120 mph, why are the rest so far behind at twice the price? Jaguar had the answer: their

The 'famous four' firewatchers at work.

The XKs of Brian Corser line up from
the right: a 120 roadster, a 140 roadster
and a 150 drop-head.

chief test driver, a figure straight from 'Biggles' called Soapy Sutton, hit 132.6 mph before an astonished bunch of journalists on the Jabbeke motorway in May 1949. In the best British tradition, 120 mph had been an understatement. And of course Lyons would have no trouble keeping the price down to £998 ($4000 at that time). He could sell his new cars by the boatload. With the anachronistic MG TC, the extraordinary XK was the car that took export markets by storm. From a vision of a couple of hundred cars, production ran to more than 30,000 and Jaguar could never make enough.

The performance was no flash in the pan. Within a year of production getting underway in summer 1949, a virtually standard XK 120 was running third at Le Mans alongside, and in front of, outright racing cars. It only needed a competition version to win that great race at record speed the next year and again in 1953, Coronation Year. Like Britain herself, Jaguar were riding on the crest of a wave. The advent of one of the fastest (190 mph) and most beautiful racing sports cars, the D type Jaguar, made the little firm a household name when it scored a fantastic hat-trick of wins at Le Mans. Within a few years, Jaguar was no obscure jungle cat, but a car unsurpassed in speed, style and quality. Already the production cars embodied the lessons learned on the track: the XK 140 had its steering perfected on the competition cars, and its huge bumpers were aimed at protecting it from the ravishes of American car parking.

All this was nearly ended when an accidental fire threatened to close down the Jaguar works in 1957. Heroic fire fighters, including William Lyons (Sir William by then), stopped the flames but not before they had destroyed much vital equipment, not to mention cars ready for export. But the men of Coventry, the city which had taken everything that the war could hurl at it, were steeped in the spirit of the blitz. After a fortnight of frantic salvation production was restored, with craftsmen working uncomplainingly in the bitter cold of unheated winter workshops. 'It is pleasing to pay this tribute to another triumph of British tenacity in defeating adversity', said the motoring bible, *Motor Sport*. And so phoenix-like, the new XK 150 rose from the ashes to go even faster and stop far more effectively than any previous XK, as well as having greater comfort. This was the XK that refused to die in the flames. Almost every one had the revolutionary new disc brakes pioneered by Jaguar at Le Mans; in its ultimate form it was to be capable of 136 mph.

For thirteen years the XKs set standards that were only to be overshadowed by a new Jaguar, the E type, whereupon the XK became a never-to-be-forgotten classic. To run an XK during the years of glory was to live in the forefront of fashion, enjoying every mile of motoring in a magnificent thoroughbred. To run an XK today is to be a member of an exclusive society: the connoisseur class. But to dream of owning one is not a far-fetched fancy: they are eminently practical cars, as wonderful as the day they were made, and still give unrivalled value for money.

Four more cars in the Corser collection: from the right, a C type, D type, XK SS, and the XK's successor, a lightweight E type based on the D type.

One of the most beautiful sports racing cars ever built, the classic D type driven here by Mel Nichols.

II

The Production XKs

Classic beauties in black and white: the black 120 roadster is a standard British car; the white 120 roadster sports typical American modifications, such as side ventilators in the wings and bonnet vents.

AT FIRST GLANCE there wasn't that much to choose between the three basic XK models, the 120, the 140 and the 150. They all had a massive chassis, torsion bar independent front suspension, cart springs at the back, a sophisticated six-cylinder engine, a crunchy Moss gearbox (politely described as 'military' by one enthusiastic writer) and a beautiful body. Yet each car had a different character. The 120 was a super sports car with everything, except dependable brakes, and which embraced fixed-head and drop-head bodywork in its latter days; the 140 was an updated version with better steering and options such as overdrive and a roomier body protected by American-style bumpers; although the same size, the 150 looked a lot bigger. It was also the first XK to stop effectively with discs on all four wheels, and was eventually the fastest of the lot with an engine gradually developed to 250 bhp from the first XK 120's 160 bhp.

The early cars were an extraordinary example of what can be done in a hurry. The XK 120 chassis was simply that from the current Mark V saloon with one-and-a-half feet lopped out of the middle and the attendant bracing replaced with a box section cross-member. It was also a little narrower, with a wheelbase of 8 ft 6 ins, and a track of 4 ft 3 ins at the front and 4 ft 2 ins at the back. There was nothing new in the idea of shortening a saloon car chassis: lots of people, including MG, Jaguar's running partners in the US export race, were doing it in the late 1940s; and there was not much new in the chassis frame. It was basically a development of that used on the pre-war Jaguar saloons and well-tried as a result.

The car was of conventional ladder design with deep box-section side members, up to $6\frac{1}{2}$ inches deep and $3\frac{1}{2}$ inches wide. Two massive cross members, one in the middle and one at the front, were supplemented by a lighter box section sweeping over the rear axle, and a tube behind the axle line which carried the rear spring shackles. The side members of the chassis, over the rear axle, were parallel, swept in to the front to carry the suspension and engine mounting points. Four outriggers supported the body in the middle and a pedal box was mounted on either right- or left-hand side of the chassis. The steering box was mounted at an angle to the front hub centre line. The engine was supported from the rear by a mounting under the gearbox on to the centre cross member. The front suspension was by wishbones with long, .930-inch diameter, torsion bars at the bottom stretching back to adjusters

Rare detail of an even rarer car: provision for a starting handle on a very early 120 roadster.

Seeing double! Two superb French-registered 120 fixed-heads visit Britain for XK Day.

located on the centre chassis cross-member. A Newton telescopic shock absorber was attached to each lower wishbone and mounted on a bracket above the top wishbone. Total front suspension movement was 7 inches ($3\frac{1}{2}$-inch bump and $3\frac{1}{2}$-inch rebound). The stub axle carriers were located by ball joints and the lower wishbones connected by an anti-roll bar. The castor angle was 3 degrees, with adjustment by shims interposed between the upper wishbone arms and the ball housing. Camber was also adjustable by means of shims interposed between the upper wishbone shaft and the frame bracket, the normal setting being 1.75 to 2 degrees. The torsion bar had differing splines at each end, allowing the suspension height to be roughly set-up before fine adjustment with the screw. When correctly set, with standard 16-inch wheels and Dunlop 6.00 section tyres, there should be a clearance of $7\frac{1}{8}$ inches under the lower face of the frame side members at a point just behind the engine sump.

Luxury liner: the interior of the 120 fixed-head.

The Burman recirculating ballsteering gear was carried in a trunnion on the upper wishbone bracket on either right- or left-hand side, the XK 120 being designed to cater for the American market from the start (unlike many British rivals that still firmly believed the rest of the world would continue to find right-hand-drive cars acceptable). In fact, the steering box was mounted so high that the column ran at only 10 degrees to the horizontal. The drop arm projected forward and was linked to a corresponding slave drop arm on the opposite side of the car by the centre member of the three-piece track rod. The normal toe-in setting was between $\frac{1}{8}$ inch and $\frac{3}{16}$ inch. This Citroen-based front suspension proved to be extremely hard-wearing and smooth in use, partly due to the use of Metalastik bushes in the lower wishbone pivots and Silentbloc bearings on the track rod ends.

The rear springs had seven leaves, five of them $\frac{7}{32}$ inches thick and the other two $\frac{3}{16}$, and proved to be nothing like so reliable as the front suspension. This was chiefly because they provided all the location for the rear axle, which did a good job of transmitting the engine's considerable power and torque. The rear springs had no interleaves, but were fitted with gaiters. Both the front spring eyes and rear shackles had rubber bushes.

The springs themselves were sloped downwards towards the front at an angle of 7.75 degrees to induce understeer, and the axle was also offset towards the front of the spring, the appropriate measurements being 20 inches from the front anchorage and 24 inches to the back. As a result, constant angles were maintained between the propeller shaft joints. Girling lever-type shock absorbers were fitted to the back of the XK 120, operating through short links to the axle casing. Bump stops and check straps limited the suspension movement to a $3\frac{1}{2}$-inch bump and $3\frac{1}{2}$-inch rebound, as at the front.

The *pièce de résistance* of the car was the magnificent XK engine, of course. Not only did it look good (Jaguar chief William Lyons insisted on that) but it produced more power—160 bhp at 5400 rpm on the 8:1 compression ratio version—than any current production engine other than Cadillac's latest V8. Even the 7:1 compression ratio version (poor quality petrol was common in the late 1940s) churned out 150 bhp. The engine's vital statistics of six cylinders, 83 mm bore and

Where the power came from, in this case a C type cylinder head.

106 mm stroke, 3442 cc and twin overhead camshafts, have since become legendary. Its alloy cylinder head, which weighed only 50 lb against 120 lb for a cast iron equivalent, was its most remarkable feature; not only did it disperse heat more easily than one using more conventional material, but it was the first hemispherical twin overhead cam design to go into volume production. Its seven-bearing crankshaft with massive $2\frac{3}{4}$-inch main bearings was well-nigh indestructible; its cast iron block was of comparative light weight because it was not encumbered with camshafts and was therefore strong in the right places because it needed no compromises; it had a carefully-developed lubrication system of comparatively low pressure to reduce power-sapping oil drag; and the lightweight valve gear ensured peak efficiency. There was altogether so little compromise on this wonderful engine: just the twin timing chains to eliminate the whine set up by using one long one; and $\frac{5}{16}$-inch lift camshafts rather than ones with $\frac{3}{8}$-inch lift, to avoid the possibility of ham-fisted mechanics bending valves when rotating cams independently during maintenance. The only real engine fault was in the cooling system, which was insufficiently developed to cope with prolonged use in heavy traffic in hot areas, such as Southern California, ironically one of its biggest markets.

The gearbox, driven through a 10-inch single plate Borg and Beck clutch, with ratios of 3.375:1 first and reverse, 1.982 second, 1.367 third, and direct top, was strong, reliable and very slow to change. This difficult gear change was mitigated by the engine's torque of 195 lb/ft at 2500 rpm and evoked little criticism in its day; drivers had not been spoiled by good synchromesh then and some were even complaining about the loss of their old 'crash' boxes. The total weight of the engine, clutch and gearbox was 640 lb with the gearbox accounting for 110 lb. Early XK 120s were fitted with ENV hypoid bevel rear axles of 3.64:1 ratio with 3.27, 3.92 and 4.30 alternatives; later cars had similar Salisbury axles with 3.54 as the standard ratio and 3.27, 3.77 and 4.09 as the alternatives after supplies from ENV dried up.

SU provided the twin $1\frac{3}{4}$-inch carburetters and the single electric fuel pump mounted below tank level on a chassis member. The carburetters were supplemented by an automatic electric starting device that was frequently fitted with a manual over-ride by owners dissatisfied with the autocratic way in which it worked.

Lockheed hydraulic brakes were fitted, those at the front being of the two leading shoe variety, which gave a front to rear braking proportion of 60:40. The 12-inch diameter brake drums of copper iron used Mintex M15 linings with a total area of 207 square inches. A fly-off handbrake opposite the driver's side of the transmission tunnel and air scoops on the front brake back plates with corresponding slots in the bodywork completed the ensemble.

The body was fantastic, as much a reason for the car's success as the engine. Not only did it look good, but it felt good, offering ample protection from the elements and obviously it worked well, such was the performance of the car. The first two hundred and forty XK 120 bodies had alloy outer skins with steel inner wings and wooden internal framework. A wood and steel sill supported the centre of the body with a substantial bulkhead. The inner wings assisted in this function at the front and the back.

The first XK, registered HKV 455, chassis number 660001 (cars are normally referred to in Britain by their conspicuous registration number which normally stays with the car throughout its life, and by their chassis number in other parts of the world, where the registration plates change), looked much the same as later XKs, except in detail, as it was but a prototype. The internal body structure was modified for production, and the XK 120 had no rear bumper at first; after the first forty production cars it had a straight-sided windscreen bolted straight on to the scuttle instead of a curved one fixed on to a structure under the skin; there was no number plate plinth and the petrol tank filler was inside the boot, plus all manner of detail differences, such as the hinges and so on. Paul Skilleter wrote in *Jaguar Sports Cars*:

'The streamlined body of Jaguar's first post-war sports car brought many benefits besides a reduction in wind resistance. The enveloping body was wide by current standards, and the wooden floor of the driving compartment over-hung either side of the chassis for quite a distance, thus allowing the use of wide, pleated leather seats and providing rather more elbow room than had been available in the (preceding) SS 100, where the seats had been mounted within the width of the chassis frame. The hollow doors had use made of their thickness, being given large pockets, and they were trimmed in leather to match the dashboard. The dashboard had the usual array of instruments to be found on a Jaguar, comprising matching speedometer and revolution counter, ammeter, fuel gauge, and combined water temperature and oil pressure gauge. By pressing a button, the fuel gauge could also be made to register the oil level in the sump. All the minor controls were dashboard mounted too, except for the headlight dipswitch (floor mounted) and horn (steering wheel boss activated)....

Oh so beautiful! The 120 drop-head.

'In William Lyons's successful attempt to civilize the sports car, the XK 120 was provided with quite a lot of luggage room. There was storage space behind the forward tipping seats on top of the twin six-volt battery boxes, and a useful amount too in the boot, the spare wheel being segregated from the suitcases in a separate compartment under the boot floor.'

The first production XK 120s left the factory in July 1949, mostly in left-hand drive form, with chassis numbers starting 67; right-hand drive versions carried the 66 prefix.

It was obvious from the initial reception that Jaguar could sell lots of XKs, particularly abroad. So they had no problem getting enough steel to make bodies more suited to volume production than the first efforts in alloy. The steel-bodied XKs, produced from April 1950 (chassis numbers 660059 and 670185) looked almost exactly like their alloy ancestors, but were considerably different under their skins; the sills were complex mild steel boxes; the door shut faces were welded up from a variety of small parts; and the door hinges were boxed in by another steel structure, to their eternal detriment as you could not lubricate them properly. The bulkhead was redesigned with different hinge mounting points for the bonnet, which had frequently cracked up, it flexed so much. The bonnet, doors and bootlid were still made from alloy, however, and all cars retained their separate chrome-plated side light housings to chassis numbers 661024 and 672926. There were other internal differences, but essentially the cars looked alike.

The first major divergence was the fixed-head coupé, introduced in March 1951. It fulfilled the demand for a car as civilized as the contemporary Mark VII saloon while retaining the performance of the sports car. The XK 120 fixed-head coupé, which bore such a close resemblance to the Bugatti type 57SC Atlantic pre-war classic, did just that. It was virtually an XK 120 roadster (to use the American description; Jaguar were inclined to call it a super sports) with a pretty steel top, wind-up windows in place of sidescreens, outside doorhandles, and a well-upholstered saloon-style interior. Wherever possible it was like the sports car. The bench-style seat was retained and spats were still fitted with steel disc wheels, although they had to be abandoned if the optional wire wheels were specified because of the space taken up by knock-off hub caps. Ventilation had received special attention with quarter lights front and rear, following complaints from America and other warm countries about too much heat in the cockpit. A heater was fitted as standard, however, but small footwell-opening ventilators were also fitted to cope with hot weather, a similar modification being carried out on the roadster (from chassis numbers 660675 and 671097).

The doors were widened to $31\frac{1}{2}$ inches and wood was used extensively in the interior, just as on the saloon. Why, the fixed-head coupé even had transparent tinted sun visors, something the roadster never had! It was quite a luxury liner, and far less claustrophobic than the roadster with the hood erect. The overall dimensions were much the same, length 14 ft 5 ins, width 5 ft 2 ins and height 4 ft $5\frac{1}{2}$ ins against the roadster's 4 ft $4\frac{1}{2}$ ins, hood up: but the fixed-head coupé felt a lot bigger inside because its head was curved back slightly, with the object of giving both increased side vision and avoiding the feeling of oppression imparted by the roadster's hood. The hood dated back to the days when such appendages were used only rarely, in the most inclement weather; in fact, the design of the XK screen, a deep V only $43\frac{1}{2}$ inches wide, was magnificent for diverting most of the weather around its occupants. It wasn't until the advent of wrap-round screens that open cars became a pain in the neck. Their hoods were awful, and that on the XK 120 roadster was no

Introducing a 140 roadster at a Brown's Lane photography session.

The prototype 140 fixed-head. Note the 120 grille and 120-style sloping side pillar.

exception. They were incredible, almost skin-tight, devices that reflected the designers' inability to produce anything bigger that would not be ripped off by the airstream at 100 mph plus, the speeds that the new generation of cars, such as the XK 120, were capable of. The XK 120 fixed-head coupé was an altogether more desirable car at the time for any one other than the dyed-in-the-wool enthusiast. The feeling of space and comfort inside was increased by repositioning the dashboard an inch further away from the seatbacks. As an enthralled scribe reported in *The Autocar*:

> 'This not only increases the feeling of spaciousness in the interior, but places the clear-faced instruments a little further from the driver's eyes, thereby reducing the change in eye focus required when taking a quick glance at the dials.
>
> 'Although the width across the seats is $46\frac{1}{2}$ inches, it should be emphasized that the new coupé is still a two-seater pure and simple, the manufacturers having wisely made no attempt to alter the character of the car by either three-abreast seating or occasional rear seats. The extra space behind the squabs has, however, been put to good use by the provision of an unusually large parcel shelf on which even small suitcases can be accommodated, a neat plated rail serving to keep objects in place. The forward portion of the platform is hinged and gives access to a trough-shaped locker extending right across the car and providing storage space for all those odds and ends which one carries when touring. Ingenuity does not end here, since the vertical panel which forms the forward side of the trough is extended downwards and hinged. When the seat squabs have been tilted forward, the entire panel, complete with locker, also swings forward to give very ready access to the two batteries.'

With such an interior after that of the roadster, it was even a pleasure to top up the batteries!

Interior of the 140 fixed-head.

The fixed-head coupé was hardly slower than the roadster although it was 1 cwt heavier at 27 cwt against 26 cwt for the steel-bodied super sports and 25.5 cwt for the alloy version, because of its superior aerodynamics. Extra insulation was also squeezed into the extra inch of height and it was an altogether quieter and more relaxed car to drive.

Self-adjusting front brakes also replaced the earlier 'micram' adjusted devices and did a lot to cope with sudden fade. The air scoops on the brake back plates were also removed at about this time (spring 1951) because they proved equally efficient at letting in water as air. In any case, wire wheels were more readily available as an option to the standard steel discs, which were increased in width to 5.5 inches from 5 inches to standardize them with the Mark VII saloon. The sporty-looking 54-spoke wire wheels did a lot to dispel brake fade, allowing vastly-increased volumes of air to circulate around the hard-pressed brake drums. A tandem master cylinder was also fitted to XK 120s from this time.

Soon after, Jaguar followed the example of MG and produced a special tuning bulletin for those customers who wished to race their cars rather than see them go to tuners of often dubious ability. The list of approved Jaguar modifications showed how good the car was, for a start. They were confined chiefly to higher compression pistons (provided good enough fuel was available), higher-lift camshafts (provided sufficiently capable mechanics could be found), matching distributor, plugs and carburetter needles, a lightened flywheel, dual exhaust (which hung two inches closer to the ground because it was too big to go through the chassis cross member), heavy-duty clutch and special crankshaft damper, beefed up torsion bars and springs, and bucket seats which were alone reckoned to be worth a second a lap on an average airfield! For £160 you could have a real racer with 8:1 or 9:1 pistons, $\frac{3}{8}$-inch lift camshafts, 1 inch diameter torsion bars, eight-leaf rear springs, the engine now giving 180 or 190 bhp according to compression ratio. Extra-thick brake linings, aero screens, 2-inch SU carburetters and an undershield were also available. When fitted with extras from the initial list, plus wire wheels, the cars became known as special equipment models in Britain or XK 120Ms in America, although the M (for modified) was never an official factory designation on the XK 120.

The next avenue of development, in April 1953, was obvious: a soft-top version of the fixed-head coupé, combining the best of both worlds catered for by the spartan roadster and the luxurious enclosed XK. The drop-head coupé's hood was as good as the roadster's was bad. The driver could raise or lower it instantly without leaving his or her seat, by simply releasing three 'over centre' toggle catches and swinging the front rail back. The wood-capped cant rails were so designed that they parted neatly and the hood material folded without further help. The material itself was notable in that it was made up of three layers, mohair on the outside, with headlining for the interior and a special canvas in between for ultimate protection from noise and the elements. When erect, it was difficult to tell the difference between the drop-head and the fixed-head coupé inside, for this wonderful hood even had an interior light! From the outside, its contours were as smooth as those of a saloon and it also had a large (for the day) rear window, measuring 25 inches by $4\frac{3}{4}$ inches, which could be unzipped for extra ventilation, rather than the fixed pillbox slot

Oh to be in Britain with a new 140 drop-head!

that passed for a window on the roadster's hood. Other than that, the drop-head coupé was furnished almost exactly the same as the fixed-head, with its winding windows contained in permanent frames.

Customers more interested in competition were not forgotten. A 200 bhp C type head with exhaust valves increased in size by $\frac{3}{16}$ inch to $1\frac{5}{8}$ inches, while the inlet valves remained at $1\frac{3}{4}$ inches, and a close ratio gearbox with ratios of 2.98, 1.74, 1.21 and the same direct top were offered as options at the same time. Production of the XK 120 continued for another eighteen months until 7631 roadsters, 2678 fixed-heads and 1769 drop-heads had been made and the XK 140 took over with these three body styles in October 1954.

For a start, the special equipment car's engine was standardized on all XK 140s, with a single exhaust. This gave 180 bhp on an 8:1 compression ratio, or 210 bhp when fitted with the optional 9:1 C type head and twin exhausts. Jaguar also ratified the popular American 'M' and 'MC' suffixes, the standard XK 140 being known as the XK 140M (because of its 'modified' XK 120 engine), and the C type-headed XK 140 as the XK 140MC in America. Cars used the close ratio gearbox introduced as an option in 1953. Wire wheels were a popular option from the start of production, too.

The chassis was almost exactly the same as that on the XK 120. The chief differences were that the engine was moved forward three inches to make more room in the cockpit and improve weight distribution from 48 per cent front and 52 per cent rear on the XK 120 to more neutral figures; the central cross member was modified to allow a Laycock overdrive to be fitted as an option; long-lasting Girling shock

absorbers were fitted in place of the old lever arm units at the back; the batteries and bulkhead positioning were changed; and rack and pinion steering was fitted. The Alford and Alder rack developed from that used on the C type racer transformed the car in conjunction with the revised weight distribution. The huge 17-inch steering wheel still needed 2.75 turns from lock to lock, and the turning circle went up to 33 ft, but altogether the handling was better.

The battery and bulkhead changes were quite complex. On the roadster and drop-head coupé, the bulkhead was moved forward three inches in company with the engine and a single 12-volt battery hidden in one front wing. On the fixed-head coupé, the bulkhead was reshaped to sweep round the engine, giving even more room in the cockpit and less room for the battery; so two six-volt batteries were fitted as on the XK 120, except that one was placed in each front wing. Detail chassis changes included the reversion to a single master cylinder as on the early XK 120s, the tandem cylinder having been found to be of no practical advantage.

Criticisms of the cooling system were allayed by an improved radiator, water pump and eight-bladed fan, which worked within a cowl. The study of under-bonnet airflow had been in its infancy when the XK 120 was designed. A pressed steel sump of 28 pints capacity replaced the XK 120's cast alloy one, which had held up to 34 pints on some early cars.

Externally, the car looked a good deal different. It used the same body pressings as the XK 120, but had hefty saloon-style bumpers to save it from being ravished in American car parks. These bumpers increased the overall length to 14 ft 8 ins. A cheaper, die-cast, alloy radiator grille replaced the XK 120's individually-slatted grille and there was extra chrome plating—a strip down the middle of the bonnet, with a matching piece on the bootlid, meeting a new badge proclaiming Jaguar's Le Mans triumphs. Improved headlights were fitted with a 'J' monogram in the middle, and flashing indicators were added low on the front wings and incorporated in new, larger, rear lights. The number plate was moved down to a fixed panel between the rear quarter bumpers and the bootlid (which had a new push-button handle), was abbreviated just above the number plate.

Internally, the cars were very different. The changes were most apparent in the drop-head and fixed-head coupés. They had tiny rear seats which could accommodate children or, perhaps, an adult sitting sideways. The space for these seats had been created by changing the engine mountings and the revised bulkhead positions, and by moving the battery positions.

Strangely, the drop-head did not use the same scuttle as that on the fixed-head, which had a foot of extra floor space. The steel top was extended back 6.75 inches further than on the XK 120 fixed-head and the windscreen moved forward. The scuttle line was raised one inch on all models and the fixed-head's roofline was lifted 1.5 inches; its windows were bigger, too, all of which made it a much less cramped car to drive. Overall weight was up by 2 cwt to 29 cwt. This was partly because the doors (much wider now at 38 inches) were made of steel rather than alloy. The trim was similar to that of the XK 120 fixed-head coupé, except that there was more of it. Switches for the indicators and optional overdrive were mounted on the fascia.

In the drop-head, which weighed much the same as the fixed-head, the interior followed the same lines, although the cockpit was not quite so light and airy because the scuttle took more space. Raising the scuttle line meant that there was an extra inch between the bottom of the dashboard, the seat squabs (which had 7-inch

One of the first pictures of a 150 drop-head, with the Brown's Lane factory in the background before the playing fields in the foreground were used for building.

adjustment rather than the 4 inches of the XK 120) and the steering column, which had been mounted almost horizontally, was now fitted at a more conventional angle. Jaguar had been able to re-angle the steering column with universal joints between the wheel and the rubber-mounted rack.

The XK 140 roadster was like a spartan version of the drop-head, with side-screens, detachable windscreen and no rear seats. The interior trim was substantially the same as that on the XK 120 roadster and the doors were still alloy. Overall weight was 28 cwt.

This range continued virtually unchanged until October 1956, when automatic transmission of the type used on the new Jaguar Mark VIII saloon was introduced as an option on the drop-head and fixed-head. The C type head and twin exhausts were also fitted to many more XK 140s as the unit was standardized on the big saloon. The automatic transmission—which was fitted in conjunction with the standard 3.54:1 axle—was the well-tried Borg Warner three-speed box with torque converter, steering column-mounted quadrant gear selector and intermediate hold switch on the dashboard. Altogether 3347 XK 140 roadsters were made; 2401 manual drop-heads; 396 automatic drop-heads; 2365 manual fixed-heads, and 385 automatic fixed-heads before the XK 150 took over in May 1957.

The 150 introduced in fixed head and drop head coupé form at first was as near as you could get to an XK saloon. It was bigger (inside) and heavier than its lithe ancestors and, contrary to appearances, a good deal faster. This was partly because it was fitted with a new cylinder head (the B type) which gave it even more torque lower in the scale, and partly because it had four-wheel disc brakes. The top speed was marginally slower than that of the XK 140 because of its larger frontal area (18.2 square feet instead of 17.5), but it was much quicker from point

The long, sweeping lines of the 150 fixed-head.

Inside the 150 roadster.

The 150S roadster is unveiled at the 1958 Paris Motor Show.

to point, thanks to the increased torque which made up for an extra 1 cwt of body on acceleration and the fade-free brakes that inspired real confidence.

These brakes were the culmination of twelve years' research that had started on aircraft. Until 1945 planes, like cars, had been fitted with a form of drum brake on their landing wheels, but their progressively higher performance and landing speeds made increasing demands on braking efficiency which could only be met by successive design changes and continued research into new materials. With the introduction of jet engines, however, Dunlop decided that the limits of drum brake performance had been reached and a new conception of braking would have to be found. In 1945 the first disc, or plate, brake was introduced. The drum was replaced by copper rings keyed into and rotating with the wheel, friction pads were mounted on a fixed torque member and arranged to contact each face of the rings when the brake was applied by hydraulic pistons in cylinders on the torque member.

This revolutionary brake proved to be of great advantage because it weighed very little (which was of crucial importance to cars which suffered greatly from unsprung weight), and because its better cooling properties and greater swept area of contact with the linings was remarkably fade-free. There were certain points of similarity between aircraft and car development which indicated that the disc brake could successfully be adapted for the road: increased performance and aerodynamic improvements had both influenced brake design, although not for the same reasons. In the case of aircraft, improved streamlining had reduced the available space for undercarriage retraction, while on the car the air flow around the brakes had been reduced by the new all-enveloping coachwork and drum size limited by small wheels and exemplified by the XK.

Experiments with disc brakes on Jaguar sports cars are reported as having started as early as 1949, but it was not until 1951 that much progress was made. These early disc brakes were based fairly closely on the current aircraft design and showed a great improvement in performance over the conventional brake drum that was giving manufacturers such as Jaguar and Aston Martin great problems. Intensive development on the sports racing Jaguars and other cars resulted in Dunlop being able to offer disc brakes at a reasonable cost by 1956. Their introduction on Jaguar production cars was delayed by the factory fire and coincided with the advent of the XK 150. Drum brakes were also listed for the XK 150, but only a few cars were fitted with them.

The system used on the XK 150 was a good deal simpler than that on the racing machines. A single pair of calipers with circular friction pads were used to grip the 12-inch discs on all four wheels instead of the complex triple calipers on the competition cars. A Lockheed vacuum servo was used to boost brake pedal pressure because the disc wheels lacked the inherent self-servo effect of the old two leading shoe drum brakes. A separate caliper acting on the rear discs was used for the hand-brake. It lacked servo assistance, of course, and was feeble to say the least.

The rest of the chassis was substantially the same as that on the earlier XKs. Steering kick-back was further reduced by rubber cushioning around the top of the steering column and wire wheels became almost standard wear.

The standard car retained the 190 bhp dual exhaust engine, but the more popular special equipment model was fitted with the new cylinder head. This engine still produced 210 bhp, but it did it at lower revs, 5500 instead of 5750, and produced slightly more torque, 216 lb/ft against 213, at a considerably lower speed, 3000 rpm compared with 4000. A much-improved pick-up in top gear resulted, and the car was a good deal more restful to drive. The different engine characteristics were achieved by combining the larger exhaust valves of the C type head with the smaller inlet port throat of the standard head, thus combining the best features of each head. The power remained the same because of more efficient gas flow, achieved by altering the angle of its inlet valves from 30 degrees to 45 degrees and by making their faces convex instead of flat.

Under the bonnet the car looked much the same, except for a revised inlet manifold with separate water gallery on top rather than integral.

Outwardly, there were great changes. At first there were only the drop-head and fixed-head coupé body styles because the factory fire had delayed production of the roadster, besides killing the XK SS. The XK 150 looked a lot bigger than its predecessors because the interior was four inches wider. This meant changing the wings and doors to accommodate a high waistline, making extra room for the passengers within. The scuttle was raised yet again and the old-style slimline split windscreen was replaced by a bulky wraparound affair now that curved glass of the right quality was available. A large matching window was fitted to the fixed-head coupé, making it even more airy and saloon-like inside.

Cooling was further improved by a much wider radiator grille, very much like that of the contemporary 3.4 litre saloons. The alligator bonnet was widened to sweep down from the raised scuttle and round the new grille, and the front bumper was much improved in appearance with an indentation to sweep round the bottom of the grille. The back bumper was made even more formidable by wrapping it right round the flanks and across the centre. Early XK 150s had a vertically-mounted number plate, before the plinth was modified to a more sloping position on the boot-lid. The saloon cars' lovely Jaguar mascot also became available as an optional fitting on the XK for the first time. New, larger rear lights were fitted and the rare disc-wheeled cars still left the factory with spats, although these were frequently abandoned by the owners.

Changes inside the body were just as evident. Raising the scuttle and waistline made the interior much bigger, and the feeling was heightened by the new bonnet. The seating arrangements were similar to those of the XK 140 coupés but the dashboard and fascia were different. Gone was the elegant figured walnut in light or dark shades which had graced the earlier coupés; no doubt because of complaints from humid export markets about how quickly this deteriorated. Leather took its place although, ironically, this was to prove hardly longer lasting than wood in places such as Singapore. The top of the fascia was also covered in padded leather and the mirror moved to the roofline instead of the scuttle to take advantage of the large rear window. On the early XK 150s the indicator switch was mounted on the top centre of the dashboard, which also had a prop for the bootlid. However, all drop-head coupés used an anodised aluminium dash panel rather than the leather centre of the fixed-head.

What the spare wheel well should look like in a 150S fixed-head.

Few people complained about the bulbous appearance of the XK 150; most appreciated its greater comfort. However, Jaguar had no intention of letting anybody catch up with the performance in their price bracket. Once the factory had recovered from their near-crippling fire, they introduced in March 1958 the XK 150 roadster, together with the more powerful engine as an option. This was the XK 150S, with yet another revised cylinder head and triple 2-inch SU carburetters. On this head the ports had been straightened for better gas flow at high revs, which, in conjunction with the larger triple carburetters, produced 250 bhp at 5500 rpm, and 240 lb/ft of torque at 4500 rpm. Stronger big end bearings, clutch and lightened flywheel were fitted along with twin SU fuel pumps.

The brakes were also improved with square, quick-change pads developed from the D type racer, in place of the older round pads. The advantage with the new pads was that it wasn't necessary to strip the caliper to change them—they just slotted in. The improved brakes, with other detail changes, such as stronger sixty-spoke wire wheels and a strutless spring loaded bootlid, were carried throughout the XK 150 range of 190 bhp standard roadster, drop-head coupé and fixed-head coupé; 210 bhp special equipment models and 250 bhp 3.4-litre S types. Wire wheels became standard on the special equipment models and overdrive on the S type, which was not available in automatic gearbox form. The roadster closely resembled the fixed-head and drop-head coupés, but there were subtle differences which many people considered improved its appearance.

The curved lower line of the screen dropped away to merge with the gentle

The most powerful standard engine
used in the XK, from the 150S model.

hump of the rear wing. The top of the steel doors, chrome trimmed, sloped down with it, and there was no upper sill, as on the other body styles. The curved screen was the same shape as that on the coupés, but there were no quarter lights and the side windows wound down flush into the doors. The hood was much simpler than that on the drop-head, but it was a good deal better than that on earlier roadsters and featured a zip-out rear window. There were no rear seats, but there was quite generous luggage room as a result, and an upholstered cover had been fitted over the transmission tunnel, on which it was possible to sit a child. A tonneau cover was supplied as standard.

Meanwhile the 3.8-litre version of the XK engine had been under development and made its appearance with straight port head in the XK 150S in October 1959. It was also available with the B type head and the resultant list of Jaguar options became quite confusing, as 7:1 and 8:1 compression ratios could still be specified as options to the 9:1, catering for the poor petrol still encountered in many export areas. The new 3.8-litre engine produced 265 bhp with the 9:1 straight-port (or gold-painted) head, and triple 2-inch SUs; 220 bhp with the 9:1 B type (blue-painted) head and twin 1.75-inch SUs; around 10 bhp less with an 8:1 compression ratio and another 10 bhp less with 7:1. The larger capacity was the result of the bore being increased to 87 mm with dry liners rather than boring out the 3.4-litre block, which was a risky business. The new block's water passages were improved at the same time.

In this form the XK entered the last eighteen months of its life before it was superseded by a car as compelling as the XK 120 had been in 1948. This was the E type Jaguar, the final embodiment of the competition cars described in the next chapter.

III

The Extra-Special XKs

IT ALL STARTED one weekend in June. William Lyons was watching the twenty-four hour race at Le Mans from the pits with Bill Heynes, his chief engineer, their attention focussed on their three XK 120s. One of them looked all set for third place when its clutch packed in, after twenty-one hours. The others finished twelfth and fifteenth. Disappointing? Not on your life! The XKs were virtually standard cars, many of the rest were racers. Heynes was sure they could win next year if they built some special cars based on the standard components. The boss agreed. It was the dawning of the glory years, the years in which the name of Jaguar swept the world, gaining an unparalleled reputation for speed, quality and style. And it was Heynes's extra special XKs, the C type and the D type, which established that reputation.

The C type was amazing, it was produced in such a short time. Heynes was so busy finishing off the new Mark VII saloon when he returned from Le Mans that he didn't get down to work on it until five months later, in October 1950. There was so much he wanted to do: increase the engine's power; reduce the drag; improve the braking; cut the car's weight; *and* make it handle better! And there was so little time. The new XK 120C (the C stood for competition) had to be ready for Le Mans next year. That was the one and only reason for building it, to win at Le Mans. Nothing else mattered to Lyons and Heynes.

Now take that engine. As described in the previous chapter the cylinder head was improved, and used with a 9:1 compression ratio, because they were sure they would get good petrol for the big race. Two larger carburetters (2-inch SUs) were fitted with their inlets breathing from the front of the car through a balance box, which was itself fed by ducting from the front of the car, so that the charge would be denser than if the carburetters were inhaling the hot air under the bonnet. This was all good for an extra 25 per cent of power, 210 bhp instead of the 170 or so of the Le Mans XK 120s. The sump was improved on those racing C types at the same time, with a lot of extra webbing to increase its rigidity. They were, after all, going to have a hard time, hammering along at more than 100 mph for a whole day and night.

The exhaust system also had something to do with the extra power: it was a better shape and emerged from the car under the passenger's side, because there was now room in the new body and frame. And what was that? A new body and

Jimmy Stewart in Ecurie Ecosse C type leads an Allard J 2 X and Tony Rolt in another C type at Goodwood on Easter Monday 1954.

frame—just when everybody had decided the XK 120 was the best thing they had ever set eyes on. Heynes wasn't one to live on past glories; he considered that the XK needed a new body and frame if drag was to be reduced and handling was to be improved. His concept of the new chassis bore no relation to that of the production car except in its overall dimensions and front suspension, which he had only just designed in any case. Bodies took care of themselves in those days with the bare minimum of aluminium to save weight and frontal area on competition cars. This principle was followed on the C type, which was all-enveloping to cut the drag of wheels exposed by cycle-type wings, which were being outlawed from international racing in any case. But it was that frame, and the rear suspension, that made the C type so different from the production XKs.

It was a tubular structure with a new steel scuttle, rear bulkhead and drilled chassis members to stiffen it. The lower and main tubes were 2 inches in diameter, the upper ones 1.5 inches and the connecting struts, 1 inch. The main tubes tapered towards the front, where the virtually standard front suspension was carried on a cross-braced member. A further light framework supported the forward-hinging bonnet, which lifted in one piece, wings and all, to give excellent accessibility to the engine and front suspension. So racing really does improve the breed. It was the first Jaguar where you could get at everything without having universal-jointed arms.

The rear suspension was based on that of the Citroen Traction Avant which had influenced car designers throughout the world since 1934. It was the first mass-production application, although torsion bars had been used for a suspension medium for years by such notable engineers as Parry Thomas with the Leyland Eight of 1920 and Porsche with his designs of the 1930s. In Heynes's application of the Citroen rear suspension, the C type's frame was ended just behind the driver's back with the second of two bulkheads. That formed the mounting for the Jaguar version of the de Dion rear end which would be needed to improve handling. Now Heynes could have gone for the conventional, fairly heavy and complicated set-up: but he reckoned that he could improve on that, and used the Citroen-based design, which worked extremely well on the smooth surfaces for which he had designed it. He threaded a torsion bar through a tube fixed to the bottom of the rear bulkhead, anchored the torsion bar in the middle and attached an XK 120 rear axle to it by a pair of trailing links. Then, on the offside, to counteract the natural tendency of the right wheel to lift under acceleration (you could see it happening all the time on hard-used XKs), and to locate the axle laterally, he used an A-bracket upper link. The result was much improved adhesion and no more wheelspin than you would get from a limited slip differential, which was not readily available then. Drag had been reduced by 20 per cent with the racing body, the weight cut to 20 cwt, and handling was much better thanks to the new back suspension and rack and pinion steering. It did not matter that the rear suspension was not fully independent; the C type was only designed to win at Le Mans, where this was not necessary at the time, because of the long straights, sweeping corners and smooth surface.

That left only the braking to be improved. This was achieved by the use of wire wheels, which allowed cooling air to circulate around the 12-inch drums. The light alloy-rimmed wheels were 16 inches all round with 6.00 section tyres at the front and 6.50 tyres at the back. The braking was further improved by a self-adjusting mechanism at the front to take up the relatively rapid wear of the linings while racing.

Two gearboxes were available with wide (3.31, 4.51, 6.59 and 11.2) and close (3.31, 3.99, 5.78 and 9.86) ratios with 2.93, 3.54, 3.75, 3.92, 4.09 and 4.27 ratios as options for the normal 3.31 rear axle ratio. A 40-gallon fuel tank in the tail, which was quickly detachable for maintenance, and a 12-volt battery in the sill under the driver's door completed the specification.

This was the stark, simple, aero-screened car that was to win at Le Mans in 1951. Much of the winter and early part of the 1952 season was devoted to intensive development of the new disc brakes in which Jaguar had been interested since 1949. The chief problem at first was vaporization of the brake fluid, caused by intense heat from the discs under braking being soaked up through the linings and operating cylinders. A lot of research was needed into lining life, too. *Practical Motorist* reported:

'It is an interesting sidelight that when fitted to the XK 120 Jaguar coupé, the brakes gave an indicated life of about 30,000 miles, although at Rheims (racing circuit) they were found to have a life of less than 400 miles. Under road racing conditions at the Mille Miglia, the brakes were sufficient for the whole race.

'Obviously, in racing on open roads in which the circuit is covered only once, brakes are not used to the same degree as in short circuits, where the driver knows the circuit so well that he leaves the application of the brakes to the last possible moment on all corners.

'It was also revealed that foreign matter such as oil and grit could enter the bore of the caliper around the brake pad, damaging the bore and resulting in piston seal damage. It was also considered undesirable to allow the pads to rub when the brakes were "off" as it resulted in heat build-up, unnecessary wear, as well as absorbing considerable engine horse-power at high speeds.'

Such was the time taken by brake testing that few other changes were possible for 1952. In any case the previous year's winning combination had proved that the C type could out-handle and out-perform everything else. But last minute changes to the aerodynamics to improve top speed at Le Mans were disastrous. The three works cars (chassis numbers XKC001, 002 and 003) were fitted with long, drooping noses and tails to match. This meant that a new radiator had to be fitted with a separate header tank behind the engine to allow the bonnet line to be lowered at the front. The piping between the tank and the smaller front-mounted radiator was too narrow and the air intake didn't help, being much reduced. In addition, C types were not fitted with cooling fans, to save power, and the water pump rotor wasn't doing its job properly and had to be subject to extensive development. As a result, all three cars overheated and retired.

Meanwhile, during the winter of 1952 and spring of the next year, the disc brakes were redesigned. The hydraulic mechanism was completely divorced from the caliper, which now acted as a stress member and guided the brake pads. The cylinder blocks containing the operating piston were mounted on pedestals to obtain the maximum heat insulation and the pistons were fitted with effective dust and dirt

The ill-fated 1952 Le Mans C type. Note the bulge on the bonnet to accept the standard C type radiator.

Ian Cummins's C type, XKC037, pictured at Centennial Park, Sydney, in 1976.

seals. The brake lining was attached to a plate which was fitted with a retraction device to remove the lining from the face of the disc when the brakes were off. Several thousand miles of testing followed on one of the works cars and Jaguar and Dunlop were happy to find that all the previous shortcomings had been eliminated. Even the original design target of a pad life of 3000 miles on a racing circuit (the length of a Le Mans race with a bit to spare) had been comfortably exceeded and the works cars were promptly fitted with discs all round. A servo was also fitted to give added power to the braking system and save strain on the drivers, because these new-fangled brakes did not have the self-servo, or binding, effect of the old two leading shoe front drums.

Now that the brake development was complete, Jaguar had more time to devote to improving the rest of the C type. For a start, there was much lightening to bring the car's weight down to around 19 cwt. Part of this was achieved by flimsier construction of the body, which kept the same lines as the original 1951 cars. More weight was saved by using lighter gauge frame tubes, 18 swg instead of 16. In fact, Jaguar had wanted to use the lighter tubing originally, but it had not been available. The alloy fuel tank, which had been prone to splitting, was changed for a lighter, more reliable, flexible aircraft-style 50-gallon bag tank; and 53 lb was saved by using lighter wiring, battery, dynamo and starter!

Three twin choke 40DCOE Weber carburetters on a new manifold replaced the twin SUs following parallel development by John Heath on his Jaguar-powered HWM special. This improved maximum power by 10 bhp, but the most significant advantage was in the extra power (25 bhp) imparted to the middle of the range. A new crankshaft damper was made in steel to withstand high revs and Dykes top rings were fitted to the pistons to combat crankcase pressurization. The new water pump, which prevented cavitation above 5000 rpm was also used, in addition to a new alloy radiator which had a 30 per cent better water flow.

Cockpit of the production C type: note the hand-operated dipswitch. There was no room for one on the floor!

The old 10-inch Borg and Beck solid centre clutch was replaced by a $7\frac{1}{4}$-inch multi-plate racing unit that was reliable, if somewhat sharp on take-off. On the rear suspension, the A-bracket was replaced by a single cast torque arm and a Panhard rod because it had been prone to failure on rough surfaces. In this form, the C type was campaigned with total success as development proceeded on what was to become one of the greatest Jaguars ever, the D type.

The first D type was essentially the C type with a completely new body–chassis unit; this achieved 178 mph during the Jabbeke demonstration of October 1953. Its design was based on aircraft practice, which was hardly surprising considering that the genius behind it was Malcolm Sayer, who had worked for Bristol Aircraft as an aerodynamicist. His body–chassis unit was really quite like an aircraft's fuselage. Its centre section consisted of an elliptical tube into which were cut suitable openings for the driver and (theoretical) passenger. The fuselage, or monocoque, which formed the entire car between the scuttle and the C type-style rear bulkhead, was stiffened by massive L-section pressings riveted to the main section so that they formed, in effect, two tubular members, or sills, roughly triangular in section. The

front and back of the monocoque was boxed in by double-skinned bulkheads with a large opening in the front one for the engine and transmission and a small opening in the rear for the propeller shaft. The front suspension and engine were carried on a sub-frame made up from four square tubes which extended back through the scuttle to the rear bulkhead. These were also welded to a front cross member with further stiffening provided by two additional square-section tubes which ran forward diagonally from the front of the bulkhead to meet in the centre of the front cross member. They were welded to the upper main frame tubes. The whole of the body structure was riveted and arc-welded from 18 swg magnesium.

The front suspension and steering were similar to that of the C type (and the production XK 140 which was under development at the time) and the rear suspension was also based on the C type system. The Salisbury axle was mounted on twin trailing links, with the bottom ones fixed to a transverse torsion bar secured in the centre as on the C type. Telescopic shock absorbers supplied the damping in the manner of the C type and an A-bracket located the axle. This was of different design to that on the C type however, with the top of the A attached to the underside of the

Functional cockpit of the production D type.

1956 D type rear suspension. Note the differential ratio painted on its housing.

differential and the extremities to the rear bulkhead.

The front of the body hinged up as on the C type and the unstressed rear coach-work was bolted on to the bulkhead so that it could be quickly detached for maintenance. The rest of the running gear on this C–D prototype was substantially as the C type, including wire wheels.

To make matters thoroughly confusing, the first four genuine D types, which followed the prototype, had C type chassis numbers! XKC401, 402, 403 and 404 were officially merely C, or competition, Jaguars until they were christened D types, apparently by journalist Harold Hastings. He was simply avoiding confusion with the earlier tubular chassis cars in his reports; but the name stuck. Two similar cars built later in 1954 bore the chassis numbers XKD405 and 406.

The first real D types were the classics that took the small Coventry firm into the realm where people gasped in admiration 'That's a Jaguar', instead of muttering 'What's that?'

They had a similar chassis to the C–D prototype with its beautiful streamlined body adapted and improved for Le Mans with a distinctive head cowling and stabilis-ing fin. Besides having a lower weight (18 cwt) and higher aerodynamic efficiency (72 per cent for the D type proper; 77 per cent for the prototype, taking the C type as 100 per cent), they had more power and a better gearbox.

The engine used dry-sump lubrication with a shallow engine sump which had the dual effect of reducing its height by nearly three inches, and of ensuring that the

bearings were not starved by oil surge, resulting from violent handling under racing conditions. This system used a scavenge pump to take the engine's oil to a large drum on the left hand side of the car with a pressure pump to return it. Both pumps were driven by transverse shafts from a worm drive on the front of the crankshaft with an oil cooler between the pressure pump and the block.

The engine was mounted in the sub-frame at an angle of eight degrees. This was advantageous not only in enabling the bonnet line to be lowered, but it gave the car a lower centre of gravity because the engine was by far its heaviest component. It was also necessary because the engine and its ancillaries could only be squeezed into the sub-frame at an angle rather than vertically. If the sub-frame had been widened to allow vertical mounting, the dimensions of the car could not have been contained to 7 ft $6\frac{5}{8}$ ins wheelbase; 4 ft 2 ins front track, 4 ft rear; 12 ft 10 ins length; 5 ft $5\frac{1}{2}$ ins width and 2 ft $7\frac{1}{2}$ ins height at the scuttle.

The cylinder head had been further developed from that on the C type by fitting larger inlet valves, of $1\frac{7}{8}$-inch diameter although the exhaust valves were unaltered at $1\frac{5}{8}$ inches. New camshafts with more overlap were fitted, which sacrificed little torque at the lower end of the scale. The same Weber carburetters were used with an airbox as before, but the inlet manifold was changed to enable them to remain horizontal on the inclined engine, and giving an effective four-degree downdraft. A similar exhaust system to that on the C type was fitted and the engine produced 245 bhp at 5750 rpm with a 9:1 compression ratio. It had no flywheel, a hefty crank-

left One of the beautiful Dunlop alloy knock-on wheels fitted to a D type.

right Powerhouse of the production D type fitted with triple Weber carburetters.

shaft damper and the weight of the Borg and Beck multi-plate racing clutch making up for that.

The gearbox was completely new. Jaguar designed it themselves with synchromesh on all four of the closely-spaced forward gears, the ratios of which were 5.98, 4.58, 3.57, direct top and 6:1 reverse. The starter motor was mounted on top of this box in front of the gearbox. A Plessey pump for the brake servo was driven by the propeller shaft at the back of the gearbox.

The $12\frac{3}{4}$-inch diameter disc brakes and back axle (which had a very high ratio of 2.79:1 for Le Mans) were similar to those on the 1953 C types. Flexible bag petrol tanks of 36.5 gallons total capacity were fitted in the tail, as on the 1953 C type. The cooling system, with a separate header tank in front of the engine but behind the radiator, was an adaptation of the 1952 Le Mans C type system. The aim was the same, a lower bonnet line, but the effect was different. It worked.

The whole car was very efficient aerodynamically, making it one of the fastest cars in endurance racing. It had a maximum speed of 180 mph on its 16-inch peg drive Dunlop alloy wheels and probably higher on the optional 17-inch versions, although Duncan Hamilton's later claims of nearly 200 mph seem optimistic. Most D types were fitted with 3.4-litre versions of the XK engine, although the last made in 1954, XKD406, had a 2.4-litre variant, with a stroke of 76.5 mm to take advantage of the handicapping system in the Tourist Trophy race. This unit produced 193 bhp at 6000 rpm and was of similar construction to the 3.4-litre engine.

In 1955, eight works cars were built with chassis numbers running from XKD501 to 508, before customer cars were built on a production line. The first three, XKD501–503, went to the semi-works teams Ecurie Ecosse and Ecurie National Belge, and the remaining five, XKD504–8, were retained by Jaguar. Outwardly the five works cars could be distinguished by their noses which were $7\frac{1}{2}$ inches longer for better air penetration, and by their brake air cooling ducts. They also had longer wrap-round windscreens to protect the drivers from buffeting at Le Mans. The overall effect of these changes was to reduce the drag co-efficient to 64 per cent, still taking the original C type as 100 per cent. Under their skins, all the 1955 D types were considerably different from the 1954 models.

'The major modification was in the frame', said *The Autocar*. 'The integral construction was found to be expensive in the event of damage, and a separate frame using the same basic tubular type of construction, but with steel tubes, was adopted. To this the main centre section is now bolted. This, as previously, is constructed in magnesium alloy with the stiffening member riveted to the skin. Also, as before, the rear bulkhead of this section forms the attachment points for the rear suspension units, and the tail section containing the tanks and spare wheel.

'This change in design means that a damaged centre section, or the frame, can be replaced as a separate unit; furthermore, it is a much better production proposition. The main frame, with engine and gearbox, and the front suspension, can be built up as one unit. Before being married to it, the centre section can also be treated as a sub-assembly, to be built up with the rear axles and

Definitive shape of the D type.

Incredible road car: the XK SS.

Rear quarter of Brian Corser's X K S S.

suspension units.

'In its aluminium form, the chassis frame was welded at all joints. Argon arc welding was used and this is a comparatively costly and slow process. When changing over to the tubular steel frame, welding at the joints was replaced by brazing. Extensive laboratory tests have proved that this results in a much stronger joint . . . by the use of steel tubes of lighter section, this change has not resulted in any additional weight, and, in fact, the new frame is not as heavy as its aluminium predecessor.'

The 1955 car's tail section looked exactly like that of the 1954 car, but was entirely of stressed skin construction like the rest of the monocoque. This meant that it did not need a supporting framework, which saved weight and allowed fatter tyres to be fitted if desired.

With the exception of XKD504–8, all the D types produced in 1955 were in effect an amalgam of the works cars of 1954 and 1955; the body and the framework were 1955 while the engine conformed—in power output—to that of 1954. The five full works cars had the body improvements and even more powerful engine.

This featured a prototype cylinder head with larger 2-inch inlet valves and $1\frac{11}{16}$-inch exhaust valves. To avoid the valves touching, the inclination of the exhaust valves was changed from 35 degrees to 40 degrees, giving rise to the designation 35/40 for this head. Camshaft lift was also increased to $1\frac{7}{16}$ inches and the timing altered. The inlet and exhaust manifolds were modified slightly and the exhaust pipes extended along the underside of the car to exit at the rear, increasing their extractor effect. These changes were worth 30 bhp more, pushing up the output to 270 bhp. In this form, with a 2.53:1 axle ratio, the works cars would pull 5600 rpm on the Mulsanne straight at Le Mans, the equivalent of 180 mph.

Jaguar had been experimenting with a de Dion rear suspension similar to that fitted to the rival Aston Martin DB3S on, first, XKC401, the D type prototype, and then on one of the 1955 cars, probably XKD504, which was the works experimental car. However, Metalastik joints used in this suspension gave trouble and it was not raced in 1955.

XKD504 was also used as a test bed for fuel injection, which made its appearance on some of the 1956 works cars, numbered XKD601–6. These machines featured the long-nose, tail-finned bodies and were around 0.5 cwt lighter than the 1955 cars because of extensive weight-paring in the body. However they were slower at Le Mans because they were forced to use an 8-inch deep full-width screen to conform to new Constructors' Championship regulations. A transparent cover from the top of the screen to the tail on the passenger side was fitted to reduce drag, in place of the old flush-fitting aluminium tonneau cover. Other changes dictated by the new rules included the fitting of a passenger door, wider seats and a smaller, 28-gallon fuel tank.

Handling was improved by increasing the size of the front anti-roll bar to $\frac{11}{16}$-inch from $\frac{9}{16}$ and joining the top rear suspension links with a three-quarter-inch anti-roll bar. XKD604 was also used as a test bed for the de Dion rear end, but survived only part of a lap on it at Silverstone before being crashed. This suspension reduced wheelspin but weighed more and was abandoned by Jaguar, who were concentrating on a completely new independent rear suspension system. The Lucas fuel injection, which had been under development since 1950, gave more power when it was functioning properly, but was not standardized because of the excellent reliability record of the Webers. Braking was further improved by the fitting of one pair of large pads and wheel cylinders to each caliper in place of the old system, which used three pairs of pads and cylinders on each front brake and two pairs of each at the back. Maintenance was much simpler with the new system and the time taken to change pads was reduced dramatically.

Customer cars, such as those initially supplied to Ecurie Ecosse, had all these modifications except for the wide-angle head and fuel injection, unless the Le Mans regulation modifications were not needed.

Despite the D type's success in endurance races and its relatively low price of £4000, Jaguar found it difficult to sell the remainder of the first batch of around a hundred production cars. At about that time, one of their star drivers, Duncan Hamilton, bought a new D type for his own use and sold his old one, XKC402 (registered OKV1) to John 'Jumbo' Goddard, after first converting it to a specification more suited to road use.

'We removed the fairing from behind the driver's head, fitted a full-width windscreen (from an Austin-Healey 100) and a hood, put carpets on the floor, and generally speaking made the car more comfortable for everyday use', said Hamilton in his autobiography, *Touch Wood*. 'When the works at Coventry saw it they promptly

What might have been with what was: the E 2 A prototype pictured beside an E type.

announced a new model: the Jaguar XK SS.'

Jaguar had time to make only sixteen of these road-going D types before the great fire destroyed vital tooling and some of the spare monocoques that had been earmarked for the XK SS. There was little apparent difference between the XK SS and a short-nosed production D type apart from a large wrap-round full-width windscreen, no headrest or division between the driver's and passenger's compartments, and proper doors on both sides. Interior trim was improved but luggage had to be carried on a rack mounted on the tail. There was no room inside.

The standard axle ratio was 3.54:1 as on other XKs, which made it one of the fastest road cars the world has ever seen.

D type development continued although the factory had finished racing in 1956 and sold the long-nosed works cars to the Ecurie Ecosse. The engine capacity was stepped up to 3.8 litres (as with the production saloons and XK 150S to follow), making the D type even faster and powering numerous Jaguar-engined specials, such as the Lister. And two new XK engines were produced for the 1958 Constructors' Championship, which carried a 3-litre maximum engine capacity rule. The first engine of 2986 cc was developed by the factory and was also featured in

Jaguar-engined specials; the second, a bored and stroked 2.4-litre saloon car based unit of 2954 cc was produced by the Ecurie Ecosse, but neither was successful. Both suffered from chronic unreliability.

Then, two years later, the last of the extra special XKs appeared. Code named E2A, it was based on a 1957 prototype sports car that bore a distinct resemblance to a D type. The chief difference between E2A and the D types it was intended to succeed was that it was bigger and that it had independent rear suspension that had been developed on the 1957 prototype. Its wheelbase was 5 inches longer than a D type at 8 feet, and 2 inches narrower at 4 feet. The overall length was 14 ft 2 ins and width 5 ft 3¾ ins. The rear of the monocoque was extended to produce a mounting for the new rear suspension which had been occupying much of Heynes's time. This system featured a rigidly-mounted differential and massive lower wishbones which, with fixed length drive shafts and cast alloy hub carriers, formed the basic suspension. Springing was by coil spring–damper units. This car was run at Le Mans in 1960 by America's Briggs Cunningham, but its 3-litre engine destroyed itself; in 3.8-litre form it proved a race-winner for a short while in the United States. However, its real significance was that it was the last of the extra-special XKs and the first of a new breed of Big Cat that was to sweep the world: the E type.

IV

What the Road Testers said

DRIVING A NEW JAGUAR was one of the highlights of every road tester's life, and none more so than John Bolster, of *Autosport*. He was lucky enough to try four of the great road-racing specials, the Lister, the HWM, the Cooper and the Tojeiro, besides a C type, D type and the standard XKs. For years the Lister was at the top of Bolster's tree, being beaten on acceleration in later years only once, by a seven-litre racing Cobra, which felt 'really sloppy' below 30 mph on its huge slicks. There was simply nothing in the same league as MVE 303, Archie Scott-Brown's famous Lister.

'It was a bit exciting on its very narrow tyres, it was enormously effective, giving me a 0–60 time of 4.6 secs and 0–100 in 11.2 secs', said Bolster. 'As a road car, it was magnificent, having perfect traffic manners and sufficient acceleration to get one clear of almost any emergency before it happened . . .

'I drove many other Jaguar-engined cars, finding a Le Mans-winning D type a perfect shopping car. Prior to that, I was at Montlhéry for the Coupé du Salon meeting, and visited the pits during the practice period. Duncan Hamilton was there with a C type Jaguar, with which he was to win the morrow's race, but he was not taking his practising too seriously. "If you can get into my hat you can have a go", he suggested, "nobody will notice".

'It was Laurence Pomeroy who offered up a prayer "for those in peril on the C". Let us merely say that the C type Jaguar had most of the performance of the D type, but none of its road-holding. At 140 mph off the banking and into the Goulet, it was distinctly alarming, while the slower corners tended to be taken on full opposite lock. It would do some modern drivers good to handle a brute like the C.'

The Motor had no complaints about HKV 455 when they received this historic car for the first full independent test in November 1949. Casting aside caution, currency restrictions and the bonds of the editorial budget, they took HKV 455 on an extended trip through France and Belgium, encompassing the Jabbeke autoroute from Ostend and the Montlhéry track in Paris. The best one-way speed was impressive: 126.8 mph, with an average of 124.6 mph, even though the hood and side-screens were kept in place. Soapy Sutton had managed only 1.8 mph faster with HKV 500, so the men from *The Motor* were well pleased, verging on the lyrical as they

It's never too late to put an XK through its paces. Here Bill Heynes (with Wally Hassan as passenger), tries out Jaguar's own 120 roadster at Silverstone just before he retired in 1969.

Hard-worked rally (and test) car NUB 120, crewed here by Ian and Pat Appleyard in the Bolton-le-Moors Rally in March 1952.

The 120 drop-head's hood, a great improvement over that of the 120 roadster.

enthused over

'acceleration such as most drivers would have never even imagined. There was no embarrassing sudden response to the accelerator pedal, but rather a docility of the power unit and a smoothness of the clutch which makes a delightful willingness to crawl in tightly-packed traffic.'

Once clear of the traffic, the power came on like a turbine, taking the XK 120 up to 60 mph in 10 seconds; 80 in 15.7 and 100 in 27.3, with the standing quarter mile taking only 17 seconds. The torque was tremendous, taking the roadster from a standstill to 100 mph in top gear in only 44.6 seconds, a real party trick! All this was with a standard 3.64:1 rear axle ratio, which gave maximum speeds of 62 and 90 mph in second and third gears. Economy was exceptionally good at 19.8 mpg from a car which weighed 25.5 cwt. The stability was exemplary: 'only a single guiding hand on the steering wheel' being needed when flat out at 124 mph, with handling to match on the corners.

'The car's precise controllability is not always appreciated at first, but once it is realised that only small wheel movements and finger and thumb are needed it is instinctive to negotiate winding roads at really high speed, audible protest from the tyres being very, very seldom heard except during violent braking.'

Surprisingly, the brakes evoked no criticism, being rated as 'magnificent'. Obviously, *The Motor* did not have to use them repeatedly, and HKV 455 must have had one of the easier Moss gearboxes, because that excited no criticism either. In fact it sounded so much better than the average, 'incorporating that sort of synchro-mesh mechanism which conceals driving inaccuracies without impeding really fast movements of the lever.' Quite the reverse of what most drivers were to find with that gearbox. . . .

The headlights and seats came in for a bit of hammer, though. The lights were good for little more than 70 mph at night, said *The Motor*'s testers, who also found it difficult to keep their places on the standard seats. They thought the steering column was a little too steeply racked, too, but they liked the odd-looking hood.

'With the hood raised, it is necessary to bow the head low when getting in, but once inside it is dry and reasonably warm, there being quite enough headroom and a great deal of elbow room. The hood, incidentally, does not flap, even at the car's very high maximum speed.'

Jaguar were not alone in using odd-looking hoods which restricted entry at that time. It would be several years before manufacturers solved the problem of making a hood big enough for comfort and small enough not to restrict performance and get torn off at the new high speeds of which cars were becoming capable.

All told, *The Motor*'s testers loved the XK 120 and said that it was destined for a 'long and honourable career'.

The Autocar were wildly appreciative when they tested the first of the steel-bodied cars, the left-hand drive JWK 675 in April 1950.

'Nothing like the XK 120, and at its price, has been previously achieved—a car of tremendous performance and yet displaying the flexibility, and even the silkiness and smoothness of a mild-mannered saloon', said their enthusiastic scribes. 'This power unit is a British achievement in which everyone in this country interested in cars of high performance may well take pride. Indeed, the XK is a prestige gainer for Britain's engineering as a whole and car engineering in particular. During a test of some 700 miles, at the beginning of which it was brand new and by no means run in, it necessarily received some merciless treatment, but showed no sign of losing tune, used very little oil and did not at any time record above 80 degrees centigrade water temperature. . . .

'Truly this is two cars in one. It can be handled quietly with very little use of the gears if the driver is in a lazy mood. Press the right foot down, however, and a different car is revealed.'

The Autocar went on to quell the fears of the diehards who claimed that synchromesh slowed up a gearbox by reporting that it did not intrude and that:

'very fast downward changing is achieved without beating the synchromesh by employing the old double-declutching technique, or more leisurely changing is made smoothly and quietly, taking full advantage of the synchromesh. Third gear is silent and can be used with tremendous effect for alternate deceleration on a winding road.'

The budget must have been a bit tighter for *The Autocar*, because they stayed in Britain and could not find a suitable piece of road for maximum speed, but their acceleration figures were around 2 seconds slower up to 60 mph and 8 seconds slower to 100; it has been estimated that the steel-bodied cars were around 1 cwt heavier than the alloy examples, and HKV 455 probably had an exceptionally good engine, having been used for racing as well as high-speed demonstrations and development work, whereas JWK 675 was still stiff and new. *The Autocar*'s fuel consumption

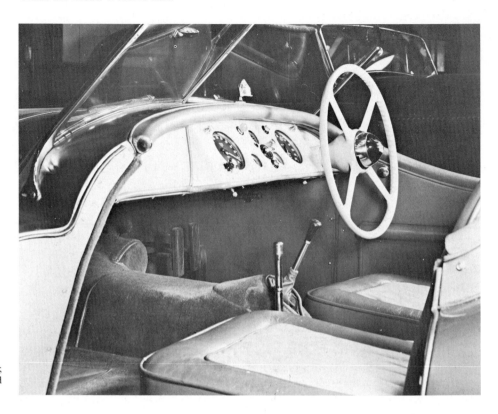

Cockpit of a very early 120 roadster;
note the rare white steering wheel and
bulge for the starter motor.

figures of between 13 and 17 mpg support this view.

The Autocar went so far as to say that the brakes did not fade, despite lapping a disused aerodrome as fast as they could. What a delightful place England must have been in 1950 with hundreds of miles of concrete runways on which to hurl your car about with complete abandon and little chance of hurting or offending anybody!

Five months later The Autocar came up trumps with a test of Ian Appleyard's famous NUB 120. The only changes from its Alpine and Tulip rally trim (reported technical editor Montague Tombs) were to the lighting and horns to make them legal for use in England. The rest of the car was untouched, even to a large dent in the offside front wing, a loose spat, battered exhaust and missing floorboards. And the only modifications were stoneguards on the headlights, a bonnet strap and vents cut in the bonnet to combat vapour locks experienced with the unaccustomed high-octane petrol already available on the Continent. An optional 25-gallon tank was used and the standard 3.64 final drive.

'The thrill of the car is in its amazing flexibility and its complete ease of handling [said Tombs]. You can do "dicing" in it if you want to. But you can also trickle quietly through a congested town, mostly in top gear, and you can handle the car just as easily as any stately saloon. The suppleness on top gear and the extreme smoothness of the engine are quite remarkable. And when you press the throttle and hear the swish of air rushing into the two carburetters, things begin to happen, and your tummy presses against your backbone as the car

Cockpit of the steel-bodied 120 roadster tested by *The Autocar*.

positively leaps into stride . . . the steering, not heavy, fairly quick, and very definite, was in good order . . . the brakes were still good enough for ordinary driving, but they would not have been good enough for dicing, for the pedal was nearly flat on the floor. Not surprisingly in the circumstances, they obviously needed adjustment. But to come away from best performance in an Alpine with any brakes left at all is something of a feat.'

And with that, NUB 120 was driven off to Coventry for servicing after 2000 miles of hammering over the rocky roads of Europe.

The Americans had to wait until May 1951 for an authoritative road test of an XK 120 although they had been buying up nearly all the production as though there was no tomorrow. *Road and Track* reported that it was by far the fastest car they had tested, with an average speed of 121.6 mph, 0–60 in 10.1 seconds and the standing quarter mile in 18.3 seconds—slightly slower than *The Motor*, but then they didn't have the benefit of an alloy racer and used a full-width aeroscreen instead of the Brooklands version on HKV 455. Power was probably slightly down, too, because the test took place at more than 3000 feet, but the great American public, who had sometimes been inclined to treat the Jaguar's performance figures with scepticism, were duly impressed. Steering and roadworthiness, continued the report:

'would be difficult to improve. The excellent seating position, combined with fast, positive steering, produces a cornering ability unequalled by any car tested to date.

'The Jaguar brakes are extremely powerful, requiring rather low pressure, and did not display any tendency to fade (apparently only severe braking, such as during a road race, tends to bring about fade on an XK). While the cooling is adequate under normal conditions, traffic driving brings a rise in engine temperature.'

Significant comments, these. The American magazine was the first to spot two of the XK's chief faults, braking and overheating. They also criticised the quality of the metallic paint used on most of the cars imported into America and pleaded for a better hood, 'a little space behind the seats' and bigger bumpers to ward off hard-parking countrymen. Lyons must have been among their readers, when you consider the XK 140 to come. Nevertheless, *Road and Track* loved the XK 120.

'Sleek as a Kentucky Derby winner, as desirable as a beautiful woman, and faster than the wind . . . here is a sports car with real personality. Your morale receives a terrific boost as soon as you sink into the comfortable leather seats.

'A real surprise is that smooth acceleration in hand at *any* speed.' And those brakes: 'although they can be faded in racing, they are real honeys in traffic.'

Road and Track were sold on the XK. So was Bill Boddy, of the equally-respected *Motor Sport*:

'It was almost immediately apparent that the engine, like a bank clerk, is quite devoid of temperament. I left it idling all the while we were in the Bayswater traffic hold-ups and I poodled along at 500 rpm in top gear without upsetting the mixture or lubricating the sparks. When a gap appeared—my word, how we made use of it.

'Even driving the Jaguar as essentially a top-gear car, 90 mph becomes commonplace in between dodging lorries along any main or secondary road, so great is the accelerative ability. No particular speed can be cited as the cruising speed—rather do you make a series of hawk-like swoops past slower traffic, punctuated by firm applications of the brakes to tuck you safely behind prevailing obstructions. . . .

'The twelve-inch Lockheed brakes normally do their stuff admirably, too. With only slight pressure and small travel on the pedal, truly powerful, progressive snag-free retardation is available, without which the XK 120 wouldn't be half the car it is. I write "normally", because I did come up against rather disconcerting fade. I had braked hard from about 80 mph—and one is so seldom *under* 70 or 80 in this car—for a minor cross roads and entered some narrow lanes, which I took at about 50, braking for the incessant corners. All of a sudden I found almost all anchorage had evaporated, just as if I'd wetted the shoes in a water-splash, only I hadn't. The harder I pressed the more negative was the effort, until negotiation of a congested high street at 20 mph constituted quite an adventure. By this time you could *smell* how hot the drums and linings were from the cockpit. After I had had lunch, temperatures (and tempers) were normal again and the brakes were as good as ever. Now this fading did not

left Factory specification aero screens and mirror cowl as fitted to a 120 roadster.

below left Luggage boot of HKV 455, the first XK to be built: it differed from the production models in its fuel filler cap, lights, boot prop, and hole for releasing the spare wheel.

below Stark door trim on the 120 roadster.

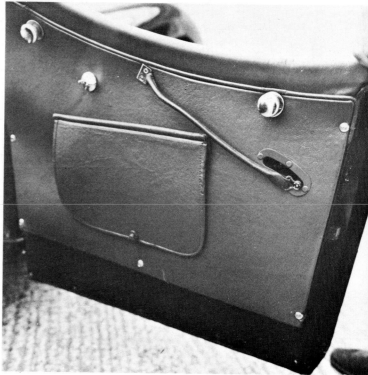

The more luxurious 120 drop-head's door trim.

Preparing for a picture session with *The Autocar*'s road test 120 fixed-head (MHP 682).

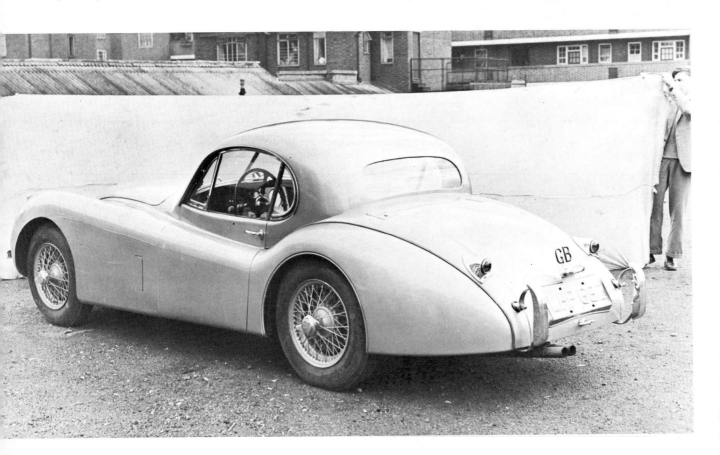

occur in really fast main road driving luckily, but I can now sympathise with XK 120 drivers who have slapped the straw during a sports car race or come down an Alp a thought too quickly.

'This suave Jaguar was so enormously quick from one place to another that to plot its true performance seemed somewhat pointless.'

Nevertheless, Boddy plotted his course to Brands Hatch and promptly lapped at 1 minute 0.5 seconds with only slightly more than normal free-movement of the brake pedal. Obviously, with steel wheels and spats, the XK 120 was suffering from under-cooling of the brakes on minor roads. With the constant blast of air on the racetrack things were not so bad, particularly with a clear track. Later XKs were much improved when wire wheels were fitted and the spats left in the garage or at the trackside. This allowed more air to circulate around the drums and fade was reduced. It was a new problem that was only just becoming apparent because almost every sports car that preceded the XK had wire wheels jutting naked in the slip-stream, which cooled the brake drums much more efficiently. The old-fashioned exposed wheels were of bigger diameter, too, allowing larger brake drums if necessary. The XK's braking problem was heightened by the all-enveloping coachwork diverting air away from the drums, the diameter of which was limited by the size of its new, small, sixteen-inch solid steel wheels. This beautiful coachwork also enabled

One of the first 120 fixed-heads to leave the factory.

the car to go much faster than the old 'square-riggers', contributing to the braking problem. It was a vicious circle that was only eliminated by disc brakes.

By 1951, numerous XK 120s were being raced in club events, with Hugh Howorth's two-tone alloy-bodied example (JWK 977) easily the fastest in Britain. Outwardly it looked quite standard, except for its lack of bumpers, screen, spats and hub caps. The more curious small boys, including myself, were intrigued to see that it had only one headlight. A grill covered the hole where the right hand light ought to have been, and large diameter trunking led to a carburetter cold air box and numerous modifications under the bonnet. Various slots and orifices in the wings admitted more than the average amount of air to the brakes.

Bolster was lucky enough to track test this projectile after a session on top of the commentary truck at Snetterton. Nowadays track tests are hardly comparable to those on the road, but in 1951, the surface of Snetterton, a wartime airfield, was probably inferior to that of many roads! In any case, Bolster noted in *Autosport* that the Howorth XK lacked temperament to such an extent that it would have been perfectly happy in London's heaviest traffic.

> 'One has often heard the expression "bags of power, old boy", but here is a case where it really does apply', said Bolster. 'The acceleration is right in the racing car class, and one seems to be up into top gear in a matter of yards, with the seat still hitting one smartly in the back. One hundred mph is left behind at quite an early stage in the game, and the acceleration remains vivid far past that moderate speed. The maximum is formidable indeed, in fact it is as high as that of some machines currently running in Formula One events.
>
> 'The engine remains astonishingly smooth and quiet apart from a rough period around 5300 rpm. It is backed up by a clutch and gearbox that do all the right things, and, of course, the pedals are properly placed for "heel and toe". The brakes are noticeably better than on a normal XK 120 and I had to use them pretty smartly when I misjudged the tremendous speed at which I was approaching a corner.
>
> 'Exactly the right degree of understeer is provided and one can use the full performance all the time without any sawing or fighting at the wheel. As a competition machine, this car has proved abundantly successful, but as a high-speed touring vehicle of impeccable manners, it would also be hard to beat.'

Bolster went on to compare the XK 120 with a vintage Aston Martin racer he tried on the same day, saying that the sports car was almost as fast round any given corner except when a sudden deviation was called for. In such an event, the Aston, much slower in a straight line, was definitely quicker than the XK 120 through a corner:

> 'The XK 120 will drift a bend in a delightful manner but it resents being flung about while it is doing it . . . that is not meant as a criticism of the Jaguar (which had a far superior ride) . . . but it simply proves, once again, that only a few independent front suspension jobs can compare on corners with the ultimate in cart springs.'

A couple of months after, in January 1952, Pomeroy endorsed Bolster's opinions on the handling in an article in *The Motor* about an XK 120 borrowed from the factory:

'I admit to feeling restrained from flinging this particular car about on ordinary roads by a number of factors, not all of which are of a truly technical nature. Even after some long acquaintance one continues to be awed by the length of the bonnet and reminded of the man who said that the worst thing about his dachshund was that when he fed it in the dining room he had to go into the kitchen to see if it was pleased.

'Similarly, on the Jaguar I felt that I was placed too far away from the accident and that a moderate change in angle on a bend resulted in very large lateral displacement of the nose of the car. This impression was heightened by the exceedingly low seating position from which one looks along the bonnet instead of looking down on top of it as one used to do on the Type 35 Bugatti and, as a further point of criticism, the seats seem unnaturally low in relation to the pedals. For these reasons I found myself taking corners at a much lower speed than was really imposed by the true road-holding powers of the car.

'I did not learn how good these really were until I, by accident, arrived on a corner far sharper than it looked and found to my surprise that by turning the wheel fairly sharply the car took me round with little ado.'

Road tests involved more than performance tests: *The Motor* even photographed their 120 fixed-head's battery compartment under the interior luggage tray.

The long, sweeping lines of the C type, driven here by Stirling Moss at Goodwood.

Later that year, in October, *The Autocar* published the first road test on the new XK 120 fixed-head coupé, and were most impressed. Their car (MHP 682) averaged just over 120 mph on the Jabbeke autoroute during a 2000-mile test, thanks to its special equipment 180 bhp engine compensating for its extra weight. This car also had the wire wheels which had become optional the previous year and much better braking as a result. *The Autocar* reported:

'The outstanding impression after having driven this car for more than 2000 miles is of the way it goes, and keeps on going. Even after a high-speed Continental journey, and also a complete road test on a Belgian motor road, the car had no feeling of tiredness, nor was there any noticeable falling off in its sprightliness. This ability to go and keep on going can also be applied to the chassis components and, in reverse, to the brakes, which will stop and keep on stopping. Those fitted to this particular model are Lockheed hydraulically operated (with automatic adjusters at the front), and during the whole time that the car was on test no manual adjustment was made to the brakes nor was there any apparent increase in the free pedal travel.'

Sadly, though, the advantages of the fixed-head coupé from the point of view of comfort of travel were marred for *The Autocar* by the driving position. They found the positioning of the pedals difficult for a tall driver and thought that the seats could have given a little more support for the leg muscles. It would have been an advantage, in their opinion, for the fly-off handbrake to have been placed further forward. However, they liked the car so much that they tempered this criticism by saying that:

> 'it must be realised that with a car of this type, in the interests of performance it is necessary to reduce the frontal area to a minimum; consequently, the overall height must be as low as possible, and this factor alone makes it very difficult to adopt what may be termed the ideal position.'

Acceleration figures were excellent, 60 mph being reached from rest in 9.9 seconds, 100 in 28.2 and the standing quarter mile covered in 17.3 seconds, almost exactly the same as the 160 bhp roadster.

The American magazine *Auto Sport* had tested a car with similar equipment (dubbed the XK 120M in the States) in wet weather and really appreciated the comfort of the fixed-head.

> 'It points up the virtues of a vehicle that combines most of the sporting characteristics of the XK roadster with most of the comforts of home: wind-up windows; adequate heating; panoramic visibility to the rear (which the roadster doesn't have with the top up); freedom from wind roar, side-curtain flapping and drumming; and a modicum of protection in case you manage to stand one on its head.
>
> 'Normally you might be able to add "no drafts" but it wasn't strictly true in the case of this sample: one of the chilliest little drafts in North America came helling out of the side ventilator and through the brake and clutch holes in the floorboards to converge on the driver's ankles. . . .
>
> 'The engine changes used to be considered strictly for competition stuff and you might expect the M to be a bit hot for town driving. Not at all: our coupé moved off smooth as silk—no roughness at idle, no hawking and spitting while waiting for stoplights, no flat spots in carburation. The steering was light and precise (more so than the standard edition), the shift through the four gears solid and quiet (you don't necessarily have to use low), the clutch firm but soft (though it still has that dreadfully long stroke characteristic of Jaguars). . . .
>
> 'The steering is, oddly enough, easier than standard, but with less self-centering action. The front shocks and torsion bar springs have been beefed up slightly, so there is less roll and the front wheels seem to adhere a good deal better under really high-speed cornering. None of this affects the ride adversely —if anything, the M type seems to ride better.'

Auto Sport were well aware of the reputation of the earlier roadsters for brake fade and considered that the new wire-wheeled model was much better. 'There was never any indication of fade despite some fifteen minutes of continuous hard use on a fast-dropping mountain grade,' they were happy to report. Performance figures were

almost identical to those recorded by *The Autocar*.

Road and Track, who tested a nearly-new XK 120M fixed-head coupé at about the same time made similar points to those of *The Autocar* and *Auto Sport* staffs and emphasized the appeal of the fixed-head coupé for women. 'They seem the less able of the two sexes to withstand the appeal of the British hardtop', said *Road and Track*. Later they reported that 'a feminine passenger applied lipstick without a trace of smear' while the car was in motion—a 'difficult operation in a soft-sprung vehicle'. Ah well, a man may think only of himself when buying a sports car, but sooner or later he will want to share it with a woman.

Soon after the driver and his mate could have the best of both worlds, an XK 120 drop-head coupé as tested by Bolster in May 1954.

'With the top down, this model resembles the well-known open sports, except for the neatly folded hood under its closely fitting envelope. In closed form it is, in my opinion, the best-looking Jaguar that has yet been made', the outspoken Bolster informed his dedicated following in *Autosport*. 'The head is padded and lined, and the operating mechanism is completely concealed. Compared with the open car, the whole interior is more luxuriously appointed, and the walnut dashboard, with large round instruments, is a joy to behold. I must confess that the metal and plastic dashboard of the average modern car, with its dials of various tortured and non-functional shapes, is something that always saddens me. I am glad that Britain's best manufacturers still scorn this jukebox fashion.'

He considered that some of the controls

'would benefit from a little re-positioning. The steering wheel is adjustable for length of column, but is, I thought, too close to the legs if a heavy overcoat be worn. The foot pedals, too, might be adjusted to give easier "heel and toe" for simultaneous braking and changing down. As, however, these trifling alterations could easily be made to suit the individual owner, this is not a serious criticism.

'The seats are extremely comfortable, there is excellent forward vision, and the beautifully made body is free from objectionable wind noise at even the highest speed. The rear quarters are somewhat blind, as is unavoidably the case with all convertible bodies, and the back window is smaller than that of a hardtop. . . .

'This is one of the finest high-speed touring cars that has ever been made.'

Praise indeed from the scourge of the motor manufacturers, although his description of the rear quarters of the drop-head coupé as being somewhat blind must have ranked as the understatement of the year.

Bolster made the drop-head perform as probably nobody had before. Despite a 160 bhp engine and 0.5 cwt weight penalty, he held *The Autocar*'s fixed-head 180 bhp figures up to 80 mph and came within 0.5 mph of 120. Needless to say, the fuel consumption shot up to 14.5 mpg from 16.2 by *The Autocar*, because of the hammering, but even then Bolster deemed his disc-wheeled car's brakes to be adequate. Incredibly, he did all this in the midst of a thunderstorm on the Silverstone Club circuit, suggesting only that the handling could have been improved by the Special

opposite Who could resist testing a D type?

right and opposite The 140 fixed-head with all the options tested by *The Motor* and *Autosport*.

Equipment package, but quickly pointing out that the hood let in no water. Jaguar were getting everything right.

Throughout the years from 1952, the lives of motoring scribes were punctuated by periods of wild excitement as they were given racing Jaguars to test on the road. The first of these epics involved a 'production' C type loaned to *The Motor* in October 1952. Needless to say, with a maximum speed of 144 mph, it was the fastest car they had tested. This redoubtable beast weighed 24 cwt all up, carrying no less than 40 gallons of petrol in its tail, yet managed 0–60 in 8 seconds, 100 in 20, and the standing quarter-mile in 16 seconds. Amazingly enough it could still produce 16 mpg on average despite additional tests such as climbing a 1 in 10 hill at 100 mph!

The Motor crew had been somewhat apprehensive when approaching the car for the first time for their full Continental test.

'The problem of luggage stowage at first appeared to be an insurmountable one. The forty-gallon petrol tank occupies the whole of the tail, and the two cockpit seats have no appreciable space behind them, but the body sides which constitute the driver's door and the passenger's elbow room proved so commodious that all the impedimenta of a prolonged trans-Continental journey could be housed therein leaving additional room for a quantity of waterproof clothing rendered

necessary by the absence of hood and normal windscreen. . . .

'Bearing in mind the necessity for maximum possible performance from such a car, the amenities are attractive and well-planned. The driver and passenger sit well inside the Jaguar and despite pouring rain very little road dirt penetrates even when the car is driven fast. . . .

'Let there be no mistake. The Jaguar 120C justifies absolutely the overworked term of thoroughbred. A stranger taking over the car for the first time at the height of a Brussels rush hour finds a docile and tractable machine completely without temperament, ready to trickle through the traffic and proceed along slippery paving and wet tramlines with most of the silence and comfort of the modern touring car. . . .

'The highest praise must be given to the steering characteristics of the Jaguar. This rack and pinion mechanism is not only light and responsive, but sufficiently high-geared for the driver to change direction more by wrist action rather than arm movement. Additionally, the car must be one of the truest "straight-line" runners the world has yet seen.'

Obviously *The Motor* considered their C type to be a fabulous road car, but perhaps wisely they refrained from exploring the full extent of its handling capabili-

A novel angle on the 140 drop-head.

ties on the road. Perilous though it might have been, the C type did have some safety devices.

'A very desirable attachment to the car under test was an additional switch on the right-hand side of the body which brought into action, until reset, the horns of the car, thus leaving the driver free to deal with other matters when over-taking at very high speeds. The switch is supplemented by a normal horn button placed so that either the driver or the passenger can reach it quickly and on the left-hand side of the scuttle there is a group of separate lighting switches. . . .

'Both bucket seats look alike but are somewhat different in construction. That of the driver is exceptionally luxurious and although a little narrow across the hips, gives excellent support in the right places and is high enough from the floor of the car to overcome the unpleasing impression of sitting with legs stretched straight out in front. The passenger seat covers a large tool box wherein lies all the necessary equipment for wheel changing and other deeds, but this makes the cushion very shallow and considerably less comfortable than the driver's version. The passenger also sits a little higher than the driver and so needs goggles at any speed in excess of 50 mph. It is noteworthy that the driver can achieve double this figure without having to protect his eyes in this manner.'

Then *The Motor* went on to praise the C type's excellent fade-free brakes, and once again emphasized the quality of its road holding, in strange contrast to Bolster's memory. *The Motor* rated their C type test as a 'great and memorable experience', although perhaps they were on the verge of something when they said that 'beyond 130 mph, the car does tend to feel a little light, but a curious sense of becoming faintly airborne is offset by no loss whatsoever in directional control.'

John Bond was quite happy with his drive in Masten Gregory's C type for *Road and Track* in August 1953. Their car, which had just won the Golden Gate road race was fitted with a 3.92 axle ratio which gave it 'acceleration figures almost beyond belief', said Bond. Needless to say, they were the best recorded by the august American journal, with 0–60 in 6.6 seconds, 0–100 in 16.8 and the standing quarter-mile in 15.15. Obviously the low gearing helped make the car faster off the mark than *The Motor*'s car, and it seems likely that the British car also had a weight penalty from extra petrol and equipment.

Top speed could only be estimated at 141 mph with a more normal ratio, although Gregory asserted that he had seen 6600 rpm in one race—something like 150 mph on a 3.31 axle. As for the handling *Road and Track* did not have a chance to explore it beyond 100 mph, so the mystery remained.

Next year, in November 1954, Maxwell Boyd of *Autosport* was one of the first journalists to have a drive in a D type, although only a short one at the Guild of Motoring Writers' test day. The car taken down to Goodwood for the tests was OKV 3, which had been driven by Wharton and Whitehead in long-distance racing and is still campaigned in historic racing today. Said Boyd:

'It will be a long time before I forget the thrill of settling down in the cockpit, behind the severely practical wood-rimmed steering wheel and pressing the starter button. The whole car quivered as the engine roared into life, and at such

Show time for the 140 fixed-head.

a moment who of us would not wish he was a Moss or a Hamilton and be able to drive such a car for hours on end?

'And you need hours on end to learn how to get the best from a D type, of course. All I had was three laps, the shortest three laps I can remember. But if ever a car inspired confidence on short acquaintance, this was it. The steering, accurate to a degree, and oh, so positive; the gearbox, with its lever exactly where the hand felt for it, just four short, sharp, satisfying snicks from bottom to top, and the brakes . . . well, all journalists know they must be careful scattering superlatives without due regard, but the D type's servo-assisted disc brakes have a stopping power with the lightest of pedal pressures that simply defies description or comparison . . . and then, of course, there is the engine, simply bursting with b.h.p. to such an extent that getting away to a clean start, via the use of the rather vicious, but very necessary multi-plate clutch, is something to be practised and learned.

'Perhaps the power of the D type's engine and the superlative efficiency of its brakes is best illustrated by the fact that on our last lap we recorded 4600 rpm in top on Lavant Straight, before braking for Woodcote, and rounding the corner in a sage and orderly fashion. . . .

'Of the roadholding it can be said that not once did this even begin to let me down, although I was not sufficiently used to the car to attempt any Moss-style cornering. However, even on such short acquaintance I could imagine that a racing driver might well have a case in pleading for some sort of independent rear suspension so that cornering might be faster, and inherently safer, at very high speeds.'

Short though Boyd's test was, it was one of the best, and his point about the rear suspension was to be proved true in years to come. Boyd's colleague, Bolster, did not mind the back suspension when he tried out OKV 3's sister car, OKV 1, a couple of months later. Bolster reported:

'The rear end skittishness of the C type has been eliminated, and once one is out of bottom gear, wheelspin is no longer a problem. The acceleration is deceptive, because it is just one smooth rush.

'As 120 mph is there for the asking on any short straight, there is work for the brakes to do. The famous disc brakes are immensely powerful, and, of course, they are more than adequate for the hardest of driving. What is more important, though, is that that they are entirely progressive, and one feels at home with them immediately . . .

'The steering of the D type is light and accurate, nor is one kept so busy at the wheel as in the case of the C type. It feels a much smaller and lighter car than its predecessor, as indeed it is; and the shape gives the driver something to aim.'

Bolster left the car thanking Duncan Hamilton for letting him try it and bitterly regretting there was not time for a full test.

However, Bond talked a Californian racing driver called Pearce Woods into

An XK prototype roadster showing the fold-through luggage compartment. Production cars had matting in the boot instead of the rubber strips shown here.

There was nothing in the same league as the Lister–Jaguar MVE 303, tested by Bolster.

The Series Two Cooper-Jaguar.

providing performance figures on the road with his 'production' D type in May 1956. Like Boyd, they found the clutch difficult for consistent starts, recording a variety of times. From 0 to 60 mph averaged out at 4.7 seconds with a best of 4.2; 0–100 at 12 seconds and the standing quarter-mile was covered in 13.7 seconds, with a best of 13.5. Top speed was no less than 162.16 mph with an unaccompanied driver, and 155.17 mph with Bond braving the slipstream! 'The wind blast was terrific but I was so busy concentrating on the tach (it hit 6600 rpm) and on catching an accurate time that I scarcely noticed the road or the flying telegraph poles', said Bond, who nevertheless declined a second run.

Road and Track's American rivals on *Sports Cars Illustrated* were stung into action by this report and managed to borrow Jerry Austin and his D type for a much longer test in August 1956. Russ Kelley of *SCI* said:

'The delivery of the horsepower is fantastic. The D has lead the pack into the first corner from the start more often than any other car on the coast. In southern California there is perhaps as representative a collection of going cars as in any place in the world, but the only sports car here that can out-accelerate the D is a 4.9 Ferrari.

'How about keeping the D in tune? Jerry Austin, the only driver to carry the checker in the D on the coast and who made this car available to *SCI* for the driver's report has never had to do so much as change the distributor points. . . .

'Is the car temperamental? This word has become almost synonymous with racing sports cars, but it certainly doesn't apply to the D. One West Coast owner bought his D in Pennsylvania and drove it to LA and has consistently raced it since.

'So far the D sounds like the ideal private owner racing car, but what about the handling? Obviously, this is the $10,000 question.'

Kelley chose the 2.4-mile Willow Springs course near Lancaster, California, to try to find out why the D type had won only one race despite being so fast. Austin did not know whether to blame himself or the car:

'You should see a Ferrari Monza go through the corners from where I do. It slips by me so easily on the inside it isn't even funny. Are the Ferraris that much better? Or is it the difference in drivers? I certainly wish I knew.'

So Kelley had a try after Austin had warmed up with a lap of less than 1 minute 50 seconds.

'The first corner off the pit straight is a left hander taken in third in the D', said Kelley. 'It is so dependent on the driver's judgment in braking from the straight and on getting just the right approach that it would be grossly unfair to judge the D's character here. This corner can be deceptively narrow when you're in a hurry and you tend to teeter delicately along the edge repeating "oops, oops, oops" to yourself.

'Turn two is of a constant radius; it is extremely long and comes up rapidly after the first. Since the car is still accelerating in third, it's only a question of lifting your foot and going in; no braking is necessary. Its combination of length and radius make it a favourite if everything goes nicely, but if you get slightly out of shape at over 90, it seems to go on for an awfully long time. With the D here maximum road speed is in the neighbourhood of 90 to 100 mph and it lacks something of being comfortable; the car refuses to retain its attitude in relation to the corner as chosen by the driver. You must constantly correct the car's tendency to straighten out. The corner's length and the fact that it is uphill cause the car to lose momentum rapidly. The application of more power to compensate for this makes necessary more rapid corrections and loss of responsiveness in the steering.

'The third corner is to the left and steeply uphill. Second gear is used here and it is perhaps the slowest corner on the course. Turn three can all too easily start a chain of approach problems because turn four follows immediately, dipping sharply downhill and leading directly into a series of right-left-right bends that constitute the slow section of the course. All this section is negotiated in seconds in a fast car. In turn three the D again attempts to straighten itself out and pushes its front wheels to the outside, leaving you with a poor approach to turn four. Obviously, there is only one thing to do and that is to slow down to make sure that your exit from this right-hander leaves you in position to deal with the right-left-right S further down the hill. If you decide not to lift your foot, your attitude to each corner would only get progressively worse, until desperate measures would have to be taken to avoid spinning out on the left hand portion of the S.

'After the S-bend comes a right-hand jog on a slight rise and then a short straight to the last two corners on the course. These last corners could almost be called one, except for a slight, almost straight relief in radius before entering the last bend on to the main straight. This last section is very fast and the short relief in radius gives you a chance to decide how bad you want to look coming into the main straight. If you decide you don't care, and don't lift your foot a little, the decreasing radius is not so great that you won't get a glimpse of the main straight, but it might be discouragingly far to the right and heading in quite a different direction than you thought it should.

'Once out of the tight corners and into this section of the course, the character of the D changes completely. This Dr Jekyll–Mr Hyde transformation comes with a real thrill. The slightly rising approach to the right-hand job after the S-bends is full-bore in second. The change into third comes breathtakingly with the crest of the rise and the turn. The fact that your confidence returns on the headlong full-bore plunge in third and fourth gears towards the sweeping corners is a real tribute to this car.

'Speeds up to 140 mph were indicated here on entering the first part of these bends and although the car has a light feel that some drivers might find objectionable, it is beautifully manageable. Austin summed it up nicely with the statement: "It's your nerve that limits you here, not the car." Except for the handling in the tight corners, it's almost unbelievable that this car can be bought over the counter.'

Unbelievable . . . that's the word Kelley's countryman, Bond, used to describe his D type's acceleration, and, understeer or not, Kelley was adamant that this D 'just might be the greatest thing since bottled beer'.

John Bentley, of the American magazine *Sports Illustrated* was almost as enthusiastic about his test of an XK 140MC roadster in April 1955. It was the fastest standard XK yet tested with a 0–60 time of 8.5 seconds against the 10 seconds of *The Autocar*'s special equipment fixed-head XK 120 in 1952. The XK 140 MC had the same options as *The Autocar*'s machine, plus, of course, a C type head. Bentley would have liked the overdrive soon to be fitted as an option and commented favourably on the steering. 'It was light, positive and accurate', he said, 'and what's more the decreased angle of the universal joint on the column provides better vision over the top of the wheel. It also affords two inches more space between the bottom of the rim and the seat.' He also appreciated the redesigned cooling system: 'Gone is the annoying tendency to overheat in traffic which once plagued XK owners', he said, much to the relief of export customers planning to buy the new Jaguar.

He still managed to make the brakes fade, though, despite the wire wheels and recommended the optional Alfin cast iron lined alloy finned, drums, much beloved by the racing fraternity of the day. He also accused Jaguar of 'gooking-up' the styling, but wound up by saying:

'The debits against the XK 140MC are insignificant besides its credits. It is a wondrous machine—docile, fast, quiet, flexible, comfortable and easy to drive. It has almost everything the enthusiast could wish for and it has it at a price that makes the Jaguar one of the best sports car dollar values on the market.'

Road and Track were full of wholehearted praise for their XK 140C two months later. They said it was Coventry's finest formula and proceeded to compare it with the XK 120 which they had held to be the best in its field for six years:

'The 1955 car seems easier to drive in traffic and there is more leg room. The shift lever seems "freer" but the leftward bias of the pedals feels awkward, at least for a few miles. The engine is quieter and smoother than before with one exception. Under full throttle there is perhaps a shade of roughness as a result of the vastly increased horsepower....

'As exhilarating as it is to drive a car such as this in traffic, only on the open road does it really begin to come to life. The new rack and pinion steering is without fault ... and it is one of the easiest and safest automobiles to drive being built today.'

Obviously the rack and stiffer springs were much appreciated.

Road and Track returned similar acceleration times to *Sports Illustrated* with a standing quarter mile in 16.6 seconds, nearly two seconds faster than the XK 120 roadster. Top speed was 121 mph, although *Road and Track* estimated that it could have reached 125 mph with more running in:

'With performance per dollar excelled by no other car, the nicer details of finish and fittings on the XK roadster come as a pleasant bonus. The quality of finish is immediately apparent on the outside, but a look under the hood shows attention to detail that is in marked contrast to that found under a domestic product.... The rearranged and larger luggage compartment is a very worthwhile improvement and most Americans will accept the larger and more massive bumpers as a necessary evil, for self-defense. In our opinion the "standard of the world" has been, and still is, the Jaguar—in the sports car category.'

Praise indeed from a magazine that was fast becoming the American sports car lovers' bible.

No British magazine tested the rare right hand drive roadster, but *Autosport* and *The Autocar* managed a crack at a fixed-head XK 140 with all the options: wire wheels, overdrive and C type head. John Bolster was most impressed with this car, registered RHP 576. He started off by wondering if it was possible to improve on the XK 120 and went on to say:

'Now that I have driven the XK 140, I can state categorically that it is a great improvement in every respect....

'On taking one's seat, it is at once obvious that the driving position is far better than that of the previous model. The accelerator and brake are arranged for "heel and toe" and the clutch pedal has a space on its left to permit the foot to be rested. The steering column is adjustable and there is more leg room than before for a tall driver. The windows are exceptionally deep, which avoids the claustrophobia that coupés often give, but their curved shape disguises the area of glass.

'Above all, the body is exactly the right size. It feels a narrow car to drive,

All-enveloping HWM–Jaguar, pictured at Shelsley Walsh hill climb in August 1956.

and yet there is enough width for two hefty individuals in heavy overcoats. The rear seats are for children or for adults on short journeys; they are very handy for occasional use.'

He found it easy to induce wheelspin, but could not make the clutch slip. RHP 576 had the 4.09:1 axle ratio that went with its overdrive, and Bolster said:

'This adds immensely to the pleasure of driving, for the top gear acceleration is really brilliant, and the flexibility notably improved. . . . The sheer performance of the car is immense. However, that is only half the story. The new steering utterly transforms the handling, and the suspension has also been revised. The XK 140 is, in fact, quite firmly sprung, and all the "float" of the 120 has gone. There is a wonderful feeling of complete control, and this is one of these very rare cars that seems to help the over-impetuous driver out of his difficulties. The rack and pinion steering gives beautifully precise control, and one can fling the 26 cwt car around like a $1\frac{1}{2}$-litre machine.'

Surprisingly, the hard-driving Bolster did not manage to fade the brakes.

'Perhaps the greatest improvement of all is in the braking department', said the former Grand Prix driver. 'With the new racing linings, it is possible really to drive on the brakes without inducing fade. Repeated applications from two miles a minute produce a choice scent of hot linings, but this has no detrimental effect, nor is adjustment required after quite a useful milage.'

Bolster wound the XK 140 special equipment model up to 121.6 mph in the space available (although on other occasions he saw 135 mph on the speedometer) with a 0–60 time of 10 seconds and a standing quarter-mile in 16.8 seconds. His fuel consumption figures worked out at 17.5 mpg, somewhat heavier than the often-seen 20 mpg for an XK 120, but better than the 14.5 mpg he recorded with his equally hard-driven XK 120 drop-head coupé. *The Autocar* achieved no less than 21.7 mpg from the same car a month later, although their acceleration figures were not quite so good. They obviously found a longer road than Bolster for their high speed tests, recording no less than 129.5 mph! A run in the opposite direction on a Continental motorway was only fractionally slower, so conditions must have been ideal and a combination of the two sets of figures is probably a true reflection of an XK 140's ultimate performance. Fuel consumption, obviously, varied with the driver and conditions.

The Autocar shared Bolster's enthusiasm for RHP 576, but thought that a brake servo would have been a worthwhile fitting. To sum up, they said:

'The number of cars capable of reaching 100 mph has increased in the past few years. There are very few which can reach this figure in under 30 seconds, as the XK 140 does with ease. More important, it can be held in overdrive to become a comfortable cruising speed with very low throttle openings and to record a fuel consumption of near enough 22 mpg. That these figures can be achieved in a car whose comfort and safety are superlative implies the highest praise for the team responsible for its creation. When these qualities are related to its price, there is no other car which can approach it in the high performance sphere, and it is a fine advertisement for the British automobile industry.'

So were the four main species of Jaguar Special, the HWM, Tojeiro, Cooper and Lister. They were among the last of the traditional racing sports cars which could be driven on the road, and Bolster completed a remarkable series of tests of these vehicles *on the road* between 1955 and 1957. The first of these unique tests, of the HWM-Jaguar, in April 1955, yielded some startling performance figures. Clad in deerstalker, tweed jacket and goggles, the fearless Bolster hit 145.1 mph in this first road test with a standing quarter mile in 15 seconds! The actual machine was the original HWM 1 raced by George Abecassis, that had been developed from one of the tiny firm's Formula Two single seater chassis. It had transverse leaf spring front suspension with torsion bars at the back, and weighed a good deal more than later HWM-Jaguars. One of the chief benefits of this early model was the quick-change Indianapolis rear axle ratio. This featured spur gears which could be readily slid off the final drive to change the ratio in a matter of minutes. Bolster put this device to good effect, using a 4.11:1 ratio for his acceleration tests and a 3.48 version for top speed!

'Using the relatively low ratio, the liveliness of the car is difficult to put into words', said Bolster. 'One can positively fly up hills in top gear, and the gear lever need seldom be used. When drifting along on a whiff of throttle at 100 mph, a touch of the pedal gives kick-in-the-back acceleration. Like all Jaguar engines, this one is so smooth that the relatively high revs involved are not readily apparent.

'The standing quarter-mile figure of 15 seconds is the best I have ever recorded. It speaks volumes for the de Dion rear end, which ensures that the wheels get a real grip on the road.'

With the substitution of the 3.48 rear end, the machine, Bolster continued,

'became less flexible, though it was still marvellous to drive on the road. Completely equipped, and with a full-width screen in place, I recorded a mean timed speed of 145.1 mph on this gear. Once again, this was the highest speed yet achieved in an *Autosport* road test.

'The straight-cut gears emit a high-pitched whine, but this has the same exhilarating quality as the song of a blower, and takes one back to the Alfas and Bugs of one's youth.'

The HWM was a good deal more comfortable than the vintage Alfa Romeos and Bugattis, although the ride was 'fairly firm'; and there was 'no appreciable roll'. The heavy rack and pinion steering inspired confidence; 'the car can be driven with one hand at nearly 150 mph and curves may be entered at this sort of velocity without drama.' The HWM had considerable understeer, but plenty of power to counteract it. And 'perhaps the extreme steadiness at very high speeds is the most impressive feature of all', said Bolster. The 'huge' Girling drum brakes were also brutally effective and the overall result after several days' motoring in the HWM was that 'I was with difficulty restrained from writing this report in poetry!'

Eighteen months later Bolster tested his second Jaguar special, the Tojeiro, at 15.5 cwt, 1.5 cwt lighter than the HWM. It also had more power from a full D type engine instead of the modified C type unit fitted to the HWM. Apart from that, the Tojeiro shared many of the HWM's features, including a tubular chassis and de Dion rear suspension. But it had a limited slip differential and put its power down even more effectively to record a 0–60 time of 5.4 seconds; standing quarter-mile in 13.6 seconds, and no less than 152.5 mph flat out. You could not change the rear axle anything like so quickly as that on the HWM, though, and 'I do not doubt that something like 170 mph would be available with a "Le Mans cog" in the final

The XK SS as tested by *Road and Track*.

drive', said Bolster. However the rear suspension and disc brake operation were still in need of development and Bolster found that the cornering and stopping powers were not up to the standard of the acceleration. Nevertheless, he had a wonderful week in the car. 'Some of my passengers became highly emotional when I first pressed that little pedal on the right, for really such acceleration is a somewhat startling experience', said Bolster.

Nine months later, he had a fully-developed car—a mark two version of the space-frame Cooper–Jaguar: the biggest and last of the front-engined cars to emerge from John Cooper's Surbiton workshops. 'What a touring car this is!' said Bolster of Michael Head's successful dual purpose road and racing machine.

'The acceleration bears no relationship to any normal experience, and a touch of third speed caused the seat back to give one a real kick in the spine as one rockets past the 100 mph mark. Once under way, the independent suspension permits the full power to be used without a trace of wheelspin. The Cooper–Jaguar is, however, a very difficult car to take cleanly off the mark.

'This is because there is a normal differential instead of one of the limited slip variety. Thus, unless the two wheels are on a road surface of completely uniform grip, one tyre may start to spin and the getaway is ruined. It is tricky to choose between too much wheelspin on the one hand, and two few revs for the Webers to pick up cleanly on the other. I covered a standing quarter-mile in 14.8 seconds, but excellent though that time is, I could certainly beat it with a little more practice, I feel.'

Maximum speed was dependent on gear ratio, of course, and with a short circuit ratio fitted, the Head car showed 136.3 mph 'but obviously well over 150 mph could be achieved with a higher "cog"', said Bolster.

He had only a couple of months to wait for his next (and most fantastic) experience: the Lister–Jaguar test. Bolster never got the really high cog he wanted for a projected 200 mph test, but he had no trouble clearing 140 mph on a circuit racing ratio that gave an extraordinary 0–60 time of 4.6 seconds and standing quarter-mile in 13.2 seconds. As the HWM and Tojeiro had been before it, the Lister was clearly the fastest car *Autosport* had tested on the road. What's more, it was easier to drive than the Cooper!

'On moving off, one is at once impressed with the comparative smoothness of the clutch, which one does not normally expect from a three-plate racing assembly', said Bolster. 'First speed is much higher than usual, for it is intended to be used on sharp corners, and its engagement is consequently synchronised. Nevertheless, it gives a most stirring getaway, and the machine runs remarkably straight without correction if too much wheelspin is accidentally induced.'

The traction was so good that Bolster 'habitually used full throttle on all four gears on every sort of road surface'. He was equally enthusiastic about the road-holding: 'There is no roll, the car simply remaining level and answering perfectly to its light and accurate steering.' He found it a 'sheer delight' as a road car with

'stupendous acceleration that rendered it extremely safe. Overtaking can be done so rapidly, and the left hand side of the road can be regained very quickly indeed. . . .

'Archie Scott-Brown has already proved that the Lister–Jaguar is Britain's fastest sports-racing car. I have now proved that it is an admirable sports-touring car, and that all its racing virtues make it a better and safer machine. Boy! What a week-end!'

The fastest of the production XKs, the 150S 3.8-litre, as tested by Bolster.

The Autocar was one of the few magazines lucky enough to test an XK SS, and was as enthusiastic as Bolster had been about the Lister. *The Autocar* found the cockpit very small, but said: 'It is surprising how small an enthusiast can make himself when offered a ride in a car like this Jaguar!' They found the performance 'highly impressive' despite a slipping clutch and managed a standing quarter mile in 14.3 seconds with a top speed on its 3.54:1 axle ratio estimated at 144 mph.

'The car's natural gait for steady driving is 20 to 30 mph higher than for fast cruising in a less ambitious sports car. Driving in comfort and without haste, 100 to 120 mph showed on the speedometer on each clear straight, and yet the braking power was such that the car nosed into successive bends at 60 to 70 mph without apparent braking effort after the bursts of speed. Just as impressive as the breathtaking acceleration is this smooth power of the brakes.'

However *The Autocar* warned that the 'steering is very light and high geared, so that the tendency of the inexperienced is to be clumsy with it . . . a grip lightly technique is required, to give the requisite precise guidance without being heavy handed. . . .

'The wind noise and the general effects of the engine and exhaust are not nearly so fierce as one might imagine or as they are remembered from earlier experience with the C type, which had only a racing screen. When the XK SS gets really wound up, the occupants feel even more a part of the car, for a warm blanket of air wraps the cockpit and the cold slipstream rushes around the shapely contours, avoiding the interior like a static charge. . . .

'It is difficult not to run out of superlatives when describing such a car. . . . Outstanding memories include the tremendous push in the back when accelerating hard; other traffic appears ahead, is overtaken and fades away in the mirror as if projected in the opposite direction. Also, the steering and roadholding qualities are such that they tend to take care of the shortcomings of a driver new to the car.'

For their test *Road and Track* pounced on their XK SS with all the speed of a Big Cat. It was a new model just delivered to one Robert Stonedale of Houston, Texas—the first in America. They were much impressed by the performance: 0–60 in 5.2 seconds (wheelspin allowing), and an estimated 149 mph flat out. But they were unimpressed by its potential as a dual purpose machine (drive to the office all week, race all weekend). They found the clutch too heavy for traffic driving, four inches too far away, and considered there was something like a foot too little leg room. The far-too-noisy side exhaust also made the toeboards unbearably hot and the racing generator proved impractical for road use. On the credit side, the brakes were 'extremely impressive', as was the thrill of driving the car on the open road. 'Even though one is unfamiliar with the car, 100 mph is so effortless that is seems like 50 mph.'

They were equally quick off the mark with their test of an XK 150 fixed-head coupé in November 1957. It was a special equipment model fitted with wire wheels and a 210 bhp engine, and seemed to have had a hard life as the American magazines were of the opinion that it would have been capable of 10 mph faster than it showed:

0–60 in 9.5 seconds, a standing quarter-mile in 17.1 seconds and 121.6 mph top speed. They were unsure about its appearance, considering that it now looked more like a mature mother cat than a lithe young huntress; and it needed a 'customising' job at the back to get rid of the excess chrome plating (surprisingly enough intended to appeal to the Americans!). However, *Road and Track* readily admitted to liking the extra four inches of interior width that went with the change in lines and extra visibility afforded by the new glass. Minor points they considered needed improving included interior door locks, resiting of instruments in front of the driver, door checks and better-placed ash trays.

The Autocar had a much better time with their XK 150 fixed-head. It was a similar special equipment model to that tested by *Road and Track* and was obviously in better tune, recording 125.5 mph flat out with a 0–60 time of 8.5 seconds, and standing start quarter-mile time of 16.9 seconds. Thus, although it was a little slower than the near-130 mph XK 140 it had much better acceleration, despite its weight (nearly 29 cwt). The engine came in for no criticism, but the gearbox was already upsetting the testers: *The Autocar* considered the gap between the lower two ratios to be 'noticeably large', and the synchromesh to be 'scarcely adequate'. The clutch travel was considered to be on the long side and axle wind-up was becoming evident with the dated chassis design and additional power. However the overdrive was worth every penny of its cost' and helped the car achieve more than 18 mpg despite long periods cruising the Continent at 115 mph. The servo brakes 'behaviour was superb'. However the handbrake power 'was not up to the high standard of the footbrakes'. These niggles aside, they considered it to be

'undeniably one of the world's fastest and safest cars. It is quiet and exceptionally refined mechanically, docile and comfortable. . . .

'Suspension is free from roll and pitch, and on smooth roads the ride is comfortable at any speed. . . . On rough roads some feed-back is transmitted through the steering wheel, but not to an unpleasant degree. The first-class steering is positive and reasonably light, with immediate response to the driver's movements; at slow speeds there is little self-centering action. At high speeds, the directional stability adds to the crew's confidence.'

Naturally, *The Autocar* liked the extra room inside the car but found the doors rather irksome. 'On level ground, clearance of the tips of the doors is 9 inches unladen; camber and weight of crew reduce this to only 3 or 4 inches', they reported, complaining at the same time about the lack of interior door locks, pulls and check straps. However, upon due consideration they decided that 'As with most cars, there are a few body details which could be improved, but we do not know of any more outstanding example of value for money.' A familiar Jaguar tale.

Bill Boddy endorsed *The Autocar*'s remarks with his test of an identical 3.4-litre fixed-head coupé in *Motor Sport*, adding that the steering was

'. . . very heavy for parking, lightening up at speed.

'The suspension gives a rather dead ride, but effectively kills road shock, yet is firm enough not to promote excessive roll when cornering fast. However,

Interior of *The Motor*'s 150S fixed-head.

there is a sense of vintage-style flexibility about the chassis and although norm-ally not noticeable, over really rough or ripply surfaces the back axle makes its presence felt, a reminder that the action of the rear wheels is not independent. This may be because half-elliptic springs are employed at the back, not the quarter-elliptic springs and ingenious linkage found on the 2.4 and 3.4-litre Jaguar saloons. The hypercritical may perhaps feel that the Jaguar chassis is not so advanced as the splendid power unit. In general, however, the XK 150 handles splendidly, especially in the hands of big-boned, bowler-hatted Britishers.'

SCI were first off the mark with a test of the XK 150S, appropriately enough a roadster. Their technical editor, Stephen Wilder, headed straight for the Lime Rock race course in August 1958 and reported that the car had 'all the comforts of a fast coupé with the splendid out of doors feeling of a raceworthy roadster.

'Steering is just a shade on the strong side, as befits a car of this size and speed. It is precise and quick, two virtues which go well with the ever astounding power available at the rear wheels. This is one of the few reasonably-priced sports cars in which you can hold a four-wheel drift on sharp turns for any length of time without losing most of your headway. And to utilise this ability, you need the quick steering which the XK provides. The clean response to the throttle helps, too. . . .

'Wheelspin can easily be provoked from a standing start and in these rather sophisticated days, it seems to us that better location of the rigid rear axle would more than justify the expense involved.

'Once under way, the acceleration is really sparkling, as a glance at our chart (showing 0–60 in 9.2 seconds) will show. A standing quarter time of 17.3 seconds is no mean feat for a car that would be just as happy trickling down Main Street.'

Top speed of *SCI*'s XK 150S roadster was disappointing at around 120 mph and it was returned to the workshop to find out why. Wilder estimated the maximum should have been nearer 135 mph, with the top up.

'Speeds and acceleration of this sort deserve the best in braking, and here the S is faultless', he said. 'Our ten fierce stops from sixty were made with ease, the discs being servo-assisted, and though smoke and a strong smell began to stream through the front spokes toward the last, there was never any difficulty in stopping the car.

'There's no doubt about it, the S is intended for the SCCA's Production Sports Car category, where it should polish up Jaguar's glory, now somewhat tarnished from neglect.'

Road and Track's XK 150S roadster, tested a month later, was much faster with a calculated top speed of 136 mph, 0–60 in 7.3 seconds and standing quarter-mile in 15.1 seconds. 'In our opinion, the 150S model makes a lot more sense than the SS', said *Road and Track*.

'It can sell at a profit for much less money, it is a practical and genuine dual-purpose machine and it will make a lot more friends for sports cars than the SS ever could.

'Externally the 150 is still unmistakably an XK, but the general lines and appearance have been softened and refined. More important, perhaps, the seating position has been tremendously improved, the cockpit is roomier, controls are easier to operate and visibility is better. . . .

'The seat adjustment has such a remarkable range that a six-footer cannot depress the clutch pedal when it is all the way back, and the extra cockpit width inherited from the previous 150 coupés makes it feasible to place a small child comfortably on the padded leather driveshaft tunnel, between driver and passenger. A very small open glove box in front of the driver is useless because everything except used chewing gum falls or blows out and the opposite box, with locking lid, is very little larger. There are, of course, door pockets, and a rear trunk which will hold one medium-sized suitcase.

'The new wind-up windows make the term "roadster" rather incongruous, but they are certainly an improvement over the best of side curtains. The top, at last, has truly graceful lines and it has been carefully engineered to seal properly against water entry, yet to fold easily and compactly behind the seats.

'In the final, critical analysis the new Jaguar 150 and 150S roadsters have a few faults, but among all the automotive connoisseurs we know the Jaguar still rates as the best all-round value in the quality dual-purpose sports car category.'

Next month Wilder was back with apologies for the lethargic 150S he had tested earlier and a vivid description of how to drive one in a race. It was a near-standard version raced by Bob Grossman with modifications confined to a different anti-roll bar and Koni shock absorbers. Wilder was very enthusiastic about the XK 150S's standard limited slip differential.

'The Powr-Lok is available on all current Jaguars as an extra-cost option', he said. 'We recommend it without reservation to any Jaguar purchaser. Though it's not easy to explain how it works, it does. Besides, it's cheap, unlike the German ZF device. Equipped with it, no matter how impossible an angle a car may assume (and as racegoers will testify, XK 150s corner at outlandish ones), the driver can still steer the car with a combination of steering wheel and throttle movement. Though they don't look like it, they feel very stable to the driver. So much so that we are now re-evaluating some old ideas. One was that maximum cornering power (measured in units of g) is a goal to be pursued at all costs. Costs of expense and comfort, yes, but at the cost of controllability, we must now say, no. Surely rational control right up to and past the peak of adhesion is well worth a slight reduction in the latter.

'Since this control is exercised through both the steering wheel and the throttle (or alternatively, the brake pedal), each of these must work in such a way that the driver is constantly in touch with what goes on. In the 150S, this is achieved basically through three highly developed systems: the drive train, the steering and the brakes.'

Needless to say, they all got top marks from Wilder.

The redoubtable Bolster was the first British journalist to road test an XK 150S, a 3.4-litre fixed-head registered XDU 984. He told his avid audience in *Autosport* in June 1959 that it was at once obvious that it had a very powerful engine.

'Even if top gear only is used, the car is sensationally lively, and one can over-take other drivers who are really trying, with contemptuous ease.

'Perhaps the XK 150S is at its best when driven in this way. The sheer sensual pleasure of feeling the big machine respond to the throttle is one of motoring's most delightful experiences. . . .

'If the XK 150S is regarded as an ultra-high speed touring car, it can be said to approach perfection. If it is handled fiercely, as a sports car, however, it is perhaps open to some criticism. For the man who likes to make quick, clean changes without a sound at all times, more powerful synchromesh would be a worthwhile improvement.

'The acceleration figures (similar to those recorded by *Road and Track* with a 132.2 mph maximum speed) are, of course, stupendous, and were no doubt aided by the optional limited slip differential. Even so, rear axle tramp can be induced if the full power is applied on bottom gear, and on second and

Dashboard of *The Motor*'s road test
150S fixed-head.

third speeds too if the road is wet. Yet, the car is curiously easy to control on
wet roads. The entirely conventional chassis may not have the extreme cornering power of some more radical designs, but it scores by giving the driver
plenty of warning that the limit is being approached. For this reason the
XK 150S is a particularly safe sports car, and one that may be handled with
confidence by any competent fast driver.'

Bolster found that the heavy and unresponsive steering was much improved
by higher tyre pressures, 45 psi at the back and 40 at the front. With racing tyres, he
considered a maximum of more than 135 mph practical.

Boddy used the same 3.4-litre car for a trip to Scotland to cover the RAC Rally
and reported in *Motor Sport* in January 1960 that 'on the motorway the Jaguar
settled for 120 mph on its mildly optimistic speedometer, hardly fell below 100 mph,

and went to 5000 rpm in overdrive top gear, or some 128 mph.' The only thing that suffered on this hard-worked car was an exhaust gasket, quickly repaired in Blackpool, Jaguar's ancestral home. 'The beauty of driving this fine car is that it is always well within itself', said Boddy. 'The steering is perhaps on the spongy side, but it's quick and responsive, while roadholding is eminently satisfactory, providing the necessary discretion is used with the throttle out of bends on slippery roads.' Soon after, on the way home, a rear spline gave trouble, a legacy of frequent flat-out acceleration tests, but a change to the spare wheel improved this and the car was returned 'with real reluctance' after 1750 miles of hard days and nights.

The minor troubles with XDU 984 were a natural result of the numerous road tests it survived. In the hands of *The Motor* it returned comparable performance figures to the C type they tested in 1952 with even better mid-range acceleration, thanks to its greater torque. They were prompted to point out that 'this everyday motor car . . . with complete closed car comfort and amenities' was within 11 mph of the top speed of the stark, open, racing sports car and 'If the truth of the time-worn tag about the racing car of today being the touring car of tomorrow ever needed proving, these two tests supply all the evidence necessary.'

Yet another test of XDU 984 was carried out by *The Autocar* early in 1960, with 136 mph flat out, but slightly slower acceleration times reflecting either the car's hard life or a more sympathetic tester. 'This is a driver's car in all respects', they said, 'yet the engine's exceptional flexibility makes it also a splendid ladies' town carriage. Regard the performance data, which, in stark printing ink, fail miserably to convey the sheer thrill of the real thing. When 136 mph was achieved, even the Continental autoroute seemed to have exchanged its curves for corners.'

Those were the days. Even better ones were to come, however, with the advent of the last, and fastest, road-going XK, the 3.8-litre S. It is fitting that the XK's test days should end with the man who introduced this chapter, John Bolster. He had a wonderful time in the only 3.8-litre that appears to have escaped for testing. Its engine 'is in a different world', said Bolster.

'Let's face it, the 3.4-litre Jaguar is a tremendous car, but the 3.8-litre has that extra torque just where it matters most. For example, the acceleration from 100 mph to 120 mph is not noticeably less brisk than that from 80 to 100 mph, and the car continues to surge forward even after the overdrive has been engaged at 115 mph.

'The maximum speed of 136.3 mph was timed with all equipment in place, including fog lamps, radio aerial etc. Obviously, a little cleaning up would have put a genuine 140 mph "in the bag". And in fact that speed may be touched under favourable conditions with the car in normal trim. This is an enormous velocity for a luxury touring car. . . .'

The figures speak for themselves. Maximum speed, 136.3 mph. Speeds in gears, direct top 115 mph; third 92 mph; second 60 mph; first 32 mph. Standing quarter-mile 16 seconds. Acceleration: 0–30 mph 3.4 seconds; 0–50, 6.2; 0–60 7.6; 0–80 12.8; 0–100, 19; 0–110, 22.2; 0–120, 27.8. All that without ruffling the hair of the man who drove her.

V

The Competition Jaguars

JAGUARS, particularly the XK and its variants, have been a constant source of amazement in competition. Since 1949 they have rarely been beaten for speed by anything other than the most specialized sports racers; as a result their competition history is one of the longest and most distinguished of any car. It all started with that great record run by Soapy Sutton in May 1949, ably recorded by Bill Boddy, editor of *Motor Sport*:

'At Earls Court last year the twin o.h.c. XK Jaguar took the show by storm, for this advanced and so attractive sports car was a last minute surprise and one which, by its elegance and potential performance capabilities, represented astonishingly good value at a basic price of £988. It was even rumoured by sceptical persons that the XK was too good to be true and must just be a publicity move, that Jaguar would never put it into series-production, at all events at the original price.

'For some months nothing more was heard of this exciting car, then, on the eve of full-scale production (still at £988) for the export markets, came an invitation to go out to the Jabbeke–Aeltre motor road and see what the car would do when officially timed by the RAC de Belgique. The results were astounding—no other word is adequate. The flying start two-way mile, hood and screen erect, was covered at 126.448 mph; a standard scuttle deflector was substituted for the screen and the speed rose to 132.362 mph for the flying start two-way kilometre and to 132.596 mph for the mile; the best run being a kilometre at 133.388 mph. Standing start kilometre and mile records were also established at 74.168 and 86.434 mph respectively. These are now Class C Belgian national records, formerly held by a Healey.

'For a normal 3442 cc sports car carrying full equipment even to front bumper, rear over-riders and GB letters, and running on Shell pump fuel, to officially exceed a speed of 133 mph is a truly meritorious achievement. A faired undershield was fitted, but this is a standard extra. Moreover, that the car was docile and tractable was demonstrated immediately after the record runs, when Sutton cruised slowly past the depot in the 3.27:1 top gear. The car was then handed over to two privileged daily Press motoring correspondents and it started on the starter and generally behaved impeccably. The only accessory

Soapy Sutton sets the world alight with his 132 mph record run at Jabbeke in May 1949.

which seemed to have had unfair demands made upon it was the 120 mph speedometer—but it remained unruffled! The Jaguar's convincing stability and quiet running had already shown up prominently during the timed runs. . . .

'Sutton was so modest about the whole thing that he was rather neglected during the celebration lunch in Ostend (and to which he drove in the same cream, left-hand drive Jaguar), until the Press took possession of him! It must not be overlooked, however, that his skill counted for much during the standing-start runs and that, stable as the Jaguar was, courage is needed to steer any car along a narrow road at speeds in excess of 130 mph. Aged 53, Sutton will be remembered for his exploits with Lea-Francis cars over twenty years ago and until recently was with Daimler. Today he is a member of the Jaguar Development Division. He was naturally alone in the car, the passenger's seat covered over with the normal tonneau cover, and he wore a white helmet and a BRDC badge on the pocket of his blue overalls.

'Through the initiative of E. W. Rankin, Public Relations Officer to Jaguar Cars Ltd, a party of motoring journalists and daily paper correspondents was flown out from Heathrow to Ostend in a Sabena Dakota, and taken in a Sabena Iso Bloc coach to witness the record attempts, and a party of Continental journalists joined them at the venue. There, in the sunshine, with smiling gendarme and curious Belgian peasants looking on, the RAC de Belgique officials worked efficiently in their Renault time-keepers' van and patrolled the course in a magnificent modern Alfa Romeo, while music and announcements were broadcast from a vast van akin in effect to a mobile cinema organ. Col. Barnes represented the RAC. So history was made, amid a characteristic British display of outward indifference.'

The next great publicity exercise was the BRDC's *Daily Express* meeting at

Johnson wins the XK's first race, the
Daily Express production car event at
Silverstone in August 1949. The near-
side wing is crumpled from a slight
collision with Wise's errant Jowett
Javelin.

Biondetti finishes eighth in the 1950
Mille Miglia, with Johnson's Jaguar in
fifth place.

Silverstone in August when three XK 120s (painted red, white and blue) lined up for a new form of competition: production car racing. The drivers were Leslie Johnson, Peter Walker and Prince Birabongse of Siam. The field consisted of Frazer Nashes, Healey Silverstones, an Allard J2, an old SS 100 Jaguar, Bentleys and assorted saloons. The Jaguars just walked away with it, although Bira had to retire with a burst tyre. Johnson won at 82 mph with Walker second and the world was crying out for the XK 120. It was not surprising, therefore, that nearly every XK 120 made in 1949 and early 1950 was exported; particularly to America and Australia. To help boost sales, Johnson drove an XK 120 in the Sports Car Club of America's Palm Beach races in January 1950, finishing second in his class behind a Ford-engined Duesenberg Indianapolis car, much to the amazement of the locals; soon after he received a works car, JWK 651, in company with Nick Haines; Peter Walker (JWK 977); Clemente Biondetti (JWK 650); Ian Appleyard (NUB 120) and Tommy Wisdom (JWK 988).

These cars, officially private entries, were to spearhead Jaguar's competition programme for 1950: Biondetti did well in the Targa Florio until he had to retire with engine trouble and the twelve-and-a-half hour event was won by Mario and Franco Bornigia in a 2.5-litre prototype Alfa Romeo. The result was far from a disgrace: Alfa were the current leaders in Formula One. Their arch-rivals, Ferrari (with Marzotto driving) won the Mille Miglia with Johnson fifth and Biondetti eighth in a race so rough that it was an achievement to finish.

Meanwhile in America, Erwin Goldschmidt and Robert Reider were leading the XK contingent in SCCA racing, with Tom Cole's Cadillac-Allard and Briggs

Le Mans 1950 ended in clutch failure for Johnson's XK, as close rival Norman Culpan speeds by in his Frazer Nash.

Tommy Wisdom thunders on in the 1951 Silverstone production car race, won by Walker's sister 120.

Cunningham's Ferrari providing much of the opposition. And halfway through the year, the young MG TC racer, Phil Hill, who was to become world champion in 1961, completed a six-month course at Jaguar and returned home with an XK 120 to mop up events in California. Soon after arriving on the West Coast, he became one of the first people to bore out the 3.4-litre block to 3.8-litres in the search for even more power.

At the same time Wisdom was ranging the length and breadth of Europe, gaining a notable third place in the Circuit of Oporto sports car race behind Bonetto's Alfa. Everybody was impressed, *The Motor* commenting that it 'would seem to bear out the maker's claim that their XK is the touring car with racing car performance!' Indeed, the only cars which could beat it were highly-specialized racers that cost a fortune and were made only in very limited numbers. Even the agricultural Allard was refused entry in the Tourist Trophy because they hadn't produced ten of their Cadillac-engined monsters for the British market: and the Ferraris and Alfas were even rarer.

However in 1950 the Allard was allowed to enter Le Mans and annexed the third place vacated by the XK. In fact it was a most encouraging race for the English as the third-placed car was driven by its constructor, Sydney Allard, and Tom Cole (British, although he was based in the USA) and fourth place fell to a Nash-Healey from Warwick, driven by Tony Rolt and Duncan Hamilton. Their consistent efforts did not go unnoticed by Lyons in the Jaguar pit: he hired them later to drive his cars!

Meanwhile, Lyons's son-in-law Appleyard was storming to a second Coupé des Alpes in the tough Alpine Rally with NUB 120; his first award had been gained with a Jaguar SS 100 rebuilt by the factory, in 1946, LNW 100. This was a truly significant success as it showed the XK to be a really versatile all-rounder, especially as two XK 120s finished second and third in the Swiss Grand Prix behind an Alfa Romeo at the same time!

Then came that year's Silverstone production car race with entries so numerous that it was divided into two events, for cars up to and over two litres. Once again it provided Jaguar with a win, in its class, although one of the XK 120 team cars, driven by Peter Whitehead in place of Tazio Nuvolari who was too sick to start, blew oil all over the track to the consternation of other competitors! Nevertheless, Peter Walker was first, Rolt second and Hamilton third in a Healey.

'Now came Britain's great classic, the RAC Tourist Trophy race', reported the emergent magazine *Autosport*. 'The weather did the dirty however, and spoilt things, though nothing, it seemed, could have stopped Stirling Moss's magnificent drive with an XK 120 Jaguar. There were no foreign entries, which was regrettable in that a British victory lost its point. The new Ulster TT was a three-hour event, and as it rained continually, perhaps radio listeners at home that Saturday afternoon were best off. Johnson's white Jaguar led Moss's green one for lap one, but thereafter it was Moss all the way.'

Moss who had been refused a drive by all the big manufacturers in the Silverstone event because of his 'lack of experience' considers this event (in which Tommy Wisdom lent him his car) to have been his big break in motor racing. It was also Jaguar's first post-war long distance victory, Moss having covered a total of 225.45 miles at 75.15 mph in dreadful conditions. In fact, there was more than one reason to celebrate: the day after was Moss's 21st birthday. Jaguar and Moss, who was signed on the spot, had really come of age.

His first 'semi official' works drive was in good old JWK 651 (Johnson's car) at Montlhery. Between them they lapped at 107.46 mph for twenty four hours with a fastest lap at 126.2 mph. The object was to average more than 100 mph for a day and a night, not bad practice for Le Mans! Five months later, in March 1951, Johnson revisited the Paris track in JWK 651 to average 131.2 mph for an hour. Obviously Heynes had been 'breathing' on the car and it is reasonable to surmise that it incorporated engine modifications he had been working on since October. During that winter, the first XK 120 to be imported into New Zealand was sold to A. J. Roycroft, whose son Ron raced it with considerable success. It passed through many owners' hands before being bought by Grant McMillan (see Chapter X).

By the winter of 1951, XK 120s were being hammered round race tracks all over the world and they were becoming the most popular car in the rally field. NUB 120, with the Appleyards driving, finished second behind Geoff Holt's MG TD in the *Daily Express* 1000-mile event, despite conditions so foul that competitors had to rub their screens with sour milk to ward off the mud.

The Appleyards followed this up by winning the Tulip Rally, losing no points over a very tough road section. The runner-up was a Swiss-entered XK 120 driven by Habitsreutinger and Horning. The French international Rally du Soleil was dominated by XKs with Perigreaux and Girier in first place and similar cars in second, third, fourth and sixth places.

Meanwhile Boddy had been over to the States and watched SCCA racing with considerable interest, noting particularly the success of XK 120s driven by Hill and Jack McAfee. This keen observer also noted that they were prone to run out of brakes, a handicap that was becoming apparent elsewhere. Nevertheless, Boddy was one of the first to air his criticisms in print, telling his audience in *Motor Sport*:

> 'The showing of the XK 120 Jaguar is magnificent. Its very rugged engine gives away nearly two litres to the Cadillac-powered cars, yet develops the same 160 bhp. The Jaguar is some 3 cwt heavier than the Allard. Its ability to go is the more meritorious for that; it would do even better in those fierce little USA races if it would stop when told to.'

The variety of cars in these SCCA races reflected the sports car boom which was sweeping America. At any major road race there would be many Cadillac and Chrysler Allards, XK 120s, and Ferraris. There would be one or two hybrids, like Briggs Cunningham's Buick-powered Mercedes (the Bumerc) or a modified Indianapolis car such as the Duesenberg, driven with great success by George Huntoon from Florida. In the smaller categories would be found sprinklings of DB 2 Aston Martins, 328 BMWs, HRGs, Cisitalias, Alfas, Jowett Jupiters, Morgans and so on. But above all there were the MGs. Between them, Jaguar and MG dominated the two classes of SCCA racing.

In England that year, 1951, Grantham put up the best performance in the Yorkshire Rally in his XK 120, with Appleyard winning a similar award in the Morecambe Rally. Half the unlimited classes in these events were made up of XKs. Johnson and Moss were less fortunate in the Mille Miglia: they crashed, but Moss was back on form for the Silverstone production car race. He led in Dodson, Hamilton, George Wicken and Johnson in that order with Holt and Wisdom

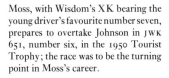

Moss, with Wisdom's XK bearing the young driver's favourite number seven, prepares to overtake Johnson in JWK 651, number six, in the 1950 Tourist Trophy; the race was to be the turning point in Moss's career.

The most famous XK rally car of all, NUB 120, storms the Gloss Glockner pass during the 1951 Alpine Rally.

One of the most successful XK rally drivers, the Swiss privateer Habits-reutinger, roars up the Italian side of the Grand Saint Bernard Pass in the 1951 Alpine Rally.

Hamilton racing home to win the William Lyons Trophy at Boreham in 1951.

The true British spirit personified by Major A. MacGregor Whitton in the Bo'ness hill climb in July 1952.

following an Aston Martin which had interjected itself into the line-up. In the same month of May, Leslie Wood walked away with the Scottish Rally in his XK 120, even winning the concours, and the Finnish Grand Prix sports car race was won by the local driver Keinanen in an Allard with an XK 120 second.

Soon after Belgian racing driver Johnny Claes won the Spa production car race in his XK 120 and Walter Scherrer won the equivalent race in Switzerland. Meanwhile John Fitch was emerging as one of the fastest drivers in SCCA racing with his XK 120.

British drivers were beginning to get their hands on more XK 120s as Jaguar fought to fulfil orders in strict rotation, some of which, for 'a sports car', dated back to 1946. In fact there were enough XKs on British circuits for a special race to be organized for them with the William Lyons Trophy as top award at Boreham. 'With all drivers in cars, identical, externally at least, it was interesting to note how the various odds stood with the bookmaker installed in the paddock', said *Autosport*.

'Hugh Howorth and Duncan Hamilton were evens, Roy Salvadori, making a return to the wheel after a crash at Silverstone, was at three to one, and Mrs Nancy Binns shared six to one with J. Craig, J. Swift and others. Though the rain had eased off for a while, the course was streaming wet as the Jags, all ten of them, shot off the line to a welter of flying spray. Round they came, a kaleidoscopic stream of red, blue, green, black and silver, Howorth leading Hamilton by a couple of lengths, then L. Wood; J. Craig whipping past Salvadori at Gilhooley, and J. Swift; in their wake came E. Farrow, his Jag much dented,

and which, on reaching Gilhooley promptly spun with a squeal of protesting tyres. Lap two and Howorth still led, and still Hamilton tailed him, followed by Wood and Craig. One car did a *tête à queue* at Orchard. "Too darned quick to see who it was", said the observer, "but he was driving an XK 120 Jaguar!" S. Powell only just held it at Gilhooley on one lap and J. Swift, approaching the bend too fast, braked hard while still in a straight line and got round safely. Craig and Wood came round late, their cars bearing dents eloquent of involuntary contact somewhere. Lap seven was unlucky for Howorth, who lost his hard-won lead by spinning round at Gilhooley, sending oil drums and straw bales flying. One drum was trapped beneath the body, against the rear wheel, its extraction causing much delay. Hamilton, his line into the corner altered perforce, slid, held his car and was away into the lead, Swift streaked past into second place and Salvadori also passed the unfortunate Howorth before he got going. And thus they finished, averaging 73.57 mph for the ten laps.'

A minor race perhaps, but a glorious illustration of what XK 120 racing was all about in 1951.

Meanwhile, back in Coventry, Jaguar were putting the finishing touches to the new XK 120C, plus four XK 120s with lightweight bodies in case they could not make Le Mans in time with the C type. As it was they finished the C type in good time and three of the lightweight XK 120s were sold to a dealer in America and the spare body left in a corner of the development shop.

The C type's debut at Le Mans was to be sensational. The new Jaguars not

It's Le Mans 1951 and the winning C type driven by Whitehead and Walker stops for fuel with Lofty England on the left directing operations from their pit counter. As Walker prepares to leave the car, Whitehead waits on the counter.

only revealed themselves to be extraordinarily good-looking, but to possess a performance to match. Despite the success of the XK 120 in competition, the general public knew that British racing cars were a disaster; they had all backed the BRM, been told it was more advanced than anything else in the world (quite true) and then seen it stutter and die in successive clouds of smoke. So Jaguars were fast, they looked good, and they were cheap. But what had they won that the general public had ever heard of? Within twenty four hours everybody was to know that Jaguars were world beaters. Rule Britannia.

Moss was the pacemaker from the start. Inside five laps he had taken the lead from the Pampus Bull, Froilan Gonzalez, in a thinly-disguised Grand Prix Talbot. The much-feared Ferraris were falling behind already. Within four hours the Jaguars were 1–2–3 until drama intervened. The second-placed C type of Italian veteran Biondetti and Johnson rumbled into the pits with a broken oil pipe, caused by severe vibration. All Britain was on tenterhooks as they listened in on the radio; it was tantamount to Britain losing the Ashes by one run. Obviously the same fault could strike again. By midnight it had, with the leading car of Moss and Jack Fairman stopping in a pool of oil. Could the two Peters, Whitehead and Walker, hold out in the remaining C type? The Talbots of Gonzalez and Rosier had already gone, victims of Moss's scorching pace. Ferrari had lost Chiron and Hall. The cumbersome Cunningham of Fitch and Walters thundered on at great speed down the straights and fought its drivers all the way through the corners. The Astons were screaming away to 1–2–3–5–6 in their class, but miles behind. One Talbot was still running second although its drivers, Meyrat and Mairesse, knew that if they tried to catch the Jaguar they would blow up like their team mates.

W. C. N. Grant Norton's 120 roadster displays rally equipment typical of the early 1950s at Goodwood in the RAC Rally.

They were all outclassed to the end. The Jaguar won by seventy-seven miles, the modern era of sports car racing had begun, and with it its greatest success story.

After that, anything else might be seen as an anti-climax, but winning the Liège-Rome-Liège Rally could never be called that. Claes and Belgian technical journalist Jacques Ickx (father of the Grand Prix star) finished what must have been the world's roughest road race—it was hardly a rally—in first place unpenalized, with another XK 120 driven by Herzet and Baudoin second, and a third, crewed by Laroche and Radix in fifth place.

Britain's classic circuit race, the TT, took place in September sunshine for a change and the works team of C types had things all their own way. Moss led throughout to win for the second year in succession, with Walker second and a reserve, Rolt, fourth after taking over Johnson's car when he felt sick. It was like a lap of honour after Le Mans, and confirmed Rolt's place in next year's team because he set the lap record. Moss kept the English public happy by winning a couple of minor races at Goodwood in the autumn—something of an exhibition.

As ever Boddy summed it up in *Motor Sport*:

'The XK 120 took the competition world by storm. Its good looks, its speed, its acceleration, all belied its exceedingly modest price, and it was still sufficiently far ahead to win for Moss at Silverstone this year. It possessed rather supple suspension and its cast-iron brakes were next to useless when hot, but it proved to be able to win classic races. . . . High praise, then, should be bestowed on Jaguar for going on from there, instead of resting on well-worn laurels. The result is the C type, a competition car of which Britain is justly proud, a car, which using the same fine engine as its forerunner but further developed, stiffer suspension very cleverly contrived at the rear, better brakes and a truly wind-defeating body, won the great Le Mans race on its first appearance. Here is a car about which there are no "ifs" and "buts".'

Needless to say, all the world wanted a Jaguar. But the Appleyards, despite their connections, were happy with old NUB 120. They won yet another Coupé des Alpes, the first competitors to do it three times in a row. No husband and wife combination could have become more famous in the rally world than Ian and Pat Appleyard. Pat Moss and Erik Carlsson were famous as individuals, not as a team from the start. The secret of the Appleyard success story lay in their meticulous preparation, and ability to anticipate the strength of the opposition. When it came to actual driving, their teamwork was matchless, Pat always being able to keep going under the worst possible conditions, leaving Ian fresh for the special-stage stuff, speed events, tests and other rally features of which he was one of the world's masters.

Over in America, a Beverly Hills wheeler-dealer called Charlie Hornburg, who had lined up the Jaguar distributorship for the West Coast when the XK 120 came out, bought two of the lightweight XK 120s built as Le Mans stand-bys. Even if the action on the coast was amateur by European standards, it was enthusiastic and it was wild. And two of the drivers who supplied much of the action were Hill and George Malbrand. It was natural that they should get a ride in these cars, the next best thing to C types.

Hill has a vivid recollection of his ride in the 120 at Elkhart Lake in December 1951. 'George ended up in the bank building with his car (he was all right) but I don't think they were as quick as my 120. And they wouldn't stop. They just wouldn't stop.' He had cured this problem by fitting Borrani wire wheels to his car, but still faced problems when he drove the lightweight out west. 'Then we had this weird overheating problem', he told *Car and Driver*. 'I ran at Reno and Palm Springs and finished second to Bill Pollack's J2 Cad-Allard. Last time we ran them was at Pebble Beach in April and Pollack won again.'

In the same month, in cold wet Scotland far from the sunshine of the West Coast of America, the Ecurie Ecosse was formed. This private Scottish motor racing stable was to uphold the honour of Jaguar even after the factory had stopped competing. Needless to say, their first cars were a fleet of four XK 120s. Club racing had been dominated by Howorth in the bigger production classes, with competition from Bill Black among others. And in the Argentine, the local hero was one Roberto Mieres, whose XK 120 was a stepping stone to Grand Prix stardom.

Moss was also heading for Grand Prix stardom as a result of his prowess behind the wheel of a Jaguar. He provided the chief attraction at Goodwood on Easter Monday, 1952, in his C type, although he was handicapped down to fourth place. Nevertheless Holt's private XK 120 won the handicap. On the rally front, Mary Newton won the ladies' prize driving an XK 120 in the RAC event, with Ian Appleyard doing well, supported by none other than Leslie Johnson in JWK 651 — it really was a most versatile car!

Moss, who was later to emulate Appleyard with a hat-trick of coupés in the Alpine with Sunbeam, tried his hand in the Lyons–Charbonnières event with a brand new green-and-white XK 120 fixed-head, registered LUC 345. He was supported by another XK 120 fixed-head coupé, the Oblin–Jaguar of Herzet, whose special bodywork bore a close resemblance to a Ferrari.

Soon after Moss comfortably won the Silverstone production sports car race

Jaguar's chief test driver, Norman Dewis, is congratulated by England at the end of the Jabbeke runs in October 1953 in which he achieved a mean average speed of 172.412 mph over a flying mile. Tyre expert 'Dunlop Mac' is patting Dewis on the back; aerodynamicist Malcom Sayer is just visible over England's shoulder.

The XKs of Peter Sparacino and Lesko lead off the line at the start of the 1954 Sebring twelve-hour race.

Dick Protheroe demonstrates that a well-prepared 120 could lead a C type, even if Rolt, seen on his tail at Goodwood on Easter Monday 1954, did get past in the end.

Col. Michael Head in his immaculate
C type, registered MDU 212.

in a C type and a supporting celebrity race (in which all the drivers used left-hand steering XK 120s), from Swiss Grand Prix ace, Baron Emmanuel de Graffenreid. It was called the Race of Champions and emphasized that Moss was a champion already.

Although they had the best drivers, Hamilton having joined the team by then, it was not a good year for Jaguar. Moss was deeply involved in testing disc brakes on the C type with Norman Dewis, the works development driver who had taken over from Soapy Sutton, and they were lying third in the Mille Miglia when they crashed with only 150 miles to go. At Le Mans, the overheating Jaguars were vanquished by the might of Mercedes, who were nothing like so fast as Moss has reported after seeing them in the Mille Miglia. It was one of his rare mistakes which panicked the factory into turning out the more streamlined C types at the last moment. If it had been anybody but Moss who had said the Mercedes were so fast they would have stuck to their 1951 shape and stood a good chance of winning.

Meanwhile, Col. Michael Head was in Finland, establishing Jaguar's name there by mopping up sports car races with his immaculate white XK 120, and Sir James Scott-Douglas scored a class win for the Ecurie Ecosse in the British Empire Trophy race on the Isle of Man, besides finishing third overall behind the handicap winner, Pat Griffiths in a Lester-MG. That year the Monaco Grand Prix was held for sports cars, and naturally Jaguar were keen to do well. The famous event attracted a fine field of sports cars, as Grand Prix cars were in the doldrums that year and all the best racing was in the sports category. Ferraris fielded their usual strong team, Aston Martin had open DB3 sports racers to replace the DB2s (dubbed saloons at the time), Wisdom and Moss were there with C types, and Manzon was entered in a Gordini. Most of them collided at Sainte Devote corner with Moss being disqualified for accepting help to straighten his radiator grille. Wisdom survived to take sixth place.

A week later, at Hyères, a few miles down the Riviera, Heurtaux won the twelve-hour race in his X K 120. The grand old roadsters would not lie down yet.

Soon after, Moss was again locked in battle with Manzon's Gordini in the Grand Prix at Rheims with the French car leading until a wheel bearing seized. It hit an electricity pylon with drastic results to the local supply: Moss assumed the lead in his C type, holding it to the end from Mairesse's Talbot and Scott-Douglas's X K 120. A few weeks later came the Jersey road race, another event which had switched from racing cars that year, which proved to be a benefit for another Ecurie Ecosse driver, Ian Stewart, in one of the first production C types, X K C006.

One of its principal competitors was a brand-new breed of Big Cat, an H W M-Jaguar driven by Finchley motor trader Oscar Moore. Moore was disappointed to finish third in his former Formula Two car fitted with scanty cycle-type wings and X K 120 engine bored out to 3.8 litres. He had been winning numerous club events in a car that was to set a trend as one of the first Jaguar specials. Another driver following this fashion at the time was Phil Scragg, who had transplanted the engine of his smashed racing X K 120 into a similar H W M-Alta chassis and was using it to good effect in hill climbs.

Moss or Stewart mopped up various club events in England and Scotland before taking part in a new form of racing in Britain: the Goodwood Nine-Hour. It turned out to be a spectacular event with racing by headlights really appealing to the public. It had all the attraction of Le Mans with the Ferraris and a Talbot besides works Jaguars and Aston Martins. The Rolt–Hamilton C type led at first; Peter Whitehead ran off the road in another works Jaguar, the Levegh–Etancelin Talbot also retired, and then Eric Thompson and Reg Parnell's Aston, lying third, caught fire while refuelling. At half distance, Moss led from Rolt, with Peter Collins (Aston) third and Salvadori's Ferrari fourth. Then the Rolt Jaguar lost a wheel

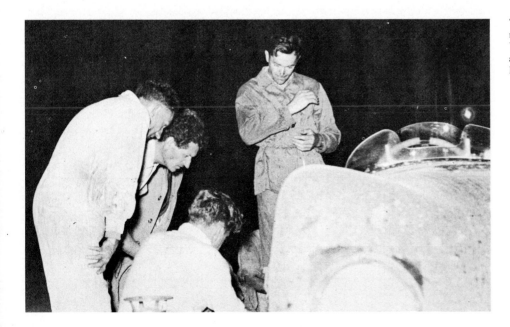

Tony Gaze watches dismayed as the mud-covered C type he shared with Whitehead and Alf Barrett slithers to a halt in Australia's first twenty-four hour race at Mount Druitt in 1954.

Le Mans 1954, and OKV 2, driven by
Moss, who had to retire with brake
trouble after being timed at 168 mph,
holds off a Gordini and passes a
Ferrari stranded in the sand like a
beached whale.

Hamilton leads Titterington in their
D types at Silverstone in 1955.

and the remaining car, Moss's, broke a rear axle A-bracket and lost a lot of time, which let Salvadori into the lead. But they were delayed in the pits by a jammed starter, which let Collins back in front with the Aston, a lead which he held to the finish. The Jaguars were beaten but their popularity had never been higher. You could actually buy a new C type then and many were on their way to America.

The first outright win to be recorded by a C type in the US was by Phil Hill at Elkhart Lake in September 1952. He was driving XKC007 and recalled:

'It was a big moment. These cars were not just a replacement for the XK 120. People expected them to be a darn sight better—the XK 120 was still very much envied for transportation but not taken very seriously as a race car.

'I was just in awe of the C type when I first stepped into it, though I could look back on it after a few years and smile.

'I remember there was a little information sheet that came along with them —a mimeographed thing. There was an adjustment for regulating the torsion bar on the rear suspension but we set them up pretty square just like they were supposed to be. It was all pretty neat. We tried some trick stuff, but it didn't work.

'The steering was light, almost scary light. It was the first car I ever drove that had a real precise feel about it—it really felt like a racing car.

'Driving it you had to behave in the same way. You couldn't just throw it around: get sideways and stay loose like the other cars we were driving then.

'It was far superior to anything else on cornering ability but it could bite; when you lost it there was not much warning.'

Soon after Fitch won the Seneca Cup at Watkins Glen in XKC008 and Sherwood Johnston, a renowned XK 120 campaigner, moved up into another C type. Meanwhile, back in Blighty, Moss and the Ecurie Ecosse continued to win club events, and R. G. Shattock in a shatteringly-fast Jaguar-powered special called the RGS Atalanta scored popular victories.

Jaguar felt that the XK 120 should not be forgotten in the competition world, however, and sent Moss over to Montlhery with a fixed-head coupé registered LWK 707. The owner of the tan-coloured coupé, Leslie Johnson, went along for the ride with Jack Fairman and pre-war Austin star Bert Hadley. They spent seven days in Paris, travelling at an average speed of 100.31 mph, to the astonishment of people throughout the world. Here was a car that could cover 16,851 miles in a week with absolutely standard equipment except for a larger than normal fuel tank and a two-way radio.

'Frequently rude remarks could be heard coming over the air', reported *Autosport*, 'but the installation was invaluable in providing the pit personnel with the necessary information relating to oil pressure, engine temperature and so on. . . .

'The ordinary driver cannot quite appreciate the sheer monotony of circulating the Montlhery saucer at such a speed. At night all sorts of things happen to disconcert the pilots. Lamps pick out rabbits and other animal life, including one fox which ended its life on the Jaguar's bumpers. Drivers imagine that armies are marching across the track, trees are falling down, and during a fearfully wet Friday night, that the entire circuit was flooded from end to end.

'Still on and on went the buff-coloured Jaguar. At the end of seven days, during which the coupé covered 27,120.281 kilometres and broke four world records, the engine sounded as healthy as when it began.'

As Jaguar's works car was racing round Montlhery, the XK 120 was still winning races, as far afield as the Singapore Motor Club's Johore Grand Prix with C. D. B. White finishing first and Saw Kim Thiat second, and in Australia, where one of the first roadsters covered 6000 miles within a week of its purchase, as well as averaging 91.3 mph for the 965 miles from Darwin to Alice Springs in the hands of owner Les Taylor and observer Dick Rendle. It was an unofficial road record for which Taylor was fined £18 with £2 costs for dangerous driving, speeding, driving without a Northern Territory licence and for driving a car not registered in the Northern Territory! Nevertheless, like all record attempts it provided unlimited publicity for Jaguar.

So, winning the classic races such as Le Mans made the works determined there would be no more débâcles like those of 1952. The Mille Miglia in 1953 turned out to be something of a development exercise with the three team Jaguars retiring honourably after much hard driving and testing of disc brakes on Rolt's machine.

It was just as well that Jaguar got their brakes right in time for Le Mans. The race of that year was to be one of the greatest seen on the French circuit, with new cars galore. The Jaguars were unfancied, having been beaten by Ferrari and Aston Martin in the International Trophy race at Silverstone just before the event. But it looked like 1951 all over again when Moss stormed past Villoresi's 4.5-litre Ferrari to take the lead on the fourth lap. It looked even more like 1951 when he pulled into the pits with fuel feed problems. But Rolt and Hamilton, laced with brandy as a pick-me-up after a monumental all-night drinking session when they thought they had been disqualified for an accidental breach of practice regulations, were equal to the occasion. The Jaguar's disc brakes helped compensate for the Ferrari's extra power and the battle continued through the night with Rolt and Hamilton allegedly taking on more medicine as their car was refuelled.

On and on they howled with the Jaguar in the lead most of the time and other cars falling by the wayside till the Ferrari was abandoned, its clutch burned out. Jaguar were back on the glory trail with Moss second, his fuel lines having cleared at last, and Cunningham third in his all-American giant. The winning C type averaged 105 mph, the first time Le Mans had been won at more than 100 mph.

What is more, they repeated the trick in the Rheims Twelve-Hour immediately afterwards, with Moss and Whitehead winning. However, their wet sump lubrication proved inadequate for the constant cornering at Goodwood in the Nine Hours and both the cars of Moss-Walker and Rolt-Hamilton retired with bearing trouble when in the lead. Once again, Aston Martin won with Whitehead and Ian Stewart's C type third and the Ecurie Ecosse cars of Jimmy Stewart and Bill Dobson, and

Hawthorn wins for Jaguar at Le Mans in 1955—a race marred by one of the worst crashes in history.

Bolton and Walshaw's 140 fixed-head circulates like clockwork at Le Mans in 1956.

John Lawrence–Frank Curtis fourth and fifth. The TT in Ulster was even less fortunate, with only one Jaguar being classed as a finisher, Moss pushing his ove. the line in fourth place with a broken gearbox. However an Ecurie Ecosse C type driven by Scott-Douglas and Guy Gale came second in the Spa Twenty Four Hour race with Dutchmen Roosdorp and Ulmen's C type third. Ian Stewart and Salvadori were second in the Nurburgring 1000 km, and already the Scottish team were starting to uphold Jaguar's honour in international racing.

In Ireland, one of the Ecurie Ecosse's four C types took second place in the Leinster Trophy in Ian Stewart's hands. In France, Armand Roboly and John Simone were second in the Hyères Twelve-Hour. In America, Johnston and Robert Wilder took third place at Sebring, followed by another C type driven by Harry Gray and Bob Gegan. In Sweden, Oscar Swahn won several races with his C type, as did John Manussis in his C type in Kenya.

Gradually more C types reached America, with Hornburg importing several, including XKCO15. The first owner was Jim Hall, who sold it to a young man called Masten Gregory. Gregory hit the Sports Car Clubs of America (SCCA) National trail with a win at Golden Gate Park, California. He then took the car to *Road and Track* for their test and was off again to Illinois, where he was disqualified for illegal refuelling, to Nebraska and a win, to Ohio and a second overall and then to New York and what was to be XKCO15's final official SCCA race. He spun, splitting the petrol tank and the car was burned out in practice. Gregory was not short of money and promptly bought a bright red C type from another competitor to replace the ashes of his white car. With his second Jaguar of the weekend he led the race until the rear end gave trouble and he moved on to other cars. That was the way of life in SCCA racing in those days. Happily, XKCO15 was rebuilt and survives immaculate today.

Bib Stilwell rounds Jaguar Corner in front of the Home for the Insane at the Albert Park Circuit in Victoria. His D type was the first to be raced in Australia.

It's all efficiency as Ninian Sanderson and John Lawrence refuel at Le Mans in 1957 with their second-placed Ecurie Ecosse D type.

The SCCA XK 120s were still being modified and, as a result, another up and coming young driver called Walt Hansgen was able to win the Watkins Glen Grand Prix with one. In other spheres, George Abecassis was successful with the works HWM-Jaguar, winning at Goodwood, and the Bill Lyons Trophy went to Ian Stewart's Ecurie Ecosse C type from the hard-driving Howorth whose car had by then acquired many C type parts, including the complete rear suspension, grafted on to the XK 120 chassis!

Jaguars were still active in the world of record breaking, too. In October the motoring world was shaken by the news that an XK 120 had been timed on a two-way average of 172.412 mph on the Jabekke motorway, by far the highest speed ever recorded by a production vehicle, or any vehicle bearing the slightest resemblance to one. Dewis's car was a standard special equipment roadster fitted with undershield and a Perspex bubble cover for the driver's head, with a 2.92:1 axle ratio.

'The opportunity was also taken to test a prototype XK 120 competition Jaguar', said *Autosport*. 'This is a development of the Le Mans-winning C type and appears to be a considerably smaller machine. It was timed over the flying mile at the astonishing speed of 178.383 mph.'

Kiwi enthusiast Harvey Hingston wins the Urenui hill climb from another 120. 'He was the better driver,' said Harvey, 'but my C type head and 2-inch racing SUs just tipped the balance in my favour'.

It really was an astonishing car, and was the forerunner of the D types.

As development continued on this car, the XK 120 reigned supreme in rallies with Appleyard winning the RAC Rally, and Jaguar taking the team prize: hardly surprising as they were by far the most popular entry. In France, Peignaux and Jacquin won the Lyons-Charbonnières Rally with a very potent XK 120 which sounded exactly like a Le Mans C type. Bomber pilot Dick Protheroe was a rising force in club racing with an XK 120 called the Ancient Egyptian (he had bought it in Cairo) and C. F. Pople won the Singapore Motor Club's Johore Grand Prix in a modified XK 120 from Au Nai Fai in another XK. In Canada, the leading lights of club racing included XK drivers Von Boch, Vern Jefferies and Bill Robinson.

XK 120 drivers who had progressed to successful C types included Irishman Joe Kelly, Hansgen and Sherwood Johnston in SCCA racing, and Scott-Douglas who had been giving a distinguished account of himself with the Ecurie Ecosse XK right until the end of the year.

By 1954, the Ecurie Ecosse were getting quite ambitious. With donations from wealthy Scottish supporters, prize money, starting money and bargain basement prices from Lyons, they bought the previous year's works C types, XKC051, 052 and 053, and entered the Buenos Aires 1000 km race. The two Stewarts, who were not related, although Jimmy's little brother Jackie was later to become world champion, were driving one car, Ninian Sanderson and Scott-Douglas the second, and Mieres and another South American driver the third. Only Sanderson and Scott-Douglas finished, fourth, with Gregory's American C type fourteenth. However, it was to be the Ecurie Ecosse's most successful season in terms of outright wins, with twelve victories, and eighteen places from seventeen events as far afield as Zandvoort and Barcelona as well as Buenos Aires.

Two other highly-successful private entrants were Hamilton, when he wasn't driving a works car, in OVC 915 (chassis number XKC038) and Head in Wisdom's old car, MDU 212 (XKC038). Between them they roared all over the Continent with their wives and carrying a few spares in their racing cars. Hamilton won in Paris and at Aintree and Head made a speciality of Scandinavia, with victories in Helsinki, Lapeenranta, Hedemora and Stockholm.

This happy tale continued with C types as the latest thing in racing sports cars until Le Mans. Jaguar became instant favourites with their beautiful new car, which rendered everything else obsolete overnight. It really was a considerable advance in the C type with its monocoque like an aeroplane's fuselage and dry sump engine. Once more the chief opposition came from Gonzales, driving a 4.9-litre Ferrari with Maurice Trintignant. Once more Moss took the Ferrari for the lead in the early stages; then Rolt came into the pits complaining of fuel starvation. Eventually the trouble was diagnosed. A fine grey dust had entered the pit tanks and was clogging the D type's filters. Then Moss had to retire with brake failure and the third D type, driven by Ken Wharton and Peter Whitehead retired with mechanical disorders. This left Rolt and Hamilton hammering on, gradually reducing the Ferrari's lead. Once more they lost time in the pits repairing damage after a brush with a Talbot, and the frantic Ferrari pit had trouble restarting their car. But Gonzales hung on to the end, finishing 105 seconds ahead of Hamilton. The 5.4-litre Cunningham of Johnston and erstwhile SCCA Jaguar driver Bill Spear was third and the Ecurie Belge's C type driven by Laurent and Swaters was fifth.

Jaguar took revenge by winning the Rheims Twelve-Hour which followed with the Whitehead–Wharton D type finishing ahead of Rolt and Hamilton, pushing their vehicle over the line to second place after being rammed by Behra's Gordini. However they were not so lucky with the handicap in the TT with the best of their 2.5-litre D types, that of Whitehead and Wharton finishing fifth.

All this must have seemed like a joy-ride compared to Whitehead's experiences in Australia's first twenty-four hour race held on the Mount Druitt circuit in New South Wales. Incessant rain covered parts of the old airstrip circuit in thick mud, the worst quagmire being in the pits, an area of grass with naked electric light bulbs strung across it. The entry ranged from Whitehead's C type and an XK 120 fixed-head driven by the 'mature' Mrs Doris Anderson, to a Humber Hawk and a Fiat 500. The C type, co-driven by Tony Gaze and Alf Barrett, howled away from the opposition, horn blaring and lights flashing every time it lapped baulking backmarkers. Mrs Anderson's XK, co-driven by Bill Pitt, sounded to be over-revving all the time. Ray Lewis's stately Mark V Jaguar saloon spent much time in the mud of the pits having repeated bearing changes. Eventually it was forced to complete twenty of the twenty-four hours running on only five cylinders, the offending piston, con rod and bearing having been removed. An MG TD went off course by twenty-four miles for the driver to buy a new clutch, fit it and return to the race. Meanwhile the C type thundered on through pot holes and mud, averaging 57 mph. Then the hard-driven XK coupé's engine moved so far forward in the chassis that it cracked its carburetters against the steering column. An appeal over the public address system brought forward a spectator whose XK was stripped for spares. Then, after eight hours, with the C type miles ahead, it suffered repeated A-bracket failure. Meanwhile the XK coupé, still revving furiously, with wheels spinning in the mud, moved up into the

The works 'knobbly'-bodied Lister–Jaguar MVE 303 howls through the chicane at Goodwood in 1958.

lead, as Dick Shaw's Holden bent a stub axle on a rough section.

'And as the chequered flag fell with Mrs Anderson victorious, several tired cars which had been sitting drunkenly in the pits lurched over the line so that they, too, could claim that they had finished the arduous test', *Autosport* reported. 'Amongst them was Whitehead's Jaguar which took sixteenth place and won the over 3000 cc open car class.'

Whitehead subsequently sold the C type before returning home, as was his habit. It went to New Zealand to be campaigned by Jack Tatton. Many cars, when no longer competitive in top European events, were raced by their owners at some of the more important meetings in Australia, then sold to local teams.

Other cars were consigned to British club racing, including one of the light-weight XK 120s built for Le Mans in 1951. This car, registered MWK 120, was raced successfully by Jaguar publicity man Bob Berry. Abecassis and Gaze raced HWM-Jaguars to great effect, even venturing as far afield as Hyères, where they were unlucky to be disqualified for a minor infringement when lying second to Trintignant's works Ferrari.

Monte Carlo or bust! McCracken heads south in his 150 drop-head in the 1959 rally.

Gerry Dunham and Manussis in their C type provided much of the opposition to the Ecurie Ecosse in Britain; Charles Wallace, Charles Sarle and Ernie Erikson took up the cudgels for Jaguar in modified XKs and a C type in SCCA racing; Laurent, van Dieten and Thielens did the same in the equivalent Continental races. But the most impressive performances were by young Bill Smith whose C type beat Desmond Titterington's D type on handicap for the Ulster Trophy and by Roger Irving who took his 1949 XK 120 (the ninth imported into America) into seventh place in the US Grand Prix at Watkins Glen behind the might of Ferrari and Cunningham works teams! In the rally world, the XK was becoming outmoded by the new Triumph TR 2, but Appleyard continued to campaign another XK 120, registered RUB 120.

Gradually the Australians acquired faster Jaguars to replace the 120s that had started their post-war sports car racing with the hordes of MG TCs. Lex Davison bought two HWM-Jaguars, winning the 1954 Australian Grand Prix with a D type engined open-wheeler and sports car races with the other. Dr John Boorman imported the ex-Manussis C type and drove it in local races, crashing twice. In America Wallace and another doctor, Dick Thompson, started to do well in SCCA

Eric Brown's famous racing XK, I ALL, wins at Crystal Palace in 1964 with world champion-to-be Jackie Stewart at the wheel.

racing with their new XK 140s.

Back at the factory, Jaguar were sufficiently well advanced with their 1955 cars to sell XKC402 (registered OKV 1) to Hamilton who passed on his C type to Dan Margulies for club racing. Broadhead bought XKC403 (registered OKV 2) for Berry to race and Mike Hawthorn, signed from Ferrari, drove XKC404 (OKV 3) in British early season events. Hamilton celebrated by racing at Agadir (where he later retired) with Margulies seventh in his old car; then took third place at 122 mph behind two Ferraris in the Dakar Grand Prix. Hawthorn did better, winning at Sebring with Walters, although protests over lap scoring took eights days to resolve and took the edge off Jaguar's glory.

It was probably fortunate that they did not enter the Mille Miglia in April 1955: Moss was at the peak of his prowess, winning at record speed for Mercedes, with *Motor Sport*'s Continental correspondent Denis Jenkinson as passenger, working a revolutionary system of pace notes that has since formed the basis of modern rallying technique.

Meanwhile Hamilton won the Coupé de Paris at Montlhery in a D type, with Head repeating his customary Scandinavian wins in another Hamilton D type.

Le Mans followed with a thrilling duel between Hawthorn and Juan Manual Fangio's Mercedes. But this was completely marred by tragedy as Levegh's Mercedes bounced off Macklin's Austin-Healey and into the crowd, killing eighty-two people. Moss took over Fangio's Mercedes and Ivor Bueb Hawthorn's D type, but the race was never the same. Gradually their rivals, Castellotti's Ferrari, Walter's Jaguar, Brooks's Aston Martin, Maglioli's Ferrari, Beauman's Jaguar, Salvadori's Aston Martin, Chapman's Lotus and Trintignant's Ferrari departed the sickening spectacle. Then Mercedes withdrew, leaving the D type five laps ahead of Valenzano's Maserati. Rolt and Hamilton retired and only Collins and Paul Frere in an Aston, plus Claes and Swaters in a Belgian D type, were within striking distance. They finished in that order, but Jaguar's great win had been clouded by the disaster.

Numerous races were cancelled on safety grounds, including two world championship events, so the next round, the TT at Dundrod, assumed major importance, with all the top teams competing—this time on a straightforward scratch basis. Handicaps had lost popularity. Jaguar fielded one D type, for Hawthorn and Ulsterman Titterington. Three drivers died in fiery crashes but the Jaguar stormed on either leading or holding second place until it seized up on the last lap. Mercedes finished 1–2–3 as Hawthorn walked home. Moss was the winner and he repeated this victory in the Targa Florio, putting him on a pinnacle above other sports car drivers. In lesser races, the Ecurie Ecosse continued to score, with Titterington and Sanderson second in the Goodwood Nine Hour and a D type driven by Berry and Dewis came fifth.

In America, Johnston won the Watkins Glen Grand Prix in his D type and finished third in the Bahamas; Wallace won the SCCA C production championship for the second year in his XK 120; and in Australia, a brilliant young engineer called Frank Gardner bought Boorman's wrecked C type and started rebuilding it to further his own driving career. Peter Whitehead took his Cooper-Jaguar to Australia, hoping for more success than he had in Britain with it. He finished second in the New Zealand Grand Prix before selling the car. Gaze, who was making a habit of importing European sports racing cars to the delight of fellow Australians, won at Christchurch in an HWM-Jaguar.

The works Jaguars started well in their 1956 season, or at least for the first six hours during which Hawthorn and Titterington led at Sebring in a fuel-injection D type before having brake trouble. However, Indianapolis winner Bob Sweikert finished third with Jack Ensley in a D type. A sad note was struck when John Heath, who constructed HWMs and did much for British motor racing after the war, was killed when he crashed his works car in the Mille Miglia. Meanwhile, the Ecurie Ecosse continued to mop up wins and places in smaller events.

In major events, the works team completed a wonderful hat-trick by winning the Rheims Twelve-Hour (Hamilton–Bueb were first), and filling the next three places thanks to the Scottish team's help. The Ecurie Ecosse went one better at Le Mans when two out of the three works cars crashed on the first lap! This left Hawthorn and Bueb in the lead until dirt in the fuel, their old enemy, delayed them. Sanderson and Flockhart took over the battle against the works Aston Martin of Moss and Collins, and won with Swaters and Rouselle fourth in the Belgian D type and Hawthorn–Bueb sixth. Scotsmen throughout the world celebrated wildly and Jaguar were thankful for the intervention of the blue cars.

Amid all this excitement, a rather ordinary-looking XK 140 fixed-head coupé had been circulating like clockwork. It was a private entry by Messrs Bolton and Walshaw, very definitely amateur, and the 25,000-mile old car had but one week of preparation at the factory. After a wet night and twelve hours, *The Motor* reported

Brian Abbott's extraordinary mod-sports 120 fixed-head at Silverstone in 1970. It was later written off at Thruxton.

that 'to our surprise, the Jaguar XK 140 was not only still in the race, but running fourteenth in the general category.' On and on went the XK 140 until regulations stopped it in the twenty-first hour. Apparently amateur pitwork had allowed it to be refuelled too early—a sad end to a gallant drive.

In the club world John Ogier kept his Tojeiro–Jaguar on the road long enough to beat Abecassis and Noel Cunningham-Reid in HWM–Jaguars and Gillie Tyrer in a C type at the Brighton Speed Trials; Mike Salmon in an XK 120 and a C type fought it out with Protheroe's Ancient Egyptian; Johnston, Fitch and George Constantine were the D type stars of SCCA racing; Harry Carter still hounded them with an XK 120; and D types reached Australia.

'Sports car racing was transformed by the arrival of three D types and some very fast Ferraris and Maseratis', said Les Hughes years later. One D type went to Melbourne car deal Bib Stilwell, who campaigned it most successfully throughout the year before selling it to radio personality Jack Davey. It was smashed up a couple of times and sold to Frank Gardner, who had sold his C type when he rebuilt the D type. Then it went to Frank Matich for racing.

'The second car went to Bill Pitt, who raced it for Mrs Anderson, who had retired after a bad accident in the Mount Druitt winning XK 120. This D type had some fierce battles with Bib Stilwell's car until it had a monumental accident and Matich rebuilt it.

'The third car was used for many years on the road by the rally driver Gelignite Jack Murray, so called for his methods of removing obstacles en route!'

John Pearson's fearsome 120 drop-head, with the entire body, including the hood, made from fibreglass.

Modsports men travel light. They save so much weight at odd points that they have to move around the components that are left to keep their wheels on the ground. Hence 'Plastic' Pearson's radiator in the floorless boot of his XK!

Yet another D type to end up in Australia was OKV I, sold by Hamilton after he had converted it into the first XK SS. The buyer, Jumbo Goddard, was still driving it twenty years later.

By December 1956, the Ecurie Ecosse were taking over the works D types, now that Jaguar had retired from racing in an official capacity. They kept one of the old short nose cars, XKD501, to make up their team with XKD504, XKD603 and XKD606. The idea was to use two cars in each of the world championship events, involving a third in strict rotation, with the old short nose car as a reserve. With the cost of such a programme in mind, Sanderson and Mieres drove 'steadily' to fourth place in XKD603, although Flockhart crashed the other car in practice. XKD605 went to Briggs Cunningham and was driven by Hawthorn and Bueb into third place behind the Maseratis of Fangio and Behra and Moss and Schell, despite suffering from a broken brake line. This was the first of the 3.8-litre D types, the result of intensive development by Cunningham's ace tuner, Alfred Momo. Hansgen and Fitch continued to do well in American racing with the D types, with XKs driven by Carter and Kessler emulating them in production events.

In Britain, the spring of 1957 was notable for the emergence of the Lister–Jaguar driven by Archie Scott-Brown. Clutch trouble eliminated him from his opening event at Snetterton, won by Protheroe's Tojeiro–Jaguar, but the tiny Scottish driver made up for that in the British Empire Trophy at Oulton Park. He vanquished the works Aston Martins and continued to do so for the rest of the season; Hamilton's D type and Leston's HWM–Jaguar suffering similar fates. In all, Scott Brown won twelve out of the fourteen races entered, finished second in one behind Salvadori's Aston Martin and retired at Snetterton. Meanwhile, on the world championship trail the Ecurie Ecosse picked up a few places until Le Mans.

Their two cars (XKD606 with fuel injection for Flockhart and Bueb; XKD603 on Webers for Sanderson and John Lawrence) dominated the event, finishing first and second with Frere and Freddy Rousselle fourth in the Ecurie Belge D type and Hamilton and Gregory sixth in Duncan's latest car (this was fitted with a 3.8-litre fuel injection engine like the winner). It was not as though the opposition was weak, except in reliability. Aston Martins, Ferraris and Maseratis which had been beating the D types in shorter events couldn't last the twenty-four hours. It was our greatest hour, said the Ecurie Ecosse's patron, David Murray.

Soon after the team sportingly took part in the Monzanapolis event, heavily weighted in favour of a squadron of Indianapolis cars, on the Monza track. It was supposed to be a race of the best from Europe versus the best from America, but the Grand Prix teams boycotted the event because their tyres were not suited to the bumpy high speed circuit, and the American cars couldn't be driven on anything else. As it was, tyre trouble kept the D types down to fourth, fifth and sixth places, which might have been first, second and third if the event had been run as a straight five hundred miles. It was split into two parts because of the toll taken by the bumps, and comprehensive rebuilds were allowed for the American cars in between. The Jaguars had raced with hardly more than a plug change since Le Mans.

The Scottish team fared badly in other world championship events, but Le Mans made up for that. Hamilton continued to have a fair measure of success in his private D types, and Scott-Brown took the Lister to Australia and New Zealand in the winter, beating all the opposition, including Maserati 250F Grand Prix cars in the Lady Wigham Trophy race at Christchurch. Whitehead's Cooper–Jaguar was also used to good effect by Stan Jones, father of the Grand Prix driver Alan Jones, and the Tojeiro–Jaguar followed the same path to the antipodes for Frank Cantwell.

The success of these Jaguar-engined specials with independent rear suspension was such that orders poured in for the most famous, the Lister, for the 1958 season. More than twenty were built for such distinguished teams as the Ecurie Ecosse and Ecurie Nationale Belge, besides private customers including Briggs Cunningham.

Scott-Brown took his Lister to Sebring with the Ecurie Ecosse's D types, but the Jaguar-powered machinery failed and was beaten by Collins's Ferrari. He also finished third in the British Empire Trophy in a car (registered HCH 736) borrowed from customer Bruce Halford, despite having to sit on several cushions to reach the pedals and see over the scuttle! However, back in the works car (one of a number registered MVE 303), he was a convincing winner at Aintree in April from Salvadori's Aston Martin and Gregory in the Ecurie Ecosse's new Lister. However, Gregory got his own back in the International Trophy meeting at Silverstone in May, beating Scott Brown into second place with Hawthorn's Ferrari third. The crowds loved it.

This neck-and-neck rivalry continued at Spa when continental race organisers allowed Scott-Brown, handicapped by an unformed hand, an entry for the first time. Sadly, he was caught on a corner by one of the circuit's notoriously sudden showers, and crashed, dying soon after being extricated from the burning Lister. Gregory,

Martin Crowther jumps to safety after his 120 roadster catches fire during a thoroughbred race in 1975. Car and driver survived to race to numerous victories.

Club racing in the late 1960s: John Harper's modified 120 fixed-head takes Peter Hull's 150 estate!

The 'flat iron' Lister–Jaguar HCH 736 leads a historic racing field.

who had been in the lead, won the event but wished it had never been run.

Bueb, then Moss, and then Hansgen continued to win the big events in Listers, with John Bekaert becoming the uncrowned king of the Silverstone club events with his HWM-Jaguar. Jaguars and Jaguar-powered machinery met with less success in international events, the three-litre XK engine produced to meet new regulations proving to be highly unreliable. The Ecurie Ecosse D type, which had been so reliable at Le Mans in 1957 could last only three laps before retiring with piston trouble. Similar trouble struck the D types of Lawrence and Fairman, while those of Charles and Jean-Marie Brussin crashed, the latter's with fatal results. Hamilton lasted the longest, hoping for second place when he crashed in a blinding rainstorm. His last big race was to be in the TT with Peter Blond, finishing sixth.

The XK 120 wasn't finished yet in competition, though. American Don Delling won his class in the Sestriere Rally, in his fixed-head, beating all the works teams, including Mercedes, in a snow-packed round-the-houses race which made up the last stage. And in club events, world champion-to-be Jim Clark became the man to watch in a D type or Lister.

The Ecurie Ecosse went as far as to have a special Lister–Jaguar built for the Monzanapolis event, with a possible Indianapolis entry in mind. But this bulky single seater did not come up to expectations, and was not reliable either! It expired while being driven by Fairman in the second of three heats of the 1958 race. And Pat O'Connor tried a Momo-tuned D type at Indianapolis in 1958, covering several laps at 129–130 mph—which was not quite fast enough to win, although highly impressive.

Cunningham entered three Lister–Jaguars for Sebring in 1959, with the fastest, driven by Moss and Bueb, leading until it ran out of petrol! Team-mate Hansgen, sharing his car with Thompson, tried to push him back to the pits but failed and retired misfiring. Moss took over the third car shared by Cunningham and Underwood but he was too far behind to get a place. Nevertheless Hansgen and Ed Crawford won numerous events in the United States in Cunningham's Lister–Jaguar.

The fortunes of Lister and Jaguar were mixed in Britain. Bueb and the Ecurie Ecosse won a few events, the Scottish team also running a Tojeiro–Jaguar. But after their past glories, it was an appalling season. In the TT, Gregory had a tremendous crash with the Tojeiro, leaping out just before the impact. He suffered a broken leg and arm, but escaped with his life as the car folded up. Jumping out at speed was a trick he had learned years before with his burning C type.

Protheroe, after spending a season with an Austin-Healey 100S, and earlier days with Ogier's Tojeiro and a C type, once again dug out the Ancient Egyptian and made it go impossibly fast in club events. It was in a strong position in the final round of the *Autosport* championship 'despite displaying an unhealthy appetite for brake drums', when it was involved in one of the many crashes which it survived throughout the years.

By 1960, D types and Lister–Jaguars were becoming a rare sight at big race meetings as more modern machinery such as Lotuses and Lolas took over. However, the Ecurie Ecosse soldiered on with one D type for nostalgic reasons. Despite its great age (for a Le Mans car), it was lying fifth when it retired with a broken crankshaft after eight hours. Cunningham also managed to race the E2A prototype at Le Mans that year but it also retired with engine trouble. The car won at Bridge-hampton in Hansgen's hands a couple of months later when fitted with a 3.8-litre engine. In South Africa, John Love in a D type and Tony Maggs in a Tojeiro had similar success with the 3.8 engine.

Lister-Jaguars remained competitive in club racing for several years into the 1960s, chiefly through the efforts of Gordon Lee with the ex-Bruce Halford 'flat iron' car and David Beckett with one of the later Costin-bodied models. Salmon mopped up minor events with his D type and Rob Beck joined the fray with another XK 120 roadster registered MXJ 954. Other notable racing XKs of that era included the 120s of Eric Brown (I ALL), Norman Watt, Graig Hinton, David Cottingham (with MWK 120, JWK 977, and MHP 682) Peter Butt and Rhoddy Harvey Baillie in JWK 650. In America, Hap Richardson was 1960 SCCA C champion on the Pacific Coast with his 120.

The best XK 140 driver of these years was David Hobbs. Actually the car was fitted with a Hobbs automatic transmission that he was demonstrating, but it certainly went fast, as did Warren Pearce in a bulbous XK 150.

Just as the Jaguar racers were disappearing, historic racing hit Britain, and Beckett was one of the first to re-enter these races in the middle 1960s with his Lister–Jaguar, which proved more than competitive. John Harper also became one of the most consistently successful drivers with Forward Engineering's Lister, while continuing to race a variety of modified XK 120s.

The most amazing XK of all however was the glass-fibre 120 drop-head of John Pearson which took lap records all over Britain in this ultra-competitive form of racing. There was little to beat it for three years until the owner moved on into other forms of racing.

Early in the 1970s, historic racing became really fashionable in Britain, with all manner of D types, Listers and XKs making a welcome reappearance. Once again there have been few cars to beat them other than the odd Ferrari (often driven by Harper!) and Maserati. In the current British thoroughbred series the winners are almost invariably the XK 120 roadsters of Harper or David Preece, with American races being won by visitors such as Martin Morris in his D type, the legendary OKV 3. It seems that for so long as there will be motor racing there will be a Jaguar winning!

Still racing: the famous OKV 3 in
Martin Morris's hands in 1976.

Chris Ball contests a historic race in an
Alta–Jaguar.

VI

Strengths and Weaknesses: Part One

EVERY CAR has its strengths and weaknesses, and none more so than the XK. Most of the mechanical parts are magnificent, but the body can be a disaster. On the surface, every XK ever made looks just great—long, sweeping wings, beautiful bonnet, perfect proportions. Underneath they are a hotch potch of nuts, bolts and afterthought welding, with all manner of edges to go rusty. Even the rare alloy-bodied XK 120 roadsters can suffer from a crumbling wooden frame and general corrosion. You have to look at an XK like some men look at women: the long, sweeping lines should be long and sweeping and not interrupted; the curves should be symmetrical; beware of ripples or wavy lines; shy away from plastic filler; and, above all, examine the car in daylight and when there is no rain on the coachwork!

The XK of your dreams should literally have a magnetic attraction except where lead filler has been used quite legitimately on compound curves. The plastic filler so beloved of bodge-up merchants will hold no attraction for a small horseshoe magnet. Prod any doubtful patches underneath with a screwdriver, because in the twenty or thirty years since it left the factory, any XK, no matter how smart outwardly, may have rusted right through at any point—and that includes the chassis.

One of the first places to check for rust is the bottom of the wings under the air intakes. Mud and debris build up here and hold moisture which is the root of all corrosion. Rust also rears its ugly head all around the headlight nacelles and sidelights. In fact, anywhere up to waist level is likely to have suffered. The worst parts are the bottoms of the wings along the sides of the car; the battery boxes; the front and rear door shut faces; the ventilators (fantastically, bad bodgers even fill these in!); and the sills, which are made in two halves and spot-welded together. It's these welds where the rust often gets its first grip; you can check them visually, but you should also employ your sense of touch when checking for corrosion here: feel all around the bottom and back of the sills with your hands for loose and rotten metal. Then look at where the sill passes through and joins the rear door shut face and peer into the wheel arch. You should spot a steel splash guard here or the remains of one. They are among the first parts to rot away, together with the shut face. Check and prod everywhere inside the rear wings because inner and outer are frequent rust traps. There should be beading between the wings and shroud, of course, but often bodgers have filled in that area. Rust is sometimes all too obvious at this point

Typical corrosion in a 150's closing plate to door pillar.

left Rot is frequently evident along the bottom of the front wings and in the vent box.

right Part of the rear section of a 150 chassis, showing rust in the spring hanger and chassis leg.

as bubbles appear on the surface. Sadly, they are often the first signs of rust as moisture penetrates beneath old layers of underseal, cannot escape, and eats its way out through the wing. Rust (and rot, with the drop-head which has a wooden frame on the top rear quarter near the door) attacks the top of the shroud, too.

Although rust attacks the chassis, it is rarely to the extent of the coachwork. The chief danger areas are the box-section rear-end of the chassis rails, in fact all

right More corrosion can be revealed when a rear wing is removed. Rust is evident in this XK's chassis and spare wheel carrier.

below left Where the trouble starts on an XK drop-head. These components are part of the wooden structure which supports the hood irons. Damp penetrates this area, the wood absorbs the water and rust gets a grip on the surrounding metal.

below right A 150 door partially stripped. Its tiny hinges can be seen on the left.

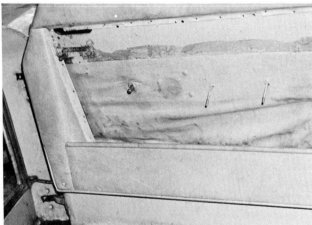

around the petrol tank and its straps, which can let go! Rust in the front of the chassis, anywhere oil has been thrown around, is uncommon, but nothing should surprise an XK owner, or potential owner, so it is worth checking, particularly in the vicinity of the radiator.

Luggage boot floors disappear fairly quickly and so does the petrol filler cap housing on outside filler models; floor panels go rusty round the edges and although the floorboards in the occupants' area are quite strong, they do rot sometimes.

Everything which opens and shuts on the body gives trouble except the bonnet; this is a beautiful piece of work in alloy (steel would have been too heavy to lift) and is often the best part of a neglected XK's body. The doors on XK 120 and 140 roadsters were made of alloy, too, and don't go rusty, of course, but their wooden frames can warp. Warping also frequently afflicts luggage boot lids. Usually, the bigger the door, the bigger the trouble on an XK. Again, there's rust: it eats away everything a foot from the bottom. Then there's the hinges, one of the weakest points on the car.

The hinges were really inadequate for the weight and leverage of the door they supported and it was very difficult to lubricate them; thus they have been subjected to heavy wear. In the worst cases the door will sag so much that it is impossible to keep it shut. Even if you can shut it, you have to lift it into position. Hinge repairs are difficult and have often been bodged, so check for holes having been cut in the wings to get at them. The mounting plate on roadster doors can also move around, causing problems. However, the hinge problem has been so common for so long that many cars have been repaired by now. Nevertheless, check the quality of the repair by opening the doors about nine inches and lifting them up and down. There's bound to be a bit of play, but there shouldn't be much.

The quality of the interior, the rubber seals, and the hood if it is an open car, are of prime importance on an XK, because the cost of replacement or repairs is high. This applies particularly to leather parts: be hypercritical here if you are buying the car, and ultra-careful if you already own it.

On the whole, the mechanical side presents fewer problems. The engine is one of the strongest twin cams ever made, frequently requiring little attention up to 100,000 miles. Needless to say, the majority of XKs have covered more than that, so watch out for general engine wear: clouds of blue smoke indicate bore or valve guide wear, although a clean blue haze on acceleration is normal. Don't worry too much about top end noise, it is often only the timing chain, which can be adjusted. The bottom chain is much more of a problem. Two sorts of tensioner have been used: on the XK 120 and early XK 140 models it was a spring-bladed device which might have worn or broken. Later models had a hydraulic tensioner, and replacement of either involves a lot of work.

However, with the hydraulic tensioner, there can be a simpler answer if you are lucky. Sometimes sludge blocks the small hole in the timing chest through which oil is fed to the tensioner. Clearing out the hole and flushing the engine can restore it to correct working order. The time to worry is if there is no noise at the top of the engine. This means that the tappets have closed up. Tappet adjustment, once correctly set, is likely to be maintained almost indefinitely—there are only three wearing surfaces per valve. The tappet noise should only be moderate, though. A tremendous clatter also means that adjustment is vital or perhaps that (heaven forbid) the camshafts are worn. As you are listening to the engine, look for oil leaks around the camshaft covers. Early models had fewer securing studs and overtightening was more likely to cause distortion. Correct tightening is still important with the later models, of course, but not so likely to damage the cover. Bearing trouble is rare with XK engines, such is the strength of the bottom ends, but listen for rumbling all the same. This ailment should be revealed by low oil pressure—below 35 psi hot at 3000 rpm —but the situation can be confused by malfunctions of the oil pressure relief valve. The spring in this device is likely to weaken giving low oil pressure readings or a piece of debris can lodge under the valve, leading you to suspect bearing trouble;

alternatively, unscrupulous people might have fitted washers behind the spring to give false high readings; or your oil pump could be worn, giving low readings. At any rate, worn bearings rumble and you should check the oil pressure relief valve and pump before you start panicking about the rest of the engine.

There's not an XK on the road that hasn't got a bit hot under the collar at some time, so make sure there are no signs of rust around the core plugs when you are taking close looks at the engine. The engine should also sound good, with a deep *varrooommm* as it revs freely up to 5000 rpm or more. Misfiring can be caused by ignition ailments or simply worn plugs, which do not last much more than 6000 miles on some hard-driven examples. An uneven tickover is often caused by incorrect synchronization of the carburetters or worn spindles in the carbs themselves. Carburetter repairs and synchronization are not as simple as they look and should be left to the experts if you are not convinced of your own ability. Leaky exhausts can also affect an engine's tune badly, particularly bottom end torque, enough to make you think there might be some intractable racing engine under the bonnet. Don't you believe it, all XK engines should have ample torque unless they have some extraordinary camshafts from hot rod companies such as Iskendarian, which are extremely rare.

Clutch condition on an XK should be fairly obvious. The pedal has a long travel and the unit should take up sweetly and smoothly; clutch judder is bad and caused by oil on the linings, or flywheel trouble. You are not supposed to have the flywheel skimmed if it has been scored by a previously worn-out clutch; but you can get away with it if you don't mind a sharper clutch action. Beware, however, of 'hot spots' on a flywheel after skimming; these high points can lead to premature clutch wear (the clutch should last at least 30,000 miles) and cause judder fairly soon in a new clutch's life. When an XK clutch starts to slip it doesn't last long, so hurriedly check its adjustment and if this doesn't cure the condition, you need a clutch change (expensive) quickly before the flywheel is scored (also expensive unless skimmed). With automatic models the gear changes should be smooth, sweet and consistent, although you can feel each gear going in. If the box gets erratic, or is reluctant to shift, seek immediate expert help as it's an expensive unit that is too complicated to be dealt with by anybody other than an expert.

The old Moss gearbox is a fantastic bag of nails. It seems to last for ever. If you find one with good synchromesh, however, it is as rare as the Crown jewels. But providing you are willing to take your time with gearchanging, particularly down through the ratios, and make sure the clutch is completely disengaged, it will go on for ages. First and reverse gears always yowl; it's when the yowling turns to howling that can be heard for hundreds of yards that the gearbox is on its way out.

Overdrives come under roughly the same heading as the automatic gearboxes, except that you should always check the electrical side for proper functioning before being panicked into thinking that the unit has given up the ghost.

The back axle hardly ever gives trouble. It's usually just a case of sitting back and forgetting about it except for the oil level. When that piece of machinery starts to howl you can start to worry.

The brakes are a different matter. There's no half measure with them; they

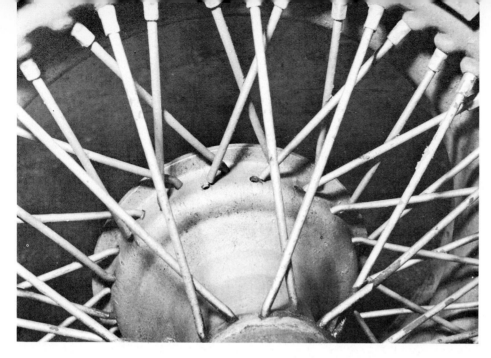

Watch for broken spokes in an XK's wire wheels.

should be in perfect working order, especially with a car as potent and heavy as an XK. Don't tolerate any corrosion on the brake pipes, any sticking in the cylinders, any rust or scoring on the discs of an XK 150, or excessive pad wear. Remember, there's always a reason for a fall in fluid level or a snatching wheel. Investigate immediately.

Check the steering very carefully. A lot of XKs have a bent track rod or two, which causes deviation while driving. Any play at the steering wheel or linkages will cause weaving. Inadequate lubrication of the ball joints or a worn rack or steering box can make the car feel as notchy as a 50p piece on corners. If the rack's rubber mountings have deteriorated, they can also cause this horrible feeling.

The suspension and wheels are equally important. The dampers don't last forever, particularly the lever arm type fitted to the back of the XK 120, which frequently suffers from poor maintenance, but can be overhauled by specialists. Rear springs gradually lose their temper, sag and break their leaves, especially on the heavy XK 150. Keep them clean and you will be able to spot ailments such as hairline cracks that can affect handling badly. By contrast, the adjustable torsion bars at the front rarely give trouble although the Metalastik suspension joints wear out. Front suspension parts are expensive so it is important to make sure that they are all in good order and that the wheels are properly balanced, as wobbling wheels cause even more wear.

The condition of the hubs is vital from the safety point of view. Examine the splines for wear and test for 'clonks' by taking your foot off the throttle at about 30 mph and then treading on the gas again.

Finally, pretend you are writing a book and get out your pen. Then, before you start to list all the other incredible things that can happen to a hard-used thirty-year-old sports car, run the pen round the splines of your wire wheels, if the car has them fitted. If they give a uniform 'ping' you should be happy. But a 'pong' noise, and rust seeping from the spoke heads, are both dangerous. They indicate loose spokes, with as many attendant pitfalls as writing a book on XKs.

VII

Strengths and Weaknesses: Part Two

PROVIDING AN XK is in good condition and properly serviced, it should give very little trouble in everyday use. The car really is one of the most reliable classic sports cars. It's when it is neglected or left standing for a long time that it poses problems. You can tell a great deal about the car by looking at it, listening to it and feeling how it handles at speed.

An XK should always look right. It should stand square on the road from every angle, poised ready to pounce like the Big Cat it is. If one haunch is lower than the other, or one side higher than its opposite, measure everything. It's quite an easy task really. Get one of those cigar packs which slide open (they're free if you know anybody who still smokes, and there's always some poor guy who'll accept the cigars if you can't face them yourself), then place the packet under one of the wishbone pivots. Extend the packet to measure the ground clearance and check that the measurement is the same on the other side. If the measurements are the same but the car still looks lopsided, carry out the same sort of check on the coachwork, except that you can use a ruler this time as there is room outside and not all cigar packets are that long! If the coachwork is lopsided, but the suspension heights are the same, you've got trouble; there's either been a mighty impact at some time, or the whole thing is collapsing (which should be obvious anyway). But if the wishbones are at different heights you don't have to worry much. You just jack up the car to take the weight off the wheels and fiddle with the torsion bar vernier adjustment till you get the ride height right both sides.

Actually, these torsion bars rarely give trouble, which is more than you can say for the leaf springs. The XK was designed in the days when there was a blacksmith in every village (and you could even find them in the towns). Apart from shoeing horses, retreading cart wheels with cast-iron slicks, making funny things out of wrought iron, and downing copious quantities of ale, these fellows were also very good at resetting motor car springs. That's all in the past now; you are better advised to replace the rear springs in pairs if they don't pass the cigar packet test. You need to check the shackle heights, of course, rather than the spring centres, because these should always be the same with the XK's old-fashioned solid axle. If the bodywork is out (which is all too common) suspect poor rust repairs to the inner wing, or wings that have not been fitted properly. And while you are scrabbling about round there check the shock absorbers, if you have an XK 120; the correct fluid level is vital in the old lever-arm shock absorbers. In fact, if they lose any oil they are on their way out and should be replaced or overhauled, otherwise the handling will deteriorate and you might fail the annual safety test in a country such as Britain. Unfortunately, these shock absorbers are fairly expensive.

Apart from these visual checks, it really does pay to examine an XK thoroughly every time you clean it, and it makes the chore a good deal more pleasurable anyway. Look for hairline cracks around the rivet holes and U-bolts on the rear springs; paint chips which could start corrosion; and fluid leaks which must receive immediate attention. Check the tyres for wear; an uneven tread pattern means that something is out somewhere and 16-inch tyres are scarce (even 15-inch E type tyres are on special order now if you have these wheels fitted). And save the last glance for the exhaust pipe(s). They should always be a pale shade of grey inside the ends after any sort of run where the engine has had a chance to clear its lungs. Black or white is bad and means your car is out of tune.

The tunes the engine plays are important, too. Listen to it every time you run it. You will be amazed at how much it can tell you. Take piston slap for instance. It is most noticeable when the engine is started from cold, before the pistons have expanded with the heat, and before the oil has started to circulate normally. During the first few moments of running the cylinder walls are comparatively dry. A quick dab on the accelerator will then produce a metallic clatter as the pistons slap from side to side in the bores. It means that an overhaul will soon be needed, while a similar sound, pinking, which occurs while the engine is hot and under load is often caused merely by the lead-free petrol we are having to use today and means that ignition adjustments are called for.

The tappets on an XK engine are prone to clatter under all running conditions with an intensity which varies with engine speed. No tappet noise at all calls for immediate attention, and equally when there is much too much. Hissing noises are made by loose manifolds or defective gaskets; you can trace leaks by squirting oil over the suspect part. Leaking manifolds can whistle, too, and you don't need a stethoscope to diagnose where the noise comes from. The only other items likely to whistle are the dynamo or water pump from lack of lubricant.

A noise somewhere between a whistle and a hiss can be caused by heavy-handed attempts to change the sparking plugs deep between the camshafts. Beware of damaging the plug body. One good blast on the throttle can send it skywards, still attached to its lead. It will come down with a thump and a bang and you'll wonder what on earth has happened. The same thing can result from cross-threading a sparking plug in that deep valley between the cam covers. The only difference is that the plug might take the threads with it leaving you with a considerable problem.

One of the best get-you-home solutions I have heard happened at Christmas time. After due consideration, the unfortunate XK's owner screwed in another plug using the lead covering from the neck of a wine bottle to jam up the damaged threads. Naturally he left the plug's lead off to minimize strain on the bodge-up, but it worked and the XK drove on until he could get a proper helicoil insert fitted.

Equally frightening things can happen when competition-minded people run

How the outer body panels of an XK fit together.

XKs without air cleaners. A cough-back in the carbs caused by something as seemingly insignificant as too little oil in the dashpots can send your beloved car up in smoke. If the excess petrol catches fire like this, restart the engine or at least keep it churning over on the staiter till the flames die or you can squirt them out with a fire extinguisher. It's one of the perils of fitting carburetters such as Webers: too many stamps on the accelerator while starting can be perilous.

So much for carburetter splutterings, which can also be caused by dirty plugs or worn valve guides. Squeaks can come from all over the place, notably a dry distributor drive. And whenever you delve down there make sure no moisture can reach the cap, from a faulty radiator overflow, for instance. Not only does damp on the cap impede starting, it can cause the cap to crack when it gets warm, which is disastrous for running, if you can get the engine to fire at all. There's only one solution to a cracked cap—buy another one, although Araldite over the crack can sometimes get you home. As any XK owner will know, the distributor is awkward to get

Plate 1 *left* Jaguar's hard-used XK 150S fixed-head coupé road test car, pictured in serene surroundings

Plate 2 *below* The XK 120 fixed-head coupé shows off its lovely lines on the famous football pitch behind the works, where so many new Jaguars were photographed

Plate 3 *right* One of the rarest XKs, the right-hand drive XK 140 roadster belonging to Bryan Corser

Plate 4 *below* The green green grass of home, and an XK 140 fixed-head coupé

Plate 5 *left* Pretty as a picture, the XK 140 drop-head coupé

Plate 6 *below* The long sweeping lines of the XK 150 roadster

Plate 7 What jolly boating weather . . .
and what jollier to take you there than
an XK 150 drop-head coupé?

Plate 8 *right* Beauty on parade: the XK 120 roadster of Bryan Corser

Plate 9 *below* Head of the line at a US concours, an XK 120 drop-head coupé with two 150s, a drop-head and a fixed-head, for company

Plate 10 *left* The car you could drive over all manner of roads and still win races in, the ex-Duncan Hamilton C type

Plate 11 *below* Bound for glory again: two D types and a Lister-Jaguar at the 1973 Le Mans historic race. In the foreground is a short-nosed car, behind it the long-nosed D type which finished second in 1957, and in the background the Lister that took over from them in 1958

Plate 12 Full-blooded power from John Harper in Paul Skilleter's alloy-bodied 120

Plate 13 The fastest Jaguar racer ever, John 'Plastic' Pearson's XK 120 drop-head coupé (even the hood was fibreglass!) pictured in 1970

Plate 14 Poetry in motion as Jens Roder speeds along a Danish road in his XK 150 roadster

Plate 15 It's concours time at Wallingford, Connecticut

Plate 16 *left* One of the most famous XKs in existence, Ian Appleyard's 120 roadster NUB 120, still bearing its Alpine rally plates

Plate 17 *below* What a touring car! The XK SS with appropriate registration number

Plate 18 *overleaf* Action all the way from John Harper in his XK 120 historic racer

Plate 19 Rare picture of an even rarer breed of Big Cat—the Ecurie Ecosse Tojeiro-Jaguar at the British Grand Prix meeting in 1959

Plate 20 OKV 3 in action at Le Mans in 1973

Plate 21 Jaguars on parade in support of the British Grand Prix: from the left, an XK SS; a D type; a Cooper-Jaguar; E2A; and a C type

Plate 22 Jaguar specials in action . . . two Costin bodied Listers

Plate 23 What an engine! One of the early XK 120 units with no studs on the front of the cam covers

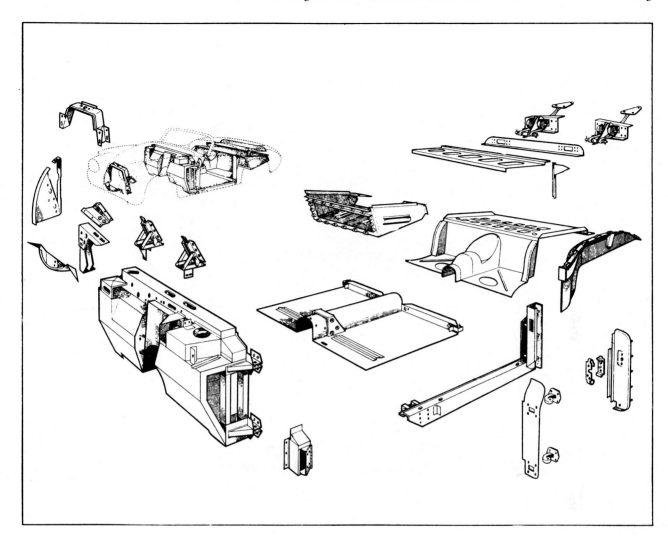

Frequent victims of corrosion: the inner body panels of an XK—in this case a 150S.

at, so make sure that the cap is seating properly, or you will get some mystery misfiring. A broken or misfitting clip can allow the cap to lift and turn slightly, resulting in a very woolly engine. As a temporary cure, you can lash the clip up with a strong rubber band.

There's a lot of strange faults that are invisible which can be cured by a spot of careful listening. Take, for instance, braided fuel pipes, which are among the greatest offenders of all. The wretched things collapse on the inside and starve the engine of fuel. You can't see the fault and it does not show up on a pressure test, which merely opens up the line again. But there is an audible diagnosis. The petrol pump stops ticking when this happens. If it ticks when the pipe is removed there must be a blockage in the pipe; if it ticks madly, but insufficient fuel gets to the engine, air can be leaking into the pipe even if there is no obvious fracture. In this case there is a fracture beneath the braiding, so squeeze all along the pipe till you find it. In the first case, a temporary cure can be made by fitting a piece of metal pipe into the fuel

The fixed-head's outer body panels—from a 150.

line and in the second case it is best to tape it up.

Clonking noises from the front can mean worn steering ball joints and Metalastik bushes. The joints tend to wear oval because they spend most of their life in a straight-ahead position. Clonks from the rear can be loose shackles and U-bolts on the springs. The cures to these ailments are obvious, but never neglect checking the hub splines at the same time. They can clonk, too, particularly when the brakes are applied hard or rapid acceleration is called for. When first heard in ageing vehicles it generally comes from the front of the car, but it can also come from the rear. H. C. Medcalf provided a graphic description in the *Jaguar Driver* magazine:

'The particular clunk I have in mind gets no better. In fact, it gets worse and louder. Exasperated owners may be seen crawling around their cars and even driving along with door open, half hanging out and accelerating madly for a second or so to the sound of loud clunks. Then temper is not improved by the thought of replacing all the rubber bushes in the front suspension, an operation which, if carried out, is likely to make this particular noise no better.

'This noise is frequently caused by worn splines on the hubs. The front ones tend to wear more than the rear ones, though eventually these too will need attention. Close examination of the splines will show just how thin the splines can wear, the very front part of the splines do not touch the wheel at all and so, as no wear takes place, comparison is very easy. When wear has reached the stage where this clunk can be heard under heavy braking then attention is called for. I would, at this point emphasise the need for attention. When one is dealing with a fine car capable of, and I hope, still traversing the country at up to 130 mph [this piece was written some time ago, but the sentiments remain], no item having a bearing on safety should be left unattended. If worn hubs are not replaced it is possible under heavy braking for the wheel to turn on the hub stripping all the splines on both hub and wheel hub. This movement, in turn, always brings off the hub cap, however tightly it is hammered on, and within a few yards the wheel falls off. Unfortunately this is not conjecture as I have spoken to someone who suffered this misfortune. Fortunately in his case speed was less than 50 mph and no injury resulted: the effect at high speeds can easily be imagined. Additionally the cost of repairing such damage is considerably higher than dealing with the hubs at an earlier date. . . .

'Removal of the front hub is comparatively simple, but a special puller is required for the rear ones. When the hubs are replaced it is also necessary to check for wear in the wheel hub . . . the aim should be that when the wheel is replaced with the car still on the jack, and before the hub cap is replaced, and with the brakes on, it is not possible to turn the wheel on the hub at all.'

Hubs are hard to get for the XK, but don't be tempted into taking such risks, thinking that hammering the hub cap on really tight will ensure you never lose a wheel. Be careful when removing a rear hub, too. Trevor Woodiwiss from South Africa nearly had a nasty experience when stripping a buckled hub on his XK 150S roadster: 'I battled for two or three weekends with a wheel puller', he said, 'and the hub eventually came off like a cannon and shot across the garden I was working in— I'm sure I would have been killed if I had been in front of it.' Obviously it pays to leave the securing nut on a few turns for safety!

There's not much more out of the ordinary to check on an XK, but always keep a close eye on the gauges. Every dial tells a tale: violent fluctuations on the ammeter mean immediate attention is needed to the batteries or voltage regulator; a fuel gauge which falls too rapidly can mean the petrol tank is leaking (seal it with Petseal if it is not too far gone); an inconsistent rev counter needle can be the first signs of clutch slip; a temperature needle that climbs in conjunction with the speedo-meter can herald a new head gasket; and an oil pressure needle that suddenly drops, without smoke from the exhaust, can be caused by a leaking sump gasket that spews oil only at high revs. Something as diabolical as that happened to Frank and Ted Walker, related in the Jaguar Drivers' Club *XK Bulletin*:

'Having had a most enjoyable run some 15 miles on a motorway at a steady

Its clunk-click every trip if your Metal-astik joints are as worn as this one.

3000 rpm and a steady 50 psi on the way to Prescott, I observed to my horror [wrote Frank] that the oil pressure was behaving in a manner somewhat similar to a British barometer. We now had a fluctuation of 10 to 40 psi. However luck was in, and a few yards up the road past the traffic lights was a filling station, on to whose forecourt we pulled.

'Hastily switching off the engine and leaping from the car, I looked under the front end of the 120 to see oil in large globules dripping onto the ground, whilst Ted lifted the bonnet in an apprehensive manner. Oil had streamed back along the chassis as far as the rear axle, and it looked extremely expensive. We removed the dipstick. It is a well-known fact that certain XK models have a sump capacity of 29 real pints, or 34 American ones, or if you wish it, 16.5 litres. On removing the dipstick it appeared that the sump now contained approximately seven real pints.

'Having looked first to see if there were any large orifices in the sump, we wiped away the surplus oil, and seeing nothing amiss, replenished the oil supply. The engine was started by Ted, and yours truly scanned the scene for the deluge. It came, from the metal-bonded flexible oil pressure take-off pipe on the top of the filter block, something that is impossible to foresee without very careful periodic inspection. These pipes become porous with age, and if you notice any sign of oiliness about them, change them. You could save yourself an awful lot of time and money. Luckily, in the case mentioned, there was no damage.'

Nevertheless, it pays to be a clock watcher with an XK.

VIII

Restoring your XK

THERE WAS A TIME when you could make rough and ready repairs on your XK and get away with it. That's just not on now unless you are stuck by the roadside. The cars are getting valuable and originality is all the rage: so you will be doing yourself no good at all if repairs are not carried out properly, even if they don't affect safety. The day of the bodge-up is gone.

The best examples of bodges used to be repairs to the door hinges. It's a fact of life that these items wear badly and allow their doors to sag. The theory of the design was that over the large area of contact between the hinge pin and the hinge arm, wear should have been minimal. In practice, the hinge pin corroded solid in the hinge arm and the bearing surfaces became the top and bottom plates of the hinge box and the corresponding surfaces of the hinge pin. When this happens, the bearing surface is reduced dramatically and rapid wear takes place because of the weight of the door, with the worst examples occurring in the 150 fixed-head, which had the heaviest doors.

Bill Lawrence, who looks after the Jaguar Drivers' Club XK register spares service, has the best method of repair that I have seen. He believes in doing jobs properly, but he is sufficiently realistic to realize that there must be a better way than removing the front wings to get at the hinge boxes; or hacking large holes in the wings in the manner of many bodgers. Certainly, many people managed to repair their bottom hinges from inside the car, but few enthusiasts are as lucky as they were now that the cars are getting older and, inevitably, the hinge pin will have become more difficult to shift.

Lawrence starts by drilling a three-quarter-inch hole directly under the offending hinge pin. It's not a bad place to drill a hole for it is practically out of sight under the wing curvature. The nut holding the bottom of the hinge pin can then be removed with a socket spanner—or not, depending on the state of corrosion. If it cannot be removed by conventional means, you can drill out the offending item to three-eighths-inch diameter. Then all you have to do is sleeve the drilled-out hole with a stainless steel bush from Lawrence and fit new hinge pins. Then fill the hole in the wing with a grommet, which is readily removed for lubrication. Alternatively you can drill and tap the hinge arm for a grease nipple and fill the hole in the wing permanently. If you are doing it this way, the bush will have to be drilled, too, and a helical oil groove machined along the inner length of the bush to serve as a grease channel. The position of the drilled and tapped hole in the hinge arm must be such that when the door is closed the grease nipple does not foul on the inner face of the wing.

Getting at the top hinge is a less dramatic exercise. You have to remove the inside ventilator panel, then the ventilator itself (I'm talking about the 150 fixed-head, but the principle is the same on the other XKs). This is secured by self-tapping screws, and you have to wrangle it over the vent arm. You can then see four quarter-inch nuts holding the vent flap, which must be removed. Then, working from the outside of the car, remove the rubber seal on which the vent door sits, and the six self-tapping screws underneath. There are six more self-tappers to remove inside and the vent assembly can then be removed. You now have access to the four quarter-inch bolts holding the rear of the hinge assembly, which are difficult to get at, but can be removed. With the door off, the assembly can then be removed for treatment like that to the bottom hinge. Watch out for shims on the hinge body; they will need careful replacement.

That's one of the easier jobs on an XK's body. The rest are rather more complicated and many need a high degree of skill. If you have to economize, it is best to decide what you can do and what is beyond you before you start. It's rather like decorating a house; most people are capable of hanging a modest length of wallpaper, but are likely to struggle when called to hang twenty-odd feet without a wrinkle beside the staircase (if you can afford more than one staircase you can afford to get a professional to restore your XK). Anyway, they paper the bedrooms themselves and call in the professional to decorate the hall. Its the same when you are restoring your family heirloom: a good compromise is to arrange for a reputable XK specialist to carry out the heavy metalwork, leaving you to refit all the little bits and pieces afterwards. You will save yourself a great deal of money doing these jobs yourself as they often take weeks or months.

If you find yourself in this economic bracket—most of us are—you have to plan the restoration carefully; not just waggle a finger at your grand vizier and tell him to get the XK restored, the Ferrari's starting to smoke.

You see, an XK is not an easy car to rebuild. You may well wonder why you didn't choose something nice and simple like an Austin-Healey or an MGA by the

It takes more than a snap of your fingers to restore an XK.

above left Plan your restoration carefully before you start or the number of parts revealed can be confusing.

above right Optimistic home restoration! Not all XKs recover from situations such as this.

The early and mid-1960s were the blackest periods for XKs. Scenes like this of an abandoned 120 roadster were common. Happily many survived.

A stripped 120 drop-head awaiting a rebuild.

time you're halfway through! Neither is it a cheap exercise, even if you do most things yourself, and beware of falling into the trap of assuming that your car won't need a full rebuild; apart from a very few freak cars, or those that have been kept in exceptionally dry climates, every XK now needs a substantial amount of work to its body if there is any sign of rust.

Before embarking on the exercise, it's worth looking at how an XK body is built. Basically, there were three major units: the big front wings, which by themselves form virtually the front third of the car, the front bulkhead which carries the windscreen and scuttle, and the rear section.

In fact, the rear end can be described as an independent component, and you can buy it complete from a number of XK specialists. It consists of rear inner wings, the tonneau panels which form the surround to the boot (or trunk) aperture, the boot floor, spare wheel well, and the rear bulkhead, which in later cars formed the 'plus two' area. The rear end is connected to the front bulkhead by means of two long sills, which themselves are mounted to the chassis with outriggers.

If you are going as far as removing the body from the chassis, it is usual for the body to be taken off in these three sections; in any case, if it's an average XK, it would probably break in half anyway if tackled any differently. But remember that when off the chassis the three main components should be supported in a way that avoids any possibility of distortion; it is worth setting up a series of trestles bound together with other pieces of wood rather like a car's spaceframe, so that the body parts are properly supported off the ground to save your back when you are working on them. There are other people who prefer to work on the body while it is still mounted on the chassis, and only then remove it so that the chassis itself can receive attention. This idea is perfectly sound providing the body is mounted properly on the chassis for a start; many have sagged.

That's the sort of work you are into when you spot a pinprick of rust in your beloved car's shutfaces. You will probably wind up having to remove the whole body to do the job properly. The job starts with removing all the minor components, work which can be done at home providing you have the patience to do it properly. Then you can clean up and refinish these items, such as chrome parts, while the heavy work, such as taking the body off, is being done by the experts. Its probably a good idea anyway; XK chromework is as precious as gold now and its safer kept under the bed than in some dim and distant workshop (at least that's what enthusiasts tell the people who share their beds!). And before you lay a spanner on the car (it's all too easy to dive in and begin ripping parts off) walk round it and make notes on what parts may be missing, or are going to need replacing; it's much easier to do this with an untouched car, when missing bits make themselves obvious, than trying to make sense out of a huge pile of rusty parts afterwards.

You should also find out which of the parts needed are readily available (ring up a specialist like Bill Lawrence) and which are going to take time to find; then plan everything accordingly, like your lady making a meal, so that it all arrives in good condition, in the right order, at the right time. And when the body's off, you can begin the normal procedure of stripping the chassis of its components (suspension, brakes and so on), after which you can take it for sandblasting. This will reveal any rust damage, which must be repaired before priming and painting. Its no good having blind faith in the substantial lines of the XK chassis; they can rust through like anything else made of steel. Its amazing how many people have stripped their cars to these last bones, then rubbed down the seemingly-massive chassis with emery paper, and refinished it to a high standard, only to find after reassembly that it was really rotten. Sandblasting, grinding, or drilling test holes is the only way to be sure that the chassis is really sound, then welding up the damage.

Meanwhile, the body itself can be repaired, and here it is preferable to replace as much as possible with complete new panels, rather than to patch. If the car is in really poor condition, the purchase of a complete new rear end is to be strongly advised; it will save hours and hours of unnecessary toil. New rear wings can be added to the ensemble if necessary; as for the front wings, repair sections for the sides of the wings can be bought. The better ones extend right up to the top curvature of the wing. But if the front wings are badly rusted or mis-shapen around the front curved portions, or full of ripples, new ones are the best cure. It's very difficult to achieve that lovely straight line down the side of the car otherwise. And that is the first thing that an expert, or a know-all, looks for when examining an XK.

Assuming that the basic shape is right, satisfactory repairs can often be made to the front wings by taking advantage of the repair kits mentioned, while you may need to fit new headlight and sidelight nacelles, which are also marketed again now. The same applies to the front bulkhead; you can now buy complete new ones, or just bulkhead ends, the triangulated portions whose lower parts so often rust away for the bottom six inches or so.

New XK sills are quite cheap to buy, but fitting them is a big job; taking the old ones out will probably mean destroying the old door shutfaces, too, so you'll need new ones (these are usually included in complete rear end assemblies). Other parts that usually need replacement on XKs are the front battery boxes, and the spare wheel well, all of which can be bought from specialists.

Rebuilding the body should normally be left to the experts; you have to be very keen and a competent welder and fitter to tackle the job alone, not to mention knowing how to lead-load the joints afterwards. So far as the chassis is concerned, any home mechanic of reasonable skill can rebuild the front suspension of an XK, as all the Metalastik joints and the two ball-joints are available. You might need the help of a garage to remove some of the old Metalastik bushes, though, and to get the new ones pressed home. A genuine factory workshop manual is an essential aid, and a parts book is most helpful, too.

When it comes to the interior of an XK, a roadster is obviously the easiest to retrim because there's much less of it. A careful home handyman can often successfully retrim such items as door panels, or even cut out and bind carpets, especially if he has a wife or girl friend sympathetic to the cause. They should be warned, though, that modern electric sowing machines do not always take kindly to stitching through heavy interior fabrics. The best machines to use are the old hand-operated Singers which amazingly can still be picked up for as little as five pounds in Britain. These wonderful little sewing machines dating back to granny's day are ideal for the slow, meticulous stitching needed with carpets, for instance. They are worth buying in any case as they will soon be antiques and start to soar in value as fast as an XK.

Stitching the seats is the biggest job in the interior once you have obtained the correct leather from Connollys, and is often best left to the experts, although their work can be expensive. While Connollys can supply exactly the right shade and texture of leather for any XK, it can be difficult to obtain the correct pattern of leather-cloth or vinyl for other parts of the interior, so keep samples of your old trim to make comparisons when you go shopping.

Another job which can be successfully tackled at home is the refinishing of an XK's woodwork, where fitted. The wooden parts should be removed according to the workshop manual (they require a fair amount of dismantling), and very carefully stripped of old varnish, taking care not to mark the veneer. Then, having made sure the surface is smooth and free from marks (staining may be required if the wood has faded), apply several coats of varnish—the polyurethene type is in general use now. You can use either a fine-haired brush, or a small spray gun for this operation.

When these first few coats are completely dry, rub down with a very fine grade of wet-and-dry paper, clean and re-coat. Continue this process until you are satisfied that you have a full, deep coverage with no brush or spray marks. Then, having rubbed down the final coat, bring to a deep polish with rubbing compound or Bluebell metal polish, then wax. This exercise should leave you with a finish that is as good as, if not better, than that supplied by the factory.

Finally, a word about jewellery, as the trade often calls the chrome trim on an XK. In common with many other manufacturers, Jaguar used a zinc alloy called Mazak for a number of their brightware castings, and this material self-destructs after about three or four years' exposure to the elements; chemicals in the air penetrate the chromium plate on the surface and attack the alloy underneath, which corrodes to form those familiar bubbles and pinpricks on the surface. XK 120 rear lights, the bootlid brightware on XK 140s and 150s, and door handles are some of the worst offenders.

Repair of Mazak castings is generally reckoned to be unsatisfactory. It seems that once the alloy has become contaminated with these impurities, no amount of re-chroming will help and the dreaded pinpricks will be back again within months. The correct alternative (once again!) is to fork out for replica parts cast in a more permanent material such as gunmetal or brass. These last almost indefinitely, and in any case can always be replated easily in future. Bonnet and bootlid badges are now being manufactured in replica form, too.

Ferrous-metal brightware is less of a problem, provided your car actually has them; XK bumpers, particularly those for the 120, are becoming difficult to

find, and expensive. If you are having your old bumpers replated, bear in mind that most of the plater's efforts are expended in polishing the old metal to a mirror finish and not in the actual electroplating process, so try to present him with the least pitted brightware possible.

First hand experiences of restoring an XK are legion, but there are few more impressive than those of David Salter, whose epic rebuild of a 150 fixed-head coupé was related in the *XK Bulletin*. While reading this account, it should be borne in mind that the rebuild took three years!

'My first task was to make the chassis sound. In order to do this the whole body and mechanics had to be removed stage by stage. After removing the rear body, I cleaned the chassis thoroughly, using a high-speed grinder and this enabled me to see where the chassis was rotten. Everything from the gearbox chassis cross-member back had to be removed, but before I did this I had to make a jig in order to line the new chassis with the front original section, which was in excellent condition due to an oil leak from the engine.

'To make the chassis, I used 18 gauge steel, shaping the metal into four box sections, welding the sections and seams together, the old chassis being used as templates. The four box sections were made into two chassis "arms" consisting of two sections each. The two completed arms were electrically welded to the front chassis. This was done by inserting the two box sections into the front chassis where the old chassis had been removed; these sections were welded in this position, then the new rear chassis was fitted over these to butt against the original front chassis. This was also welded making a strong and secure job.

'The next stage of this job was to make two cross-members to hold the spring hangers and petrol tank in position. Before these could be welded between the two arms of the chassis, the chassis arms themselves had to be sprung inwards exactly half an inch either side, by means of a carpenter's clamp. This stressed the chassis as it had been originally.

'The front wings were my next task. I again used the old wings as templates and shaped the new ones in three parts, side, top and front, using 20 gauge steel and welding all the seams together.'

This job, of course, is totally beyond the average owner, but because of the soaring value of XKs a variety of firms are now making replica body panels, as mentioned. They are obtainable through Lawrence at the Jaguar Drivers' Club, and, in fact, he makes many of the panels himself, being a skilled toolmaker. However, to continue with David's epic rebuild:

'I then decided when fitting the sidelight onto the wing to make a slight modification. Instead of flanging the sidelight into the wing, I fitted it into a triangular hole cut out of the wing and welded it in place. I then welded a false floor in the underside of the wing. This modification overcomes the usual problem of rust lifting the flanges. The headlight cylinder was fitted as the wing took shape and the wheel arch was turned and wired to shape. The wing was welded onto the bulkhead and bolted to the chassis; the same procedure was adopted for the other side. To complete the front half, the inner parts of the wings and battery

above right Typical home restoration scene.

above An XK's bulkhead mounted on its back on the bench for repairs, showing the bottom part which frequently suffers from rot. In this case, some new parts have already been fitted.

The bare bones of a restoration. Now's the time to check the chassis thoroughly.

boxes were all made to original specifications, though with another slight modification, this time to the battery boxes.

'To these I fitted rubber sealing strips between battery box and wing, to stop water and road dirt rusting the bottom of the wings. The sills were then made and bolted to the chassis.

'Next I attacked the rear of the car, the inner wings being my first objective. These were again made from 20 gauge steel, and were bolted to the chassis and sills, not forgetting the alloy spacers between chassis and wing. Over these inner wings I then fitted the valance which was made by hammering and stretching the metal to shape. The bottom part of the roof was then welded to the valence to complete the shaping.

'The inside of the boot and spare wheel compartment floor and sides were remade and welded into position before the boot lid was finally fitted. Using a new wing I had obtained as my pattern, I hammered, stretched and shaped the other rear wing. After much offering up of the two wings, I was finally able to secure them. The metal floors and back seat compartments were made and welded to the sills and rear half, and the two wooden floors were bolted in position. All metal body parts were painted with black bitumenous paint during assembly.

'The complete shells of the doors were made in several sections which were welded together.'

It should be noted at this point that kits to repair parts of the doors, particularly the bottom, are now available as frequently it is possible to salvage the top of the door. The best kits to use are the ones which extend right up to the curve of the door, where the metal is strong. A poor quality door repair will often give a 'dished' look to the panel. This is because when making body parts from smaller pieces, extreme care has to be taken when welding to avoid distortion. David then rebuilt his door hinges and 'with all the structural parts now made and fitted I could start on the mechanics', he reported.

'On stripping down the original engine I found that the cylinder bores, crankshaft and cams were in quite good condition and only needing a new set of pistons, big ends and main bearings. I assembled the bottom half of the engine and then decided to replace the timing chains and sprockets. Furthering my attentions to the head, I decided to fit all new valves and springs, and spent a great deal of time polishing the ports.

'The gearbox was also stripped down and all new gears and bearings fitted. The back axle, when examined, needed new bearings, but the crown wheel and pinion were in excellent condition and therefore did not need replacing. All the brakes were overhauled, new discs and wheel bearings fitted and all new brake pipes, including the metal ones, replaced. A replacement servo unit completed this section of the car.'

It's the brakes which seem to suffer most during a prolonged rebuild! Brake fluid readily absorbs water and the entire system can corrode rapidly. If a rebuild is likely to take a long time it is well worth while stripping the brake system to begin with, to preserve the parts from corrosion. And if the car is likely to be used only in the summer months, it is worth doing this before winter storage. The same applies to clutch hydraulics, of course. The use of non-corroding metal pipes such as Kunifers also helps to prolong the life of a system.

David's next job was to rebuild the suspension, which makes a fantastic difference to many cars' handling, and to make a new wiring loom. It is hardly worth the trouble making a new loom now that excellent replacements, complete with all fittings, are available. It is worth running a new loom inside the car, however, rather than through the chassis as originally fitted, to avoid the trouble caused here by dirt and corrosion.

'It then came to spraying the car and preparing the surface and welded seams for this', said David. 'I first covered the welded seams with body solder and then went over all the body with a fine sanding disc, to buff off the surface ready for etch priming. After applying the etch primer there came six undercoats of grey, and then six top coats, rubbing down the surface between each coat. The car was beginning to look more like a car now than it had for the last two and a half years. It was still not finished, though, for we still had the upholstery to renew. Apart from the two front seats and headlining, which were recovered and remade by a professional upholsterer, the rest was done by my wife and myself, using a very old hand sewing machine which coped very well. The final stage, before the wheels were fitted, was a complete undersealing and water-proofing of the underside of the body.'

That's the sort of thing you get involved in when rebuilding an XK! The mechanical side is quite straightforward, strictly as per workshop manual. Probably the most important aspect of running an XK, once it is in good condition, is rust-proofing. Underseal, as used by Salter, is quite efficient for about three years, if applied properly. After that is often becomes brittle, allowing cracks to form, thus letting water in behind the coating. The rust that develops from this syndrome is chronic as the water cannot escape outwards through the rubberised underseal. It therefore eats its way through the metal, appearing eventually on the exterior as pinhead pricks, which rapidly develop into bubbles as the paint lifts and eventually huge holes appear in the once pristine panel. The way to avoid this is by scrupulous maintenance of the underseal to prevent any cracks forming and to renew the whole coat when it becomes brittle.

An alternative is coachpainting the entire underside of the car and keeping it scrupulously clean, or spraying everything frequently with oil in the old-fashioned way. There are specialist firms providing these treatments and other kinds such as wax injection of box members; or you can use products such as Waxoyl yourself, injecting it into sills, head and sidelight nacelles, and wherever there is an enclosed space. But it should always be remembered that rustproofing is just part of the ordinary maintenance of a car and does not last for life. Ideally such treatment should be subject to a two-yearly overhaul.

IX

The American Scene

THERE'S NOBODY who has appreciated his XK more than the average American. From the first time he set eyes on these immortal sports cars, through the 1960s when general interest was on the wane, until today when enthusiasm has never been higher, his attitude has never changed: for him XKs are just great. For sure, many Americans thrashed their XKs during the glory years and neglected them during the bleak years, but the car was always special. Whether screaming away from traffic lights or rattling along to college, it was the XK that turned everybody's head and filled its driver with pride. And now they have become antiques, classics, call them what you like, their status is assured. However, I doubt whether anybody has loved his XK more consistently than Jack Stamp from Wichita, Kansas:

'I saw my first Jaguar in 1948 while attending the Indianapolis 500-mile race. It was an SS tourer and it was love at first sight. Having grown up in the state of Oklahoma, in the centre of America, sports cars of this type were just not seen. On a return trip to the 500-mile race in 1950, I saw an XK 120 and knew at that moment that I would have to own one.

'At that time the closest Jaguar dealer to my home in Oklahoma was 400 miles away in St Louis, Missouri. In June of 1951 I took the train to St Louis to take delivery of a bronze XK 120, number 670993, from the Clayrich Motor Car Company. On the drive back to Oklahoma the Jaguar proved to be everything I had read about it. During the next year I became active in the Sports Car Club of America, entering rallies and races. Also, as this was my only car, I drove it daily. There were only four or five Jaguars in the entire state of Oklahoma and the car would always draw a great deal of attention. The car proved to be very dependable and the fact that no dealership was within 400 miles in any direction caused little concern.

'During the 1950s in the Midwest, sports car racing was done on small airfields with little or no weekend air traffic. On some occasions, a race would have to be delayed for a scheduled flight to land, however. The cars most frequently seen at these events were XK 120s, MGs, Allards and a C type now and then. The cars were driven to the event by their owners and upon arriving, hubcaps and bumpers were removed. Headlights were taped. And after the races, the removed parts were put back on and the cars were driven home.

'At one of these races held in Okmulgee, Oklahoma, I offered the XK 120 to a tall, lean Texan called Carroll Shelby, who was just starting his racing career. He won that day and followed it with many others including Le Mans.

'In 1952, the XK 120M was announced and in August of 1952, I traded the XK 120 in for a metallic blue XK 120M, number 672539. This car was used as its predecessor, except for racing. In September 1955, I purchased one of the new XK 140 MC drop-head coupés, number 817339, the car I still own today. Over the past 22 years, the car has been used for pleasure, entering rallies, autocrosses, gymkhanas and concours. In 1956, I became a member of the Jaguar Owners' Association, which later became the Jaguar Clubs of North America. In the late 1960s and early 1970s, clubs were formed rapidly throughout the country with concours as the highlights of their activities.

'After entering two JCNA concours in 1973, a complete restoration programme was begun during the winter of 1973–4, and during the next three years the XK 140 was entered in 20 concours, winning 17 first places, three seconds and three best-of-show awards. This car has also won three national JCNA championships in its class, from 1974 to 1976, and was driven 13,000 miles to all events.

'I can truthfully say that I am as enthusiastic about my Jaguars as I was all those years ago when I took delivery of my first XK 120. At present I own two other Jaguars, besides the XK 140. My wife, Vicki, drives a 1969 XKE Two Plus Two and I drive an 1971 XJ6 in which I have covered 107,000 miles. During the past 26 years, I have driven Jaguars nearly 200,000 miles and enjoyed every one. . . .'

It's people like Stamp and Bruce Carnachan from Glendale, California, who are the greatest ambassadors for Jaguar cars. Carnachan bought his XK 120 special equipment roadster, chassis number s675728, in June 1957, from a friend who purchased it new at Brentwood Motors, Los Angeles, in November 1954. 'I used the car for rallies, time trials, gymkhanas, economy runs and daily transport until 1969, when a leaking head gasket forced me to embark on a rebuild that was to take eighteen

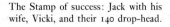
The Stamp of success: Jack with his wife, Vicki, and their 140 drop-head.

Bruce Carnachan with his great love, his 120 roadster.

months', said Carnachan. 'At that time I did not plan on making a concours special as I believe that Jaguars are meant to be driven.' Nevertheless, while rebuilding the engine, Carnachan was pleased to find that all tolerances were within factory specifications and took no short cuts in the restoration. 'That's quite something at 96,400 miles', he said.

Carnachan also concentrated on keeping the car in its original state, a pleasing trend that has developed in recent years, particularly in American restoration. Gone are the days of the tarted-up XKs with extensive chrome plating, wide wheels and maybe even a V8 under the bonnet. The people who did that to classic cars have either moved with the times and restored their beloved machines to their original specification or moved on to the custom car field, where run-of-the-mill saloons or vans are the subject of their frequently bizarre work. It must be admitted, though, that many of these old saloons and vans are better as custom cars, having been close to the scrap yard before they caught the eye of the custom car people. These people never touch an XK now because they are too expensive and recognized as glorious reminders of the past, although, to their credit, they are frequently to be seen admiring absolutely standard XKs at jamborees and shows.

Whether he intended to show his XK or not, Carnachan stuck to the original light-blue colour scheme during his retrim and respray and made a magnificent job of it. The 120 finished third first time out; quite an achievement, as American concours are of an exceptionally high standard, attracting the most fanatical of owners.

'Three second places and seven first followed before becoming the 1975 JCNA national class two XK 120 champion', said Carnachan. 'It was great to win this award, but I got more pleasure from the 1974 Western States conference meeting.'

He drove 600 miles to compete in all manner of events that day at Clear Lakes,

California, winning the concours and the gymkhana before being voted owner of the second most popular car behind a magnificent 1948 3½-litre Jaguar drop-head coupé. It was the great American dream come true: win the concours, win the gymkhana and then step back modestly to acclaim an elder.

Carnachan and his car were really living, like the time he saw 126 mph on the speedometer on the back straight at Ontario Raceway before slowing for 'other traffic' and taking turn two at 100 mph; like the time the car broke the lights at 131.2 mph, top and side curtains up, at the El Mirage drag festival in the California Desert 'back in 58. . . .' Said Carnachan:

'That was a great day and I guess we could have gone faster, but one of the top snaps blew open and I thought a tyre had gone, so I lifted off the gas with more than 100 yards to go to the timing light. The rev counter showed 5400 at the time, so I think we could have made 134–135 mph on those Dunlop tyres.

'In the same year, I ran the car in a quarter-mile drag strip event with a best run of four at something over 15 seconds with the top up and side curtains on. On this run I was paired with a '56 Corvette with V8 and manual transmission, but I only saw him in the rear-view mirror after the start.

'The 120's acceleration seems on par with my 1965 Mustang GT coupé, which has a four-throat carburetter, dual exhaust, and 225 bhp through automatic transmission. They both reach 60 mph from rest in 8.2 seconds, with the Mustang very quick up to 30 mph if you can control the wheelspin, and the Jaguar much stronger once you get into second gear above 25 mph.'

Carnachan also has an XK 140 roadster, number s810019, fitted with 72-spoke Boranni alloy wheels and Alfin brake drums from new in 1954 that he is intending to use in historic racing; and five other XKs to restore, a 120 roadster, a 120 drop-head and a 120 fixed-head, plus two 140 drop-heads! XK owners are like that, dedicated to preserving the marque.

Scottish-born Arthur Kinnear, mechanic-in-charge for Air Canada at New York's John F. Kennedy Airport, is one of the leading lights on the East Coast. He owns an XK 140 drop-head and a 120 roadster that has become a TV star! The 1951-model XK 120 took ten years to restore from a 'pile of junk' to second place winner in the 1974 national concours, before being featured in TV and magazine advertisements for men's clothing, cosmetics and so on. 'It leads me a very exciting life, and the money helps', says Kinnear. His XK 140 is in equally good shape, also winning a second place in national concours, in 1975.

'The XK 140 is the car I have owned the longest [says Kinnear], and it is still very original except for the engine, which I replaced with one from an XK 140 I found in a tree!

'I took the original 8:1 compression ratio engine out and installed a 9:1 engine with C type head, 2-inch SU carbs and close-ratio gearbox, which now makes it a very comfortable car with a most respectable turn of speed.

'A couple of years ago a few of us Jaguar owners got together and formed Jaguar Drivers' Club in the greater New York area where we meet every third

Happiness is a 120 roadster and a 140 drop-head for Art Kinnear.

Bob and Marie Smiley have a right to look confident: their competition-prepared XK is about to win its class and best-in-show award at the Jaguar Club of southern New England's concours at Wallingford, Connecticut, in September 1974.

Part of a typical line-up for an American concours.

Saturday of the month. We are trying something new this year with the rebuilding of a 3.4-litre engine during our meetings as the chief project. This enables some of our members who are not too mechanically-minded to see how it's done. We also thought it was a good idea as most of the questions we are asked seemed to centre on engine problems.'

Kinnear is president of the club; many of his club mates work for airlines and spend a lot of time travelling the world looking for XK parts. They run an extensive spares self-help service, assisting fellow owners from as far away as Brazil with parts picked up at sales in Britain and elsewhere. Kinnear is a man of many projects, including a deep interest in the Ecurie Ecosse.

'Being Scottish by birth, I have been reviewing the history and accomplishments of the Ecurie Ecosse for my personal interest', he says. 'Last year I was over in Scotland five times talking to and corresponding with people who were associated with the stable, including Lord Elgin. I was able to find a couple of Ecurie Ecosse wrecks in Scotland, the Tojeiro crashed by Masten Gregory at Goodwood and one of their old Listers . . . they will be great cars again one day.'

The American scene is not confined to concours and other more gentle club competitions, though. There are XK owners such as Bob Smiley, from Northport, New York, who actively campaign their cars in the historic racing which is rapidly catching on in the United States. Smiley got the racing bug after taking part in speed weekends at Lime Rock and Bridgehampton.

'It would irk me when at Lime Rock, after turning a particularly good time in my XK 120, I would have to listen to Al Garz say "But, of course, this is not racing; this is only high-speed touring! We are not racing." I discovered very quickly how right he was when I bought my winter project XK 140 roadster, the ex-Julian MacKay car, to the SCCA driver's school at Lime Rock on July 28, 1977. I was taking the first step towards fulfilling a dream: getting a regional racing licence.

'At the Lime Rock school, fifty-seven prospective racers began by listening to a one-hour chalk-talk where among other things we studied a map of the course and were shown "the line". I thought about how my five years' experience at this track with our club would really pay off. I knew the line already! I had trophies to prove it. Little did I realize that on this day I would only occasionally have access to the line! For in the first half-hour session on the track, with thirty-one other closed-wheel cars ranging from Corvettes and A sports racers to MG Midgets and showroom stock Hondas, driving at my old time-trial speeds, I would be mostly concerned with relinquishing the road to the onrushing Vettes or impatiently trying to pass those seemingly out-of-control showroom stockers! The line was the last thing on my mind because I was frightened to death . . . really. If at that point my crew had suggested that we go home, I would not have argued. They didn't suggest it, but they did think about it, as I found out later! But the worst was yet to come.

'I drove out for the second half-hour session feeling a bit more comfortable driving the line when it was possible, passing when it was safe, and signalling the obnoxious Corvettes to pass me when necessary. Not that they needed the signals! Their best signal seemed to be the yellow flag, under which they passed with increasing regularity. I was driving as fast as I could safely, not caring to injure my body or my car. The session over, I steered for the pits, parked the car, and headed for the spot where our group instructors were to deliver a critique on our performances. It began: "Car number 49 [me]. You didn't hit the apexes twice the same way. You're apexing too early in the uphill, too late in the downhill and not at all in turn three! Have you found the apex in the Big Bend yet? There is one, you know!" I found there was one to get in and one to get out. Little did they know that I had all I could do to control this beast, let alone steer it accurately through a turn. I felt embarrassed, defeated and insignificant. What in hell did these people know about driving an old Jaguar? Didn't they notice me driving with my right hand on the main straight, flapping my left arm over the door trying to regain circulation? It's certainly draughty out there. . . .

'The severest cut was the comment: "Car 49, you're too slow. You've got to get faster." Nobody knew Bob Smiley, but dammit, everybody knew car 49. Why had I made those numbers so large?

'Time had come for the third session. I began to drive with, I thought, reckless abandon, faster than I had ever driven. I was surprised when the wheels didn't fall off and when I didn't spin out in the West Bend, my old nemesis in time trials. I began to hear the beautiful music of the exhaust that is played on a Jaguar when the revs exceed 5500 and I was happy. I was thrilled when I discovered that for whatever shortcomings the old Jag had in handling capability, there was precious little in its class that was more powerful on the straights. I knew that when I passed three C and D production cars on the main straight, tucked in neatly in front of them and drove headlong for the apex (I found it!) in the Big Bend. I was having fun, real fun, when I suddenly discovered that I could no longer shift gears. The clutch had blown. I limped slowly round the track, down the main straight, onto the escape road beyond the Big Bend and pulled to a stop. Utter dejection! Just when I was going good. I sat there watching all the other cars finish the third session. As they came down the main straight, directly towards me, before veering toward Big Bend, I imagined they were laughing at me, especially the cars I had just passed before the clutch blew. Then came the awful ignominy . . . having to be towed into the pits by a Datsun pick-up truck, like a huge green whale being hauled to shore. What further embarrassment could I suffer?

'But at least I was driving better and faster, so on to the critique for a morale-boosting compliment. Like hell! "Car 49, you've got to get faster!" I nodded in agreement, and thought to myself that they were supposed to teach me to drive faster. Wasn't this a school? Yes it was a school, and soon I received my official report card. Average scores for judgement and technique and a poor score for lap times. Very good score for attitude and courtesy! I was delighted to learn that they thought highly of my attitude and courtesy, but I wondered how these traits were going to make a successful race driver. Especially courtesy! Finally the chief steward's official remark: "Could be faster". What did that mean? Was could a polite way of saying should? Were they being courteous too? Or were they complimenting my third session efforts and saying could instead of must? We drank some beer and I wondered whether I would ever make the next school, two weeks hence.

'But I did. After a session of twelve- to eighteen-hour work days in the 100 degree heat of early August, repairing the ravages of the first school (both physical and emotional), and after an intermediate test session on the proceeding Tuesday where we discovered numerous other problems (this is called sorting out!), my crew (my wife and MacKay) and I were out for the August drivers' school. This was to be the last school of the year in this part of the country. Six hours of driving time and approval of the observing officials are necessary to qualify for a novice permit. The blown clutch in the first school had limited me to about one and a half hours' time, and only three more hours would be possible here. Julian noted that I would need to "dazzle" the officials. He said permits were often granted to student drivers who seem to have made significant progress and appear ready for the experience of a regional race, although they might not have six hours on the course. The car ran perfectly and we completed the entire three hours without incident, while gradually reducing lap times. I don't know whether or not the officials were dazzled but they all agreed that I was much faster and smoother and ready to race. I got my permit and I was so happy I was numb!

'Experience did it. It was my second school and I had a tremendous advantage over those who were applying in their first school. That little bit of experience and accompanying confidence were all that was needed. We finished fourth in the students' race to a 400 bhp Lola, a Camaro and a Corvette, out-performing all cars in comparable classes. WE did it. I use that pronoun frequently now. When a race car is successful, it is the "we", the entire crew, that makes the success possible.

'So it really was a school! I learned that experience is a great teacher. I learned that practice makes not perfect, but closer to perfect. I learned that the efforts of many contribute to any small success an individual may achieve and that building confidence is vital to improved performance. But after all, I should know these things. I'm a teacher myself!'

But Smiley is more than that. He is one of the greatest XK enthusiasts in America, having achieved the magic 100 points at the JCNA Empire Division's concours in 1976, a much sought and rarely achieved distinction. The preparation included fitting special 'show' exhaust manifolds to his race-prepared XK 120 after arrival at a show and then replacing them with his 'travelling' manifolds, lest the heat should spoil the show pipes' finish. Now Smiley has retired this car from concours after winning five successive best-of-show awards and finishing second by 0.1 of a point in the JCNA National Challenge Trophy competition.

His contribution to the events now is a third XK, an immaculate, entirely original XK 120 roadster, looking exactly as it did when it left the factory in 1954, even to the paint and upholstery, which are unchanged. In his 'spare' time he races the 140, finishing second and third in his first two events and later gaining his regional licence before aiming at a national licence. That's the role of an XK in America today: club events, concours, racing and fun on the road. Americans have never appreciated them more.

'This is one of my favourite pictures', says Bob Smiley. You can see why. Both cars are his!

X

XKs Abroad

AUSTRALIA AND NEW ZEALAND are two of the greatest centres of interest in the XK world. The early XK 120s were greeted with wild enthusiasm in 1950; in fact, the first XK 120 to arrive in Australia was only the second production car. It was used to good effect by the distributors, Brysons, for publicity, eventually being donated as a major prize in a Sydney lottery.

As the years went by, the XKs gradually found their way on to the used car lots and by the mid-1960s enthusiasm was at its lowest ebb. You could buy a tatty old XK very cheaply, blast it all over the country, bodge it up and sell it for much the same as you paid for it. But when manufacturers everywhere were gradually forced to drop their open sports cars in face of looming American safety regulations, interest revived in the glorious XKs. Even old number two, the lottery car, surfaced again in a sorry state; it was discovered on an isolated farm on the southern New South Wales coast, with bits and pieces scattered over a wide area. The owner was totally unmoved by the most persistent pleas to sell his car for restoration. He was a 'gunner' (to use the Australian description), a man who was 'gonna restore it some day' but never would. However, while Jaguar enthusiasts know that old number two is still alive, they will never give up their attempts to revive it.

One of the greatest enthusiasts in Australia is Les Hughes, who co-owns an immaculate XK 150S fixed-head coupé with his father, who is also called Les.

'Our first real contact with XKs was in 1963', said Les junior. 'I distinctly remember my father coming home from his business bubbling with excitement after a colleague had just bought a magnificent grey XK 150S 3.8-litre fitted with D type wheels. This car was absolutely pristine, and in my father's eyes, everything a Jaguar should be. Today this car is stored in an air-tight heated box and is only used on the rarest occasions, but the memory has lingered. . . .

'Seven years later I bought my first Jaguar—the greatest and most thrilling car I had been near. Soon after, my father and myself joined the Jaguar Car Club of Victoria and dad bought a 3.8-litre Mark II saloon, while my car was a 1956 2.4-litre Mark I. The enthusiasm and "disease" soon caught us, and after several more Mark IIs, including a very fast overdrive model, we started to think of the ideal car and soon came to the conclusion that it was the one firmly imprinted in dad's memory, that XK 150S. By that time I had become a com-

The lovely 150S fixed-head owned by
the two Les Hughes, father and son.

mittee member of the club, with my 2.4-litre winning the odd concours award,
alongside the XK 150S from the airtight box, which was often voted the car of
the day. Meanwhile, Dad scoured the newspapers of several states, trying to
find an original XK 150S.

'Our clubmates joined in the hunt and eventually we asked the Jaguar
Drivers' Club of New South Wales for help. Soon after, one of their members,
John Thomas, told us of a car which had been left in a wrecker's yard with the
engine dismantled, and half of the car protruding from a shed. However, the
car had been well-maintained in its day and was just what we wanted, a 3.8-litre
XK 150S fixed-head.

'It had not been modified, and although grass had grown through the
floor and into the engine compartment, the body was not too bad and nothing
was missing. We bought the car unseen and it was transported back to
Melbourne, 500 miles away.

'Our first sight was rather disappointing for the body had several dents and
seven years' exposure to the elements had made it pretty grubby. However,
the whole car was sound and had no rust and showed no signs of major accident
repairs, although the engine was rather rough. The inside of the car was
completely original, in light grey to match the Cotswold blue exterior. We were
not too keen on this colour scheme, but decided not to change it, for the sake of
originality.

'Restoration work was done over several years, during which time the car
was never off the road for long. My father did most of the work, with only items
such as painting done outside by a professional.

'The engine and gearbox, which were original, were stripped and rebuilt, using all new parts, many of which were obtained with the help of a friend in Oxfordshire, Geoffrey Stevens, who built a unique XK 150 estate car. The front end was re-rubbered with parts which the XK Register in Victoria had discovered could be interchanged with local cars such as Holdens and Ford Falcons, plus old stocks found by Brysons, who have always co-operated with the clubs.

'Local engineering firms re-sleeved the cast iron brake cylinders, but again, mostly new parts were used. The body was stripped to bare metal and all the dents knocked out; all the chrome was re-done and new S badges for the doors were cast. After re-spoking the chrome wire wheels, we sprayed them with water and left them outside for three or four nights to see if they rusted. This proved to be an ideal way of checking the job, even if the wheel repair company did not appreciate having to do their work again on one or two occasions.

'Many other bits and pieces were replaced and the upholstery and interior renovated only recently. The leather had suffered the usual Australian problem of drying out in the intense heat unless continually fed with hide food. Countless hours were spent on detail work and the car has frequently won its section in concours events, although it has been retired now that we have found a Mark VII saloon, and haven't the time to prepare both cars. The XK, however, is still used extensively for club outings, including the 2000-mile trip to Queensland for the annual get-together each winter.'

The Hughes's XK 150S is a good example of the original cars that have survived in Australia; the XK 140 fixed-head coupé of John Smith is a typical example of the cars that have been extensively modified to keep them running. John reported in the *Jaguar Journal* of Australia:

'My car started life as a British Racing Green coupé with C type head and close-ratio gearbox. It was first used as a team support car at Le Mans and then sold to the Sultan of Johore, a noted car buff. It came to Australia at the time of the Empire Games in Perth (in 1960) and it seems that the Sultan sold it rather than have it shipped back. The car had several owners in Western Australia until it came into violent collision with a Holden in 1965. The result of this was the total destruction of the right hand front mudguard and door, a bent chassis and assorted other damage.

'At this stage the car was regarded as a write-off and was duly partly wrecked. The seats found their way into a Morgan, the engine and gearbox went into an XK 120 and sundry other items were disposed of. This process went on as the car changed hands many times until 1969 when Wing Commander Ian Boughton bought the car and started restoration. A new wing, door and grille were obtained and the chassis and body separated and straightened. Ian succeeded in fitting the body and chassis back together and setting it up with XK 150 wire wheels and disc brakes before he was posted to Singapore. The car stayed in Perth and I bought it from Ian a year later. Ian had also bought a wrecked XK 150S which had a 4.2-litre E type motor in it and the two cars were sold as a package deal.

Alan Shepherd (left) and Dave Jewell test their 120 roadster during Original Performance Day at Wangergo, Australia.

Part of the XK line-up at the Australian Jaguar Car Clubs' annual national weekend at Mildura in 1976.

'The 4.2-litre motor was fitted to the XK 140 with an overdrive gearbox with the minimum of difficulty and the clutch was converted to hydraulic operation. The XK 150 pedal and master cylinder assembly was welded to the XK 140 chassis, which gave a much better pedal position than the original 140 set-up. The twin fuel pumps off the XK 150S were fitted along with a large filter and the car was completely rewired with better fusing arrangements and all terminal blocks and fuses inside the car for easier servicing (as a consequence the car has yet to blow a fuse).

'The missing bumpers were not replaced and any other non-essential items were left out in a weight-saving campaign. The twin batteries were replaced with a single 12-volt unit which has proved quite adequate and lighter. The weight-saving campaign succeeded and the car is now about 200 lb lighter than

Some of the Australian restorations are magnificent, particularly that of this 150S.

standard and significantly faster.

'A twin two-inch bore straight through the exhaust system was constructed and though undoubtedly efficient in getting rid of the gas, its muffling ability has proved to be limited.

'Several problems cropped up on the road. One was an appetite for spring centre bolts and the other was an appetite for tyres. Wheelspin was a big problem even with the 185 x 15 Michelin X A S tyres that I had fitted on E type chrome wire wheels. A limited slip differential was duly obtained from a wrecked XK 150 and fitted. This almost cured the wheelspin problems and improved acceleration off the mark quite noticeably. Tramp rods are my next project.

'The original radiator proved inadequate and was replaced by a modern multi-tube core of heavy design and a Fiat 128 electric fan was fitted. I have never liked mechanical fans because of the power losses associated with them. At any rate, the overheating was duly banished, although not without great cost having been incurred: the new radiator cost the equivalent of £150—it must have had a gold core!

'Alfa Romeo bucket seats have been fitted to the car and are an absolute must. The true bucket design holds driver and passenger perfectly under any conditions and they must be regarded as a major improvement on the original fittings. They are also the only major part that is non-Jaguar.

'The car and I have enjoyed considerable success in club competitions since then and it is probably one of the fastest XKs in Australia; top speed has yet to be reached, but it seems likely that it is in excess of 145 mph, and a standing start quarter mile has been covered in 15.5 seconds, with more to come from better technique and tramp rods.

'On the road, the performance is belied by the greatest docility you could imagine. The engine has massive low speed torque and high revs are rarely used. Passing ability in top gear is first class and overall performance is excellent. Ride can only be described as mediocre and the noise level as high, but overall the car is as close to my idea of being perfect as the Aston Martins, Ferraris and Maseratis I have driven. It has more appeal than Jaguar's own E type, for me anyway, and I do not contemplate changing cars for a long time to come.'

It is estimated that around 600 XKs have been imported new and second hand into Australia, with most finding homes in Sydney, Melbourne, Adelaide and Brisbane, although the earliest complete example, chassis number four, has been raced by Boughton in Western Australia. Some of these cars have been found in terrible condition and more examples are being imported in all manner of states of repair and disrepair as values continue to soar. Good examples were fetching around £8000 in 1978, with the emphasis on XK 120s after years of market dominance by the XK 150.

The scene in New Zealand is much the same as Australia with two of the greatest enthusiasts there, Harvey Hingston and Grant McMillan telling how they lived with their XKs in the middle years.

'I had just turned 21 when I bought my first XK [said Harvey in *Jaguar Driver*] and my father's protests concerning the purchase of a sports car were politely listened to but not heeded. My brother and I had decided to pool our resources and buy a car that would go fast, and stand up to a "good stropping" without constant tuning and replacing burnt-out valves. We noticed that a Jaguar XK 120 was for sale at Christchurch (400 miles away), so we flew down to the Jaguar dealers, Archbalds Ltd, where the car was on sale on behalf of a client.

'The car was marked at £995, and its owner had just completed racing it successfully at local club meetings. This XK had the C type head, 2-inch SU carbs, lightened flywheel and D type exhaust system, whose contents burst into the atmosphere near the passenger's side door. The owner then took us for a demonstration, which is still vivid in my memory. What a contrast to the low-powered machinery we had been used to! The owner knew how to demonstrate the car's capabilities all right—I noticed the speedometer hovering on 100 mph in third gear within the 30 mph residential limits of Christchurch, and frankly, I was scared stiff!

'The car was duly purchased for £990 and how proud we were of our new acquisition. When we arrived home our father greeted us with the words: "Second hand raced Jaguar junk—you boys will break your necks!"

'The sprucing up scheme now began. New white enamel, new red carpets, and the seats reupholstered.

'The performance was still shattering, but the oil consumption! One quart per 100 miles. During the winter, my brother and I, armed with a factory manual, decided to take our time, and strip the engine, and, oh! what we found! Four of the pistons were cracked and only the rings were holding them together. Our financial outlay left us with insufficient cash to replace these parts, so I sold my old bicycle for £5 and my brother sold his fishing rod. Pistons were then

left Aldo Vinzio's 350,000-mile 140
fixed-head climbs the Col du Simplon.

right Australia has one of the best-kept
and most original D types in captivity:
that owned by Bob Janes.

obtained and fitted and then the cylinder head was taken to a local garage to
have the valve seats stoned. This head had valve face angles of 45 degrees and
30 degrees, but this garage (it was the first Jag head they had seen) stoned both
seats to 45 degrees and very nearly wrecked the head! However, after some
weeks the car burst into life once more, with the same bellow, but less smoke.

'The speed limit in New Zealand at this time was 50 mph (it is now 55
mph) so speeding had to be done discreetly. We used to do our speeding at night
—preferably with the hood down, and a full moon. Twice a week I used to
travel on good roads to a town 20 miles away, where there was a fellow enthusiast. On the way home, if the road was quiet, I would give the Jag its head, and
let it wind up to its 130 mph maximum. The local traffic officer (unknown to
me) knew of my nightly excursions and lay in wait just off the main road, on the
fastest straight in the journey.

'It must have been a sharp clear night, and the bellow of the Jag would
have carried for miles. My father told me later, after talking to the officer, that
he (the officer) had heard me coming and the exhaust note sounded so beautiful
as it reached its crescendo in each gear, that he forgot about the chase and
listened to the bugle cry instead. "I had my warning", he told my father, "so
next time, look out!"

'At this time my brother decided he wanted to buy a speedboat, so I bought
out his share in the car. I was working as a salesman for the local Ford dealer
at the time, who objected to his employees driving an opposition make, and as I
couldn't sell the new Thames Traders anyway, I decided to make use of my five
years at High School and enter a teacher training college.

'The Jaguar came too, and even though it was a 1951 model and eight
years old by then, it was still a force to be reckoned with. One of the most
embarrassing moments was when I was turning out of a side road into the main

road and a Mark VIII Jaguar sailed past. I accelerated hard and caught it up and noticed that it was cruising at just under 100 mph. I pulled out to pass it on a clear stretch and when I drew level in order to give the driver a friendly wave I noticed that it was chauffeur-driven and the occupants were the Prime Minister and other ministers of the crown! I hastily completed my pass and sped down the nearest side road!

'In 1959, after having the car for three pleasurable years, I was offered a clean swap by the owner of a 1956 Ford o.h.v. V8. When I found that the value of this car was in the vicinity of £1000 I reluctantly swapped her with the customline, hoping that this would be the stepping stone to a later model XK. My other friends with Jaguars greeted me and my Ford with the remark: "Gone into the trucking business again we see."

'I often wonder where that 120 is now, and should I ever see it again, I would greet it with a friendly pat, and ask its present owner if I could hear it bellow once more.'

While the XK series was current, even the earlier models fetched good prices, but with the introduction of the E type in 1961, values plunged and by 1966, the XK 120 was fetching very little, and consequently most were in poor condition. They were just not worth maintaining properly. However some enthusiasts, such as Grant McMillan and his father, felt differently. Their experience is typical, although their car was really historic: it was chassis number 660009, the first to reach New Zealand in 1950.

'It had had nineteen owners, including more than a few dealers and finance companies when we found her', said Grant. 'By then its original bronze coach-work had been red, blue, green, red again, you name it, before turning white. The Pater Parent suggested that it might be an interesting proposition for the two of us to do up a bit.

'At that time, it belonged to an architectural student who loved it, but not dearly enough, for it was costing him the earth to run. So he had to part with it, reluctantly, for the not outrageous sum of £400. As we drove it home, the rear core plug fell out and the engine was on the garage floor the next day.

'I was only 16 and on holiday from school, so I had the time to tinker and get it all back together again. The engine seemed strong, it steered well, stopped, sort of; and made the most glorious growl you can imagine. It rattled like hell, but that didn't matter either, as I drove it to Auckland Grammar.

'Cool summer nights, cloudless skies and starlight covering the hills, standing hard on the brakes into the corners, then howling up through the gears to 5500 each time, then down-shifting and sawing away at the huge wheel, wind in the hair, dust in the eyes, fire in the blood; that's what it was all about. Those are the things that stick in my memory. Hot summer days and burbling along, feeling fine. Cold winter mornings and crouched down low out of the wind, foot hard down as far as it would go and watching the speedo climb slowly and the road flash past quickly, and feeling the heart beating faster to see what you can both do. That's XK motoring: those are the things to recall. But I suppose

above left and right One of the oldest XKs, right-hand drive chassis number two, pictured at Nowra, Australia in 1973. The owner refused to part with it, saying he was going to do it up some day. . . .

The XKs line up for a concours sponsored by an Australian national TV channel.

I must also remember the odd trial and tribulation that occurred.

'There was the time when I decided to repaint it during the holidays and began dutifully to rub it down, only to find more and more colours coming through, until I could pick the paint off in thick sheets. A one-week job took three, and it looked like Joseph's coat before it thankfully turned off-white again. New upholstery, hood and carpets were added and this bit-by-bit restoration seemed like the way to go, for you could have your car and restore it. There were the shocks, too, of having the front suspension redone, and finding that all the ball joints were now oval, and that new ones were very expensive.

'The gearbox jammed once, but I managed to fix it, twice. How was I to know that the plungers were not all the same? Various little oddments were fixed from time to time and some big ones, too, like a burnt valve which also revealed an original cylinder head so corroded that it had to be replaced. The radiator was in the same league.

'Constant attacks by motorbikes and exploring the handling at the limit did nothing to improve the coachwork. Eventually, at the second attempt, I found a competent panelbeater and we got the body straight. By now it was 1968 and the summer was fine, so the hood stayed in the garage and it remained there for the winter, too, as an umbrella was adequate for sudden showers while caught in a traffic jam.

'It was a splendid car and not really a white elephant at all, despite being christened BaBa by some MG Car Club character. The name has stuck, though, as part of the story, so I cannot argue. By now I had bought the other half from my father, so that I owned every rattle in the car, plus the Odd Noises. But she still kept soldiering on, still kept running out of brakes, still kept being superb fun to drive, until one fateful evening I went for a quiet zizz —at 60 mph on the Bombay Hills. We flew through the air with the greatest of ease, but the landing was hard. I recovered sooner than BaBa (yes, you may

Harvey Hingston, from New Zealand, with his first love, a 1951-model 120 roadster.

use that name) and now it is going through its Final and Finest Restoration. It's all on a ten-year plan, and the best years have already been had, but one day, when 660009 is resplendent again, we shall both go for another drive and it will be just like it always was: up through the gears, hard on the brakes, howl, varoooom—I might even build in a few rattles for old time's sake.'

South Africans share many of the same problems as Australians and New Zealanders when it comes to owning an XK; the heat of the sun takes its toll on upholstery and even wiring looms; but their cars rarely suffer from extensive corrosion unless they have been kept in coastal areas for long. Then the salt in the air can cause as much damage as that on the roads of Britain and parts of America. Spare parts are expensive in Australia and New Zealand, but cost even more in South Africa, even if you can find them! The experiences of Trevor Woodiwiss from Marshalltown in the Transvaal are typical. He owns an XK 150 drop-head coupé that has had more than 1500 hours spent on its restoration already and is 'probably still some ten years away from hitting the road, as I can work on my cars only on Sundays.'

Trevor's other XK is one of the rare right-hand drive 150S 3.8-litre roadsters.

'When I bought it, it was original, but had been neglected [he said]. I gradually went through it, replacing gaskets and so on, which were readily available from local agents, who knew which similar-engined saloons they fitted.

'The shock absorbers were totally unserviceable, and I replaced them with local ones, which were much better. A springsmith restored the rest of the suspension, and the local machine shop worked on one of the hubs until it would run true. Getting brake pads was a bit of a problem until I took the samples into a general spares dealer and then managed to get German-made replacements. Pirare parts were used to cure a general engine misfire, but the triple SU carburetters were a real problem. I had terrible trouble getting spares for these big carburetters and had to guess at what was needed for our high altitude—we are 5600 feet above sea level and our carbs need different needles. However, I eventually managed to get it running rather well, with a very smooth and fast pickup, although the ignition is critical and it is very prone to pinking if only slightly over-advanced (our petrol is only 93 octane and my engine has the 9:1 compression ratio).

'The tyres were absolutely bald and I set about ordering Dunlop Road Speeds from England—we have only truck-type tyres produced locally for 16-inch wheels and I wanted my car to remain as original as possible. This involved getting an import permit (which I was told I would not stand a chance of obtaining) from the authorities in Pretoria. However, I managed to talk them into it and eventually got my tyres from England after a nine-month delay. Through a friend who has a Jaguar agency in Pretoria, 50 miles away, I had managed to get a set of five brand new 16-inch chrome spoked rims from the Cape Town main agents, 1000 miles away. These were fitted, with the new tyres, and the car looked pretty good.

'Throughout the rejuvenation of the XK 150S roadster and the rebuilding

It's gymkhana time in New Zealand for 140 roadster owner James Yates.

Ultimate XK? Trevor Woodiwiss's very rare 150S 3.8-litre right-hand drive roadster, hood erect, outside his home in South Africa.

of the 150 drop-head, the problem of obtaining spares seems to stem from the change in agents. This is quite apart from the general problem of all spares being scarce for any 18-year-old motor car, let alone a rare imported model.' Trevor then went on to describe a problem that is worldwide:

'When I originally started the drop-head rebuild, the agents were still a family business who had had the Jaguar agency for some years. With repeated visits, I got to know one of the chaps at the spares counter quite well and he was prepared to scratch around a bit to help. He cross-referenced to some of the saloons and very often found that he had the requested part in stock.

'Nowadays, however, even though the agent may still have the parts in stock, he doesn't realise it (or in some cases doesn't even care), and actually, a request for a part for an XK 150S is often exclaimed about as an XJ what? Generally, this comes from people now working at Jaguar spares counters who have previously been employed by Leylands with spares for Austins, and so on, and who have no knowledge of such cars as XKs.

'There are still a few people, however, who put an effort into trying to help, and recently I have found that the best method is to take a sample of the part required and say that it is for a friend who is out of town and you don't know quite which model it is for. With a bit of help and scratching around, the part often comes to hand.'

There is little that will stop a determined XK owner, however, particularly Arthur Winship, from Salisbury, Rhodesia. He had fancied an XK for years when he staked his financial future on Jaguars in 1972. Winship quit his job in Zambia, returned to England, bought a new XJ6 saloon from the factory, and shipped it to Cape Town via Southampton. Following a 2000-mile drive north he sold the XJ6 in Salisbury for three times the price he had paid for it; bought a house and cast his eyes over a forlorn XK 120 marked up at £800 on a local used car lot. Winship liked the look of the car, but his wife thought a midnight blue E type with chrome wire wheels looked even better, so he said he would buy that. Next day, when he returned for the E type, he sneaked the XK home as well! Said Winship:

'I started stripping it the day I got her, never dreaming that it would not turn another wheel for five years.

'The hot sun had shrunk the wooden frames of the alloy-skinned doors some previous owner had fitted; the car had a monstrous home-made petrol tank, and some other owner had cut across the bonnet above the radiator, bolted the front bit in permanently, and cobbled up the remaining bits of the bonnet to lift in a very shaky manner. What's more, the car had an XK 140 radiator grille fitted over the original XK 120 grille. Some people are funny.

'Eventually I obtained a new bonnet and a good used petrol tank in England, but because of the economic sanctions on Rhodesia, it was difficult to bring them home. Eventually I managed to smuggle them out inside a friend's car being shipped to Portuguese East Africa.

'During four holidays in England I have managed to obtain a new radiator grille, wiring loom and various other bits and pieces, and smuggle them out in my suitcase. This has meant abandoning most of my clothes to keep within the 44 lb baggage limit at London's Heathrow Airport. At one time, when passing through a firearms check, a bobby tried to pull a pair of XK headlamps to pieces, and he was on the point of ruining one lamp when I waved the receipt at him, telling him he could stand the cost of a replacement. He had to take my word that there was no gun or bomb concealed inside.'

Winship leads an equally adventurous life at home in Rhodesia in his XK. In recent times he has twice used its great speed to escape terrorist ambushes in out-lying regions. (He never goes out without a .303 ex-Army jungle carbine and a military-style self-loading pistol in the cockpit and a .25 Walther pistol in the glove-box.) Acquiring spare parts is less hazardous in Rhodesia, home of hundreds of ancient pre-sanctions cars. They survive by courtesy of the low humidity, which means that metal can be as good as new twenty years later, and because of the myriad small machine shops that can make almost any mechanical part for a car. Some specialize in brake parts, some in gearboxes and so on. XK owners are also helped by the fact that many Mark VII saloons are now in the scrap-yards of Rhodesia, and with local ingenuity, most of the parts can be adapted for an XK. The only thing that really suffers in this XK paradise nearly 5000 feet above sea level is the upholstery, which lasts next to no time in the burning sun.

You have to be equally determined to combat the opposite sort of problems in Canada, as Bill Heather related:

'After a series of adventures with lesser marques, I was determined to buy the ultimate, an XK 150. One beautiful April Sunday in 1959, I committed myself to a 1958 drop-head. The vendor, a physician of some repute, was glad to take my American chrome palace and some cash for his 12,000-mile beauty. I couldn't understand why he would part with such a dream, but soon discovered the answer: incredibly high maintenance costs. In the next 12 months I drove that vehicle 20,000 miles and carefully documented the $974 spent on repairs and maintenance—a lot of money in those days. This did not include the gas, oil, licence, insurance and so on. Twelve months was enough for my credit balance, so April 1960 saw the 150 passed on to another unsuspecting enthusiast. However, I did enjoy many of those expensive Jaguar miles and continued to envy their owners. It is easy to see why there are so many sad XKs about. The reasons are purely economic. Second, third and subsequent owners are often young men of limited financial means who are swept away by the thrill of owning a Jaguar. The high cost and frequency of repairs leads to a high rate of resale. Indeed, often disillusionment sets in after only a few months.

'At any rate my affluence improved slowly and in the late summer of 1964, I bought, from the original owner, a 1959 drop-head with overdrive, and 55,000 miles on the clock. It needed much bodywork and some mechanical attention, but this was allowed for in the purchase price.

'Now we drive this car less than 5000 miles a year and heartily enjoy every mile. It is stored all winter as Jaguars don't take kindly to real cold and salty roads. Running expenses are moderate, mechanical failures have been few, but combatting rust has been a continuing and very expensive problem. We hope to keep our 150 indefinitely and much care and attention is lavished on it.'

An equal amount of care has to be lavished on XKs in Scandinavia, where the clubs and owners in Denmark and Sweden work in close co-operation. One of the keenest XK owners in Denmark, Jens Roder, of Espergaerde, who has five XK 120 drop-head coupés and one 3.8-litre 150 drop-head, says:

'Spares for older Jaguars up to the Mark II are difficult to obtain (with the exception of the engine), and XK parts are unobtainable in Denmark. The club has organized, through a couple of members in the trade, more or less regular collections of spares in England, so that our situation is much the same now.

Those of us who run XKs here have found the situation to be much improved over the past few years with the emergence of the replica spares market. The main problem still seems to be chrome parts and emblems.'

Running costs are the main problem in Eire, which must be treated as a foreign country so far as XKs are concerned. One of the leading enthusiasts in Dublin, Ian Russell-Hill, who runs an XK 140 fixed-head, says:

'The road tax for a 3.4-litre car is £180 in Ireland and insurance runs at about £450. Also most parts for repairs have to come in from England and are subject to a tax of 37.5 per cent plus 20 per cent VAT. Another pitfall is the fact that a private individual is not permitted to import any car into Ireland except under the change of residence permit. At the moment we are in the process of clearing an American XK 140MC which has been off the road since 1962—a process which has taken nine months so far.

'However the pleasures of owning and driving an XK are fantastic, although my beautiful wife Maureen will not let me stop for petrol. Every time I do manage to stop so many people come over to talk to us about the car that a one-hour drive can take nearly three.'

Road tax is even higher in Singapore, as Paul Ashton relates:

'You have to be really keen, as well as lucky, to run an XK here. The tax on a 3.4-litre runs out at £900 per annum, including a 50 per cent old car surcharge. Needless to say, a 3.8-litre job costs even more.

'Connolly hide lasts no time at all in the tropics, either. All classic cars here are retrimmed in vinyl, which was often original equipment in these parts in any case. In the same way, plywood interior parts rot away quickly and good veneer is impossible to find. However, there is one compensation. The constant heat allows twelve months-of-the-year restoration without the horribly grazed

The immaculate 150S roadster of the great Danish enthusiast Jens Roder.

knuckles I used to get trying to undo plugs and nuts in winter!'

Some of the greatest enthusiasts for the marque are to be found in France and Switzerland. Parisian dentist Dr Phillippe Renault must have the biggest collection of Jaguars in the world, amounting to more than fifty cars, including a C type, two D types, three Listers, a Cooper, HWM and Tojeiro, the Emeryson, HK Jaguar and a Ghia-bodied example. And Aldo Vinzio from Geneva drives his XK 140 every day, summer, winter, to the sea and to the mountains, and in competition. In the nineteen years he has owned the car, it has covered no less than 350,000 miles with few repairs. The engine has been rebuilt only once, at 125,000 miles, and the chassis remade as recently as two years ago.

'I can point out that the gearbox, although a bit noisy, is completely original, as is the rear suspension', says the amazing Mr Vinzio, who goes on to quote from an old French magazine:

Half-Angel, Half-Beast, the Jaguar XK 140 roadster: a Love Story
'The XK is the halfway point in the quarrel between the ancients and the moderns. It is an alliance of present-day mechanical sophistication and classical beauty of sensual and uncluttered lines.

'Noble and without weakness, its design is characterized by purity, with no concession to the fashion of the fifties, since the XK 140, like its forerunner, the XK 120, is the archetypal British sports car. This car has such a personality that the driver at the wheel is in a state of hypnosis, living to the rhythm of his machine, seduced by the hollow throbbing of the six cylinders from Coventry.

'In the end, it doesn't matter which one of us chose the other, since we will never be parting. I found her in the open of a suburban yard, covered in snow, down-trodden beneath the weight of her own negligence. It was a desperate case, calling for open-heart surgery; perhaps it was a bad match, in any case the original engine, which has already produced enough to propel the monster at 130 mph had been replaced by a unit from a 12-cylinder E type, producing 265 bhp, which took the top speed to 140 mph. The acceleration was not improved, however, as the rear wheels skidded in first and second gear. After a short test over a few kilometres, I felt that this magnificent engine sent back to the children's playground the MGAs, TR 3s and Morgans, propelled as they were by engines like eunuchs is search of virility. The long, proud bonnet shelters the controlled power, and continues its long-lined shape. The extent of the detail in the coachwork, recalls to mind, like the majesty of the super-structure of the wings, the pure perspectives of ancient Greek porticos. Alas! This idea that the English formulated of the sports car has now completely disappeared, taking with it this disproportionate aesthetic appeal of two passengers surrounded by leather sitting at the back of a metal frame which protects them from the weight of tradition.

'Half angel, half beast, she is brutal and uncomfortable, but come evening . . . the XK, as you know, is a Parisian animal, who likes to show herself off, boldly moving through the Champs Elysées, provoking astonishment and envy from the gossips of St Germain when she double-parks in front of the drug store; one can forgive her anything, she has so much charm!

'Her low-cut, practical doors allow you to get out without opening them, a useful tip for claustrophobics! In summer, the XK does without a hood, which disappears behind the two black leather seats, and what a pleasure when, at Deauville or St Tropez, the Ferrari or Lamborghini owner comes across thinking (the ignoramus!) that he could buy. . . .

'No, she's not for sale, and the fickle lover who wouldn't part with her will admit ostensibly his impotence, impotence to drive her to the limit, to under-stand her, to go too far with her. . . .

'But the man who adopts her has a motor-cyclist's soul, and knows full well that, immortal as she is, she will drive him to Nirvanah, on a track that will not stop at the museum.'

C'est la vie avec une XK.

The Swiss XK Register gather on the banks of Lake Geneva.

XI
The Men Behind the XK

LIKE MANY WONDERFUL THINGS, the Jaguar XK sprang from visions in the night, the dream of four men watching for fire in war-time Coventry. They had been brought together at the SS factory in Foleshill by one of their number, William Lyons, a stylist with an unerring eye for all that was best in other people's products. His brand of eclecticism was nothing to be ashamed of; he adapted the ideas of others in an entirely original manner that made his product unique. For instance, the old name SS Cars was clearly taken from the best in motor cycles produced by George Brough; the name SS implied quality in the early 1930s, and Lyons had started as a motor cycle sidecar maker in 1922. Then, when the name SS led to feelings of universal mistrust at the activities of Hitler's pre-war storm troopers, Lyons changed the name of the cars to Jaguar, but left the company as SS. He did not sit bolt upright in his bath like Archimedes, shouting 'Jaguar!' instead of 'Eureka!' He gave the task to his advertising men. Wayne Mineau reported it all in the *Daily Mail*:

> 'One day in 1935 when the model was almost ready Lyons rang his advertising department. "Bring me a list of names", he said, "of insects, animals, birds and fish." On his desk went a typewritten array of five hundred creatures that walked, crawled, swam or flew. Within the hour Lyons made his brilliant choice. "I like the sound of Jaguar", he said. "It has everything we want—power, speed and grace."'

Although this story has been strenuously denied over the years, it has the ring of truth. That's how Lyons did things. He was the visionary who inspired his dedicated colleagues to find what he wanted. Then he made his decision and stuck to it. Eventually, after the war, he changed the name of the company too, to Jaguar Cars Ltd, leaving behind SS with its unfortunate associations. But he did not change his pre-war principles: his cars were never cheap, which made ownership of them a matter for pride; but compared to their rivals, they were an absolute bargain.

The Bugatti Atlantic coupé of 1938 that was to inspire so much of his styling would have cost four times as much as the first XK; the Mille Miglia BMW of 1940 that gave rise to the rest of the XK's immortal lines was priceless.

The slogan that launched Jaguar saloons in the 1950s, 'grace, space and pace', was taken from an advertisement before the war by Jaguar's great rivals, MG. The

Lyons 'leaned heavily' on the Bugatti Atlantique coupé for XK inspiration.

Lyons cars killed off the bigger MGs, then were the first to follow the export trail blazed by the smaller T series into America, along with Allard. Until those famous fire-watching sessions at Foleshill, SS Jaguars—they were always called that until 1945—had beautiful bodies with relatively indifferent mechanicals. The engine that Lyons visualized was to be a twin overhead camshaft unit like that of the great racing cars of the 1930s, such as the Sunbeam Tiger. It had to be designed so that it looked the high-speed efficiency unit that it was, and convey to the layman some idea of the thought and care which had been expended on the design and construction of the unseen functional parts. So said the wonderful designer, Bill 'Mungo' Heynes, who transformed everything mechanical on Jaguar cars.

Heynes also was called in for fire-watching sessions after the normal day's work of designing mundane war vehicles, along with Claude Baily and Wally Hassan. Heynes had been hired from Humber by Lyons in 1935, as chief engineer. And that year Lyons christened his cars 'Jaguar'; for thirty years after, Heynes's name was to be synonymous with that of Jaguar. 'My first job was to design a chassis for a new body that was already under way', he told the Automobile Division of the Institution of Mechanical Engineers in 1953.

That chassis, developed by Bob Knight, was to be the foundation of the XK 120 in 1948. Once that little task was out of the way, Heynes set to work on the front suspension. He based his ideas on the torsion bar set used by the revolutionary new Citroen Traction Avant (you know, the Maigret cars). Hassan, an old Bentley boy who

had produced wonderful racing cars for wealthy employers in the 1930s, actually
built the suspension in 1938, then spent the next ten years on intermittent development. The result was that Heynes evolved the use of ball-type kingpin joints to locate
and control wheel movement on independent front suspension systems, a practice
that has been universally adopted by engineers who know the work of a genius when
they see it. This system made its debut on the first post-war design, the Jaguar Mark
V saloon, the car whose chassis was adapted for the XK 120.

Then came the *pièce de résistance*: the XK engine. It was designed in collaboration with Claude Baily, who had moved over from the Morris Engines factory, with
advice from the ever-helpful Hassan. Lyons laid down the basics during discussions
in 1944 and 1945 when fires were not so frequent as they had been during the height
of the Blitz. He wanted to reduce his existing range of push-rod engines, a 1.8-litre
four-cylinder, and two six-cylinders at 2.7 litres and 3.5 litres, with only two units,
a four- and a six-cylinder. They were to be more powerful and also look the part.
Lyons wanted an output of 120 bhp; Heynes visualized 160 bhp, a figure which had
been extracted from one of the existing 3.5 litres as a result of extensive tuning.
'Sir William had always promised me a clean sheet of paper for this design', Heynes
said twenty years later in *The Motor*.

> 'With Claude Baily and Walter Hassan, I laid down the twin overhead camshaft
> design for both four and six cylinder engines. Direct-operated valves and the
> hemispherical head had always been my idea of how it should be done.
>
> 'I suppose it was a relic of my early motor cycle days, when "twin ohc" was
> a *sine qua non* among the élite. I met with opposition on this design from every
> imaginable quarter, except Sir William (the only one who mattered) and
> Claude Baily and Walter Hassan, who had worked so closely with me.'

Hassan remembered it slightly differently in *Climax in Coventry*, written in
collaboration with Graham Robson for Motor Racing Publications:

Members of Jaguar's 1953 Le Mans
team were reunited at a London reception held in their honour by the
Jaguar Drivers' Club in 1973. Standing
(left to right): Bob Penney, Gordon
Gardner, Duncan Hamilton, F. R. W.
England, Tony Rolt, Ted Brookes,
'Jock' Thomson, Sir William Lyons,
Monsieur J. M. Lelievre (Hon. President, L'Automobile Club de L'Ouest),
Tom Jones, W. M. Heynes, Phil
Weaver, R. J. Knight. Front row (left
to right): Len Hayden, Joe Sutton,
Frank Rainbow, Stirling Moss, Norman Dewis, Ian Stewart. Only two
members of that history-making team
were missing—the late Malcolm Sayer
and the late Jack Emerson.

'Mr Lyons had a great liking for a twin overhead camshaft layout, but Claude Baily and I pointed out that this would be expensive and probably fairly noisy, too. On the evidence of the engines we used pre-war, we felt we could design an engine with a simple bathtub cylinder head combustion space and with push-rod overhead valves, which would give him all the power he wanted. As far as we could see this would be easier, cheaper to make, and quieter. However, this didn't satisfy him at all, and if he wasn't completely satisfied with anything he would never agree to it. His new engine would have to be good looking, with all the glamour of the famous engines produced for racing in previous years, so that when you opened the bonnet of a post-war Jaguar you would be looking at power and be impressed. He got his way, of course—Mr Lyons always did!— but I must admit that the rest of us thought that it was rather a waste of time and money at that time.'

Three four-cylinder experimental engines were produced before the XK design was finalized; the first, a 1360 cc twin cam, code-named XF, was used for assessing the merits of the 'fire-watching' design; the second, a 1776 cc XG unit was used to evaluate the alternative of a BMW-style cross pushrod head. It turned out to be too tall, a fault shared with the Bristol engine developed from this pre-war German design; and the third, the XJ, was produced in six-cylinder form as well. After three years of development, including much gas flow work on the cylinder head by Harry Weslake, its stroke was lengthened to increase the low-speed torque, and the name changed to XK.

The four-cylinder version, mooted for economy-conscious post-war Britain, never went into production because there was such a demand for the six. But it achieved brief glory in Goldie Gardner's MG record breaker EX 135, which took Class E international records at 177 mph in 1948.

Throughout this period, 1945–48, Heynes was in charge of all engineering, Baily of engine design, Hassan of all development (which included the chassis) and Lyons in command of everything, including the body, which was considered to be a separate department at the time. He preferred to work in raw material rather than on the drawing board, although he had the services of a brilliant aerodynamicist, Malcolm Sayer, from Bristols, for that. Lyons tended to commandeer the services of a skilled operative—such as Frank Gardner, superintendent of Jaguar's sawmill, the only man he called by his first name—who could turn his ideas into a mock-up in an experimental bay. This was the secret spot in the Jaguar factory, Lyons's special place where few people knew what went on, and many mock-ups were scrapped before one was approved. You could almost hear him saying: 'Now, Frank, I want to make a car. It has to look like this BMW racing machine with a touch of the Bugatti.' Later, drawings were made from the sawmill mock-ups and Sayer rounded off the corners, making the whole concept sound aerodynamically. Lyons was a stylist of the old school, doing it all by eye, leaving the mechanics for Heynes, Baily, Hassan and company to work out later, although Sayer did some projects straight from his drawing board.

'Sir William had been working on a sports body design (the XK 120) for some

time, and it was decided to give the engine a limited run on this two-seater for a year before embarking on the main production, saloon cars [said Heynes]. We anticipated about two to three hundred cars would be sold in twelve months, but the success of the XK 120 at the 1948 and 1949 Earls Court shows was such that we had to replace the body (initially aluminium panels on a wooden frame) with an all-steel body more suited to mass production, almost overnight.'

The original XK 120, HKV 455, was built in a very short space of time. It seems likely that when it appeared at Earls Court in 1948, it had covered few miles. But throughout the following year it was driven far and fast by test driver Soapy Sutton. 'It will be recalled that the car made a successful debut at the 1948 Motor Show', he wrote later in *Autosport*, where:

'. . . although universally admired, doubts were expressed in some quarters as to whether performance would match the appearance. We, at the works, knew that it was outstanding, but had only a vague idea of the maximum speed we might expect, so the obvious thing was to find out. It was most desirable that, having named the car XK 120, that figure in terms of mph should be attained.... It would indeed have been a catastrophe had the car failed to do its stuff before the assembled multitude (at Jabbeke), so preliminary tests were carried out in this country.

'There was, however, one little matter which was secretly worrying me. My fastest ever speed had been achieved in the dim and distant past, when I clocked 112 mph at Brooklands on a Lea Francis. . . .

'Now twenty years is a long time, and another 20 mph or so on the top of 112 mph is quite a considerable step, and although I had kept my hand in to a certain extent by driving moderately fast cars in the interim, I had not exceeded

The men behind the XK: from the left, competition preparation chief Phil Weaver, engine man Harry Mundy, Jaguar chief Sir William Lyons, service and competition manager Lofty England, chief engineer William Heynes, development engineer Wally Hassan, engine designer Claude Baily, and cylinder head expert Harry Weslake.

my speed of a score years earlier, and I must confess to having had some doubts as to my ability to cope.

'It was essential that both the car and myself should be tried out before proceeding to Belgium, so I set out early one spring morning for a road where a five-mile straight was available.

'I must admit that while waiting for the dawn at a transport cafe, consuming numerous cups of tea, I was a little apprehensive as both the car and myself were unknown quantities. . . .

'However, as soon as I let in the clutch all traces of nervousness vanished. That first run certainly felt fast, very fast indeed, the road appearing to taper off to the width of a footpath, and I remember involuntarily ducking my head, as the telegraph wires, which crossed at one point, appeared to bear down upon me. . . . A quick glance at the rev counter showed the speed to be over 125 mph, but I was quite comfortable and the car held the road perfectly. . . .

'Feeling quite satisfied, I returned to the cafe for more tea, which somehow tasted much better than before.'

So that's how they designed and developed the XK 120, very much on traditional lines: build it and see how it goes. The same principles applied to C type chassis and disc brake development although the bodies were produced far more scientifically with Sayer being given his head. He gradually smoothed out the C type body till it became more and more efficient, and then designed his great work: the D type which, of course, bore such a remarkable resemblance to an aircraft. Not only was it one of the first cars to use a fuselage, or monocoque, but it had a fin for Le Mans which did a remarkably good job of keeping directional stability, one of the XK's strong points with its conventional chassis, and a weaker point with the later E type (based on the D type, but without a fin).

It took a lot of intensive work by Heynes and his team to build the C type in time for Le Mans, 1951. Details of his supremely simple rear suspension and entirely new frame have been related in Chapter III. Nevertheless, despite the workload of producing this car, the Mark VII saloon, and retooling the XK's body for production, he found time to instigate the historic adaptation of aircraft-style disc brakes for cars in 1949. The amount of development work which went into these revolutionary brakes was immense, often with racing drivers Tony Rolt (a skilled engineer) and Stirling Moss doing much of the testing with Norman Dewis. Recently Dewis, who joined Jaguars in 1952, gave a historic interview to Phil Porter, managing director of Midland Car Restorations and editor of the *XK Bulletin*. He said:

'When I first joined, the big push was for disc brakes, and that was my first project. I knew the people at Dunlops and we had a good tie-up. There was a good build-up between Jaguars and Dunlop, and Mr Heynes said to me: "You've got the car, get on with the development." The first trial disc brake was put on the XK 120 by Dunlops. In those days it wasn't the great big empire it is today, and there was probably only about five people involved. It was just a matter of test, test, test until we got it right. There were problems right at the start. Nobody had any idea of what temperature the discs would run at, or the pad material, because adapting it from an aircraft brake to a car brake was an entirely different thing. You see, on the aircraft they had what we called the "wheel slide protector" where you couldn't lock a wheel. Well, we looked at that but it was OK on an aircraft because you'd got plenty of space. A pilot just pushed on a lever and that was it, you had maximum "decel" without locking, and, of course, they only do one stop and then taxi in. So really it was an entirely different requirement for the car, and temperatures were our problem for a start. The unit was inside the wheel and we hadn't realized what sort of airflow or air-ducting we needed to cool it, so all this was trial and error. We were seeing temperatures after a few laps of 500 and 600 degrees. I could finish up with the disc glowing dull red and the fluid almost bursting into flame, but it was only then that we found out and realized we had to do something about cooling. So first we fitted wire wheels to get air from the outside and then we had ducts in the front to bring air in on the inside of the brake and gradually we got the temperatures down to a sensible level.'

The Ecurie Ecosse team pictured after the 1957 Monzanapolis event. From the left: Wilkie Wilkinson, Ninian Sanderson, Jack Fairman, John Lawrence.

Cooling, particularly that of the engine, was always one of the Jaguar team's weak spots, however, a fact which must have been obvious after the 1952 Le Mans débâcle. It was surprising that they should have been caught out in such a way after all the tales of XKs that overheated in Californian traffic jams. This was because early tests of the XK engine were carried out in a couple of hack Mark V saloons with their large air intakes, during which overheating failed to manifest itself. Not much was known about the science of underbonnet airflow at the time either.

It seems that the beautiful slim shape of the XK 120's and 140's bonnets was to blame for their overheating, however, and it was not until 1957 that Lyons (Sir William by then) could bring himself to change it. Besides, any change to the XK 140 body panels would have involved expensive re-tooling at a time when the Mark I saloon was being introduced. It was this penny-pinching attitude that had a lot to do with Jaguar's great success. A good example can be seen in the ventilator box hinge of the XK 120 and 140; the actual hinge is merely an adaptation of a three-inch door hinge obtained from any ironmonger's! Lyons saved money not only by brilliant design giving rise to long production runs which meant that development costs and tooling could be offset against a large volume of products; he saved pennies everywhere it didn't show, even in the ventilator box. This enabled him to provide quality where it did show, in the general design and in the fittings obvious to the eye, such as the upholstery, which was always real leather on the XKs.

He was a classic example of a hard-headed businessman. On the one hand—the fire-watching sessions are a good example—he never missed an opportunity to extract more work, fairly, from his staff. On the other, he was endearing, as Wally Hassan remembered:

'During the war, when things were very tight (for everybody, even motor manufacturers), he sometimes threw a garden party in the grounds of his house at Wappenbury, where he always put on a good spread and made the children very welcome. On one occasion the Hassan family—Ethel, and the two boys and myself—had cycled over from Whitnash, but Mr Lyons lent us his car to take home and the bikes had to go in the boot!'

How Lyons worked: a very early post-war Jaguar prototype showing the basic lines of the XK 120 roadster.

Again, he could be tough with his suppliers, and had to be to keep his prices in their extremely competitive bracket. One of Lyons's most valued lieutenants, the man he eventually handed over to on his retirement in 1972, was Lofty England, who as service manager and racing team manager was closely involved in the design and development of the XKs. It is a tribute to this former racing mechanic that so few changes had to be made to the XKs during their production life. And, like Lyons, he was a tough man if you did not do as you were told. Duncan Hamilton tells this story of England in his autobiography *Touch Wood*:

'Co-driving with Ivor Bueb, I won the Rheims twelve-hour race (in 1956) and in so doing had my connection with Jaguars severed. Lofty England contended that I did not obey pit signals, and no sooner was the race over than he told me that I would not be driving at Le Mans. We had a fearful row, and coming as I had, straight from the cockpit of a racing car, I was in no mood to suffer irate team managers gladly. The real trouble was that when told to slow down I had actually gone faster and faster until I had broken the lap record at the end of the twelve-hour race when my team were placed one, two, three and with no competitor within striking distance.

'That is how the bare facts appear, but it was not quite as simple as that. In the first place, I had in the back of my mind the fact that Tony Rolt and I had been robbed of certain victory during the last twelve-hour race when our back axle gave trouble right at the end forcing us to concede victory to team-mates who had been well behind. Then on this particular occasion I would have literally had to slow right down just to let Paul Frere pass me; he was too far behind to do it without my help. Had Mike (Hawthorn) been driving it would have been different; he would have gone faster and, anyway, he was our number one driver. As it was he was back in his hotel resting for the French Grand Prix which was to follow this race. I missed Lofty's first slow down signal but saw the second one. I decided to lift off early and to go slower on the straight past the grandstand down to Heliopolis. Previously I had gone full chat down this straight leaving my braking for Heliopolis to the last possible moment. Far from slowing me up my new method saw me through the corner faster than ever before and my lap times improved!'

Within two hours Hamilton had joined Ferrari but he rejoined Jaguar after England sent him a card the following Christmas . . . and that's the way they ran their racing team!

Another great name behind Jaguar's racing successes was David Murray, the Scottish accountant who ran the Ecurie Ecosse with the great tuning wizard Wilkie Wilkinson. Murray went on record in his book, appropriately called *Ecurie Ecosse*, with these two quotes:

'The years climaxing in the Le Mans and Monza glories can be classed as the upward climb during which Ecurie Ecosse rose from being an unknown shoestring outfit to becoming a well-known shoestring concern!'

'Jaguar cars remain my first and constant love. In fact years after the D type was obsolescent by fast-moving standards, one still remained on my team strength. I just couldn't part with a car which had served us so long and so well, a car which served as a constant reminder to motor racegoers the world over that Ecurie Ecosse meant dark-blue Jaguars.'

And that's the way he ran his racing team. . . .

Wilkinson went on record for the way in which his cars went. With only a small garage in an Edinburgh mews he achieved as high a standard of preparation, development and success as the Jaguar works itself! The same type of tribute should be paid to Alfred Momo, the American tuner who eventually produced the greatest XK engine of all, the 3.8-litre, after everybody had been trying for years, although he had the not inconsiderable wealth of Briggs Cunningham behind him.

In later years, John 'Plastic' Pearson followed by John Harper, Jim Tester and Ron Beaty have developed the XK even further to keep it in the forefront of historic racing. But they all take the back seat for the four fire watchers from Foleshill who turned their dreams into reality.

The great Jaguar enthusiast Briggs Cunningham.

XII

Interchangeability of Spare Parts

THE BIGGEST PROBLEM when running an old sports car such as an XK used to be obtaining spare parts. The cars, rarely maintained properly, were always breaking down as they were hammered round the countryside, followed by frantic searching through the spares departments of garages for miles around, raids on scrapyards for parts from similar vehicles, and swoops on similar-looking parts from motoring jumble sales.

Now 'the times they are a changing': XKs are valuable and rarely driven every day. The owners invariably have another vehicle and more time to locate spares. Also, because the cars are valuable, they have often been restored to excellent running order and are driven with more consideration; as a result breakdowns are fewer despite the advancing age of the vehicles. With their increasing value, it has become worthwhile for some firms to make replica parts, for the chances of finding XK parts in the average garage spares department are remote now. They've all been scoured a hundred times, or the parts were sold off to make room for later stock which will turn over more quickly. An efficiently-run spares department has to turn over its stock five times a year, which means that only specialists can keep XK parts today. This is not a bad thing—it certainly saves the customer a lot of time.

But some aspects of the situation will never change: namely, the 'Jag Swags' organized by the Jaguar Drivers' Club in Britain. With the price of new spares increasing at the same rate as most other things, these jumble sales are becoming more and more popular. They present the opportunity to sell off surplus spares for the same sort of price that is being asked for the ones that are needed, and for obvious reasons it is best to build up a stock of parts before starting a rebuild. It's here that a knowledge of the parts which are interchangeable is essential, particularly on the body side. Most of the firms selling Jaguar panels know which ones will fit alternative models, but few of the smaller vendors have any idea. If you know which parts can be swopped around you can be on to a bargain, or well on the way to finding that elusive piece to complete the rebuild.

On the XK 120 steel-bodied models, all roadster doors are the same; drop-head and fixed-head doors are similar; some of the fixed-head doors were made in alloy, some in steel. Roadster wings are not directly interchangeable with those on the fixed-head, but can easily be modified: they are also similar to those on the drop-

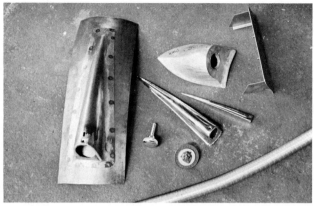

head; some roadster wings had vent boxes, some did not; the back three-quarters of the XK 120 rear wings was the same as on all other models of XK, which means that they can be salvaged for economic repairs. Most XK 120s have the same wooden floor and the XK 120 fixed-head and drop-head share the same hinge boxes with the XK 140 and XK 150. Roadster hinge boxes are different but do not wear out so quickly because they have less weight to support, although they still rust. The flat laminated windscreen glass on XK 120 and 140 fixed-head and drop-head coupés is interchangeable and all XK 150 windscreens are the same.

New components manufactured for XKs by specialists: sidelight pods, bonnet badges, breather tubes, headlight flashes, rear lights, ventilator plates, and hood retaining knobs.

More specialist body parts: headlight nacelles, sidelamp pods and aero screens, plus a remanufactured hub.

On the XK 140, the roadster doors are peculiar to that model; the drop-head's doors are the same as those on the XK 120 fixed-head and drop-head; the XK 140 fixed-head's doors fit only that model. The boot lids on XK 140s are similar to those on the XK 120, and they are shorter at the bottom edge and can easily be adapted. The early XK 150 boot lid with vertical number plate plinth is similar. XK 140 boot lids were made in alloy as the XK 120 lid, or steel as the XK 150 lid. A majority of XK 140 drop-head body parts were the same as those on XK 120 fixed-head or drop-head. The spare wheel trays for the XK 140 were the same as those on the XK 150; so were the steel boot floor, steel and wood floor assemblies and seat pans. There were three varieties of inner wing on the XK 140 and similar variations on the XK 120.

On the XK 150, all inner wings were basically the same, except for those on the S type which were modified on the right-hand side for the triple carbs and air cleaners, an adaptation that can be done on a standard wing for an XK 150S. The same steel doors were fitted to XK 150 drop-heads and fixed-heads, and the XK 150 roadster doors were only slightly modified. All XK 150 front wings were basically the same except for the S type which was slightly modified.

The XK 120 and 140 shared a similar alloy bonnet, which was similar to that on an XK 150, except that the last car had greater width, and the 150 roadster had a longer bonnet.

On the mechanical side, cylinder heads can be swopped around quite easily. There are four basic XK heads which interchange, plus the head from the later 3.8-litre E type, or Mark X saloon. The XK heads are the A type with $1\frac{3}{4}$-inch inlet valves (30 degree seats), $1\frac{1}{2}$-inch exhaust valves (45 degree seats) 10 degree by 15 overlap, $\frac{5}{16}$-inch lift cams; the B type with $1\frac{3}{4}$-inch inlet valves (45 degree seats), $1\frac{5}{8}$-inch exhaust valves (45 degree seats), 15 degree by 15 overlap, $1\frac{3}{8}$-inch lift cams; the C type with $1\frac{3}{4}$-inch inlet valves (30 degree seats), $1\frac{5}{8}$-inch exhaust valves (45 degree seats), 15 degree by 15, $\frac{3}{8}$-inch lift cams; and the D type with $1\frac{7}{8}$-inch inlet valves (30 degree seats), $1\frac{7}{8}$-inch exhaust valves (45 degree seats), 30 degrees by 30 overlap and $\frac{3}{8}$-inch lift cams. The E type head was basically the same as the B type head except that it had straight inlet ports and different port spacing.

The A type head was to be found on early Mark VII saloons up to October 1954; the C type head as an option on the Mark VIIM and Mark VIII saloons; the B type head on the 3.4-litre Mark I and Mark II saloons, the Mark IX saloons; the E type head for the XK 150S was also featured on the E types made between March 1961 and October 1964, and the Mark X saloons made between 1962 and 1964. The $\frac{3}{8}$-inch lift was fitted to all Jaguars made from October 1954 until late 1969, except the 2.4-litre models.

Carburetters can be swopped around providing you have a manifold to go with them. Triple two-inch SU carburetters on an XK, other than an S type, need a variety of modifications particularly on the XK 120, in which the steering column gets in the way, and either a Mark X or E type manifold; twin two-inch SU carbs on an E type head require fewer modifications, merely the substitution of a Jaguar 420 or early Daimler Sovereign manifold or that from an XJ 6. Twin $1\frac{3}{4}$-inch SU carburetters on an E type head need the manifold from a Jaguar 240 or 340.

Everything at the bottom end of a 3.4-litre and a 3.8-litre engine is similar, the 3.8-litre engine being fitted to the Mark IX, and X saloons and the early E type. The cylinder blocks are different, however. Flywheels are readily interchangeable and the E type part weighs only 24 lb against 28 lb for that on a standard XK. Sumps are interchangeable among XKs, some having capacities up to 24 pints. Clutches are readily interchangeable with all Jaguar models, providing the flywheel has the right drilling and tapping, but gearboxes present quite a few problems.

Early XK 120s were fitted with a single helical gearbox with the prefix SH or JH. These units were interchangeable as a whole, although they were different internally as follows: SH had cluster gears on the layshaft; JH had the same except that first speed was separately splined to the sleeve of the layshaft. Later XK 120s, 140s and 150s had a single helical gearbox with the prefix SL or JL. These were not directly interchangeable with the first two types, unless the propeller shaft was changed as well. The SL and JL units had a shorter mainshaft and no rear extension and bearing. The SH and JH, on the other hand, had a rear extension, complete with ball bearing and rear end cover, secured to the rear face of the gearbox casing. Suffix letters CR, MS or J indicated that close ratios had been fitted and JS on 150 gearboxes meant that shaved gears were used. Shaved gears could not be interchanged with helical gears, although the whole unit could be exchanged for that of any SL or JL gearbox. Gearboxes with the prefix GB were fitted to Mark I and Mark II saloons and were not interchangeable as a unit because they had a long mainshaft and extension to the rear face of the gearbox. The gears in these boxes were similar to those in the SH and SL units. The letters N, E or S at the end of the gearbox prefix letters showed that an overdrive had been fitted. This was not applicable to the SH or JH gearboxes. A particularly daunting problem that has arisen in recent years has been the total lack of new first and reverse layshafts for non-synchromesh gearboxes as fitted to XKs.

Post-1964 baulk ring all-synchromesh gearboxes as fitted to 4.2-litre E types, post-1964 S type saloons and other Jaguar saloons can be fitted to XKs with some modification, providing they are bought with their attendant bellhousing, starter motor, flywheel and clutch. Remember, before you consider fitting such a box, that the gearlever will end up very close to the dashboard as the all-synchromesh box does not have the XK boxes' remote control mechanism.

Many overdrive spares are interchangeable with those on Mark II saloons and the big Austin-Healey sports cars.

Rear axles swop around happily between one XK and another providing the ratios are not too extreme and the Powerdrive limited slip differential from a 3.8-litre Mark II saloon can be fitted quite easily to an XK Salisbury axle; in the same way wire wheels can be fitted to all XKs except those with ENV axles. Disc brakes can be substituted for XK drums (go for XK 150 parts) and quick-change square brake pad calipers fitted in place of early round-pad XK 150 units. Rack and pinion steering from an XK 140 or 150 can be fitted to the XK 120, providing all the parts are available, including the steering column; indeed rack and pinion steering is something of a necessity on a right-hand drive car when fitting triple carburetters or they will foul the steering column. Otherwise the steering column has to be cut and universally jointed. But that sort of interchangeability is included in the next chapter, on modifications.

Typical XK body parts as supplied by specialists.

XIII

Modifications

JAGUARS ARE INCREDIBLE cars: there's not a lot you can do to improve them. Perhaps disc brakes for the XK 120 or 140 and a bit of help with the cooling are just about all that makes much difference on the road, apart from radial ply tyres if you can find any. But on the racetrack it is a different tale; the racing XKs may look very much like road cars but under their skins they are extensively modified. In spite of this they can still be driven on the road. One of Britain's top drivers, John Harper, often drives to and from historic race meetings in his XK 120 with nothing more than trade registration plates and a silencer added! That's more than can be said for the vast majority of other thoroughbred racers, some of which have never turned a wheel on an ordinary road.

What are these demon tweaks that the top men use? Their engines are invariably meticulously assembled 3.8-litre E type units, producing around 300 bhp. Three 45DCOE Weber carburetters are popular wear, although Harper had been using triple Dellortos with even bigger (48 mm) chokes recently. A six-branch, 'bunch of bananas' E type exhaust manifold running into short pipes, to exit in front of the nearside rear wheel, and crankcase breathers complete the visible engine modifications. The engines use forged pistons with special crowns giving a compression ratio of about 10:1; standard 9:1 pistons have been causing a lot of trouble in recent years as the manufacturers have changed the material. Obviously, the engines are carefully-balanced and a lightweight flywheel is fitted; 11–14 lb is the lightest practical weight without inviting warp and excessive clutch judder. Competition clutches with solid centres are essential and the connecting rods are shot peened for extra strength. Cylinder heads are gas flowed and fitted with $1\frac{7}{8}$-inch or 2-inch inlet valves, special springs and full-race camshafts.

Which of these modifications are worthwhile for road use? A 3.8-litre engine or straight-port head is a worthwhile substitute in any XK; with triple 2-inch SU carburetters it is rated at 265 bhp by the factory, or 245 with twin SUs. Weber or Dellorto carburetters are attractive, but hardly worth the expense for the limited amount of extra power and torque they can produce. Solid centre clutches and E type flywheels are well worth fitting; the flywheel alone does a lot to improve throttle response with little loss of smoothness at take-off. Alternatively, 2-inch SUs are well worth fitting to 3.4-litre cars if the original $1\frac{3}{4}$-inch carburetters are badly worn; otherwise the larger carburetters are hardly worth the expense. The larger ones differ chiefly from the smaller ones in that they have manual chokes instead of the electric starting device. To get over this problem you can fit the float chamber and electric starting carburetter from one of the old $1\frac{3}{4}$-inch SUs providing it is an HD series unit; otherwise you have to stop up the hole left in the manifold and fit a manual choke. The fuel supply is critical on any racing Jaguar. One of the most experienced tuners, Warren Pearce, of Epsom, Surrey, is a firm believer in increasing the diameter of the fuel pipes to allow the petrol to get to the front of the car more quickly. That makes all the difference to power outputs, he says.

Triple carburetters on an XK need a bit of surgery on the right-hand front wing if ram pipes are used, or a lot of hacking about if air cleaners are fitted. At the same time it is a good idea to fit the hydraulic reservoirs on the back of the left-hand inner wing, making sure to use metal pipes as the heat of the exhaust can affect plastic piping. This small modification not only makes more room for the carburetter set-up, but gives more ready access to the distributor. Incidentally, racing XKs use special distributors with the advance pipe blanked off.

Few of the thoroughbred racers use oil coolers now that they compete only in relatively short races and such fittings are simply not needed on the road. An XK's oil is hardly likely to reach the critical 95 degrees centigrade danger level in anything other than an endurance race. Also, it is usually a waste of time and money expecting to make much of an improvement on a Jaguar head; they did a really good job of the castings. Before the advent of the straight port head, some XKs were fitted with wide angle D type heads and produced a great deal of extra power; but these were rare birds and worth a fortune today. The 'production' D type head offers no advantage over a standard E type head.

Over the years a variety of modifications has been tried to cure the XK's overheating problems. One of the most effective but least known is the modified thermostat. All that is done here is to enlarge the bypass hole in the top to allow more

One of the fastest drivers of the much-modified racing XKs, John Harper, hard on the tail of Austin-Healey driver John Chatham at Silverstone.

water to flow through unhindered. Providing the hole is not made too big the car will not run too cool, and the extra flow can be enough to prevent it from overheating. Another effective method used in more severe cases has been to remove the thermostat and add a radiator blind and perhaps an auxilliary electric fan, in front of the radiator.

The great enthusiast, Bruce Carnachan, has yet another method to cope with conditions in California. He says:

'The cooling problems with the XK 120 in Southern California, which has a climate similar to the Costa Brava region of Spain, are well known. But I find with a cooling system in good order, the XK 120 does not overheat as long as you can maintain progress of at least 30 mph, even when the air temperature is 100 degrees fahrenheit. Sure, the gauge might read about 82–85 degrees centigrade, but when rolling along at 55 mph [the legal limit in the United States] on an 85 to 90 degree day, it will stay at about 78 to 80 degrees centigrade.

'To aid cooling when I was caught in the daily rush-home traffic in downtown Los Angeles, I would switch on the heater and that would lower engine temperature by about five degrees, then I added a small fan in front of the radiator (an old Jaguar heater fan and motor), and I'd switch it on whenever running slower than 25 mph on a warm day.

'The next cooling modification was to add a water recovery system. I retained the 4 psi pressure cap, and fitted a sealing gasket between the cap's metal lip and the radiator lip. Then I mounted a container to catch the overflow on the left inner wing—using a quart glass jar rather than plastic, which might melt—and made a vented syphoning cap for the bottle and hooked up the radiator overflow pipe to that. Now the car does not use water—I have rarely added any in the past four years.'

Windscreen washer reservoirs from Mark II saloons make ideal overflow bottles, and neoprene fuel piping from aeromodelling shops lasts longer than the rubber overflow pipes on Jaguar radiators.

Ingenious overflow systems are used on some thoroughbred racers. The 120s prepared by Tester Engineering (for Harper), Forward Engineering, and Oldham and Crowther, have used a series one E type header tank mounted behind the engine with the flow through the water rail reversed. Other alternatives include fitting a radiator with a thicker core which means removing the engine fan and substituting an electric fan in front of the radiator.

Braking is the other area that can be much improved on the road-going XKs and has to be modified on racing machines. The simple solution is to fit XK 150 discs all round on the earlier cars. Providing you have all the parts, including the rear axle, handbrake linkages, pipes and servo, it is relatively simple to transform an XK 120 or 140. Period solutions included fitting Alfin drums and Borrani wire wheels, which proved quite effective at minimizing brake fade. However, Alfin drums are no longer available and the magnificent alloy-rimmed Borrani wheels beloved of Enzo Ferrari for so long have always been very expensive. Lifelong motoring enthusiast Derek Bovett-White had these optional extras fitted at the factory when his 'ultimate specification' XK 120 was delivered to him for use in Malaya in 1952. 'They cost £60 each even then', he recalled as he served pints at the enthusiasts' haunt, the Anchor Inn, Barcombe, in the wilds of Sussex.

> 'I could average 85 mph in that car along Malaysian roads with no braking trouble at all. It can be quite nonsensical, the purists' objections to any departure from what they regard as factory specifications. I can see no harm at all in improving the car so long as it is done with taste. And what could be more original that the modifications carried out on cars such as mine at the factory?'

So Alfin drums and Borrari wires are 'in' if you want period modifications to improve your car's braking. In fact, wire wheels can be fitted readily to any disc-wheeled XK except those that survive with one of the early ENV axles. A practical solution to the problem of originality versus performance can be fitting 15-inch E type wire wheels (they do not use the entire XK spline width, but it does not seem to matter) with readily-obtainable radial ply tyres (Dunlop SP Sports are the best compromise of cost and quality) for everyday use, and saving the original 16-inch wheels with cross-ply tyres for occasions where originality counts.

Problems occur with the fitting of disc brakes to combat fade when all the parts listed earlier are not available. The essential components are, of course, the discs, calipers and adaptors, from an XK 150, and the servo. This is essential because disc brakes do not have the self-servo effect so cunningly incorporated in the two leading shoe front brakes by Heynes. The disc, calipers and adaptors bolt on in place of the drums and back plates; the chief problem then is connecting the pipes and handbrake. The XK 120 and 140 had a Lockheed system and Dunlop made the early Jaguar disc brakes, so adaptors are needed to screw into the existing pipework (providing it is good condition) from Dunlop's flexible piping to the calipers. The problem with the handbrake, once an XK 150 cable has been obtained, is locating it on the axle. In this case, it is necessary to make two clips to encircle the axle and hold the ends of the cable sleeves. Fitting the calipers so that the discs run true through them without too much float depends on correct shimming of the half shafts and packing the caliper mountings.

An alternative set-up is to fit the discs and calipers from an XK 150 or a Mark IX saloon at the front, retaining the original drum brakes at the back. This saves a lot of work, and the original handbrake is more effective than that used on the rear disc brakes. This also eliminates the necessity for a servo, although harder-than-standard brake linings, such as Ferodo VG 95, are worth trying with this set-up.

Extensive modifications are made to the XK's suspension for the race track. In the early days 'Alpine' springs (named after the rally) were fitted to combat axle tramp; these springs had two extra leaves to increase their stiffness and are still worth fitting to XKs subject to spirited driving if they have no other axle location. Unfortunately these springs tend to make the cars somewhat tail happy and radius arms are a better cure for axle wind up. A Watts linkage to locate the axle laterally helps with hard-raced XKs.

Once the axle is held firmly where it was designed to be, there is little problem

The superbly-engineered coil-sprung rear end of Plastic Pearson's XK. The solid rear axle had to be retained to stay within British modified sports car rules.

Typical historic racing powerhouse: that from the Plastic Pearson racing XK. Note the six-branch exhaust system, triple 45DCOE Weber carburetters, complex overflow system on the radiator (front-mounted at this point) and crankcase breathers.

John N. Pearson tending his beast.

Cockpit of Plastic Pearson's modsports XK. Note the alloy floor and extensive weight-saving.

with the handling, and softer springs can be fitted to lightweight racers. This conforms to the general trend in thoroughbred racing of moving from stiffened suspension to much softer springing, using shock absorbers of larger capacity and a variety of anti-roll bars. Current developments in this vein include fitting Armstrong dampers from Formula One cars with softened springs located by a shackle at the back and trunnion at the front. Roll centres are altered and the cars given half a degree of negative camber at the front. Road-going adaptations of this school of thought manifest themselves chiefly in the fitting of Koni shock absorbers all round (special brackets are needed for those at the back of an XK 120).

Other solutions to the problem of the XK's lively axle included grafting the entire rear end of a C type on to Hugh Howorth's famous machine; and coil spring rear suspension on John Pearson's plastic projectile! Pearson's ultimate chassis was chopped off and semi-space framed at the back to reduce weight. The coil springs were attached to the axle just behind the mounting point of its bottom locating arms, which had replaced the front half of the leaf spring. The back half of the leaf spring provided the rest of the axle's location and the coil spring units, from a Lola T142, incorporated the dampers. This car was fitted with 15-inch wide Lola wheels for modsport racing. Six-inch wheel are the maximum allowed for current thoroughbred racing and are the widest practical for use on the road.

The steering of any XK 120 is immeasurably improved by fitting the rack and pinion, complete with linkages and steering column, from an XK 140 or 150, a standard race track modification, that works just as well on the road. Some thoroughbred racers have been fitted with phosphor bronze bushes in place of the rubber elements of their front suspension to improve response; but this is at the expense of comfort on the road. In short, they can be painful to drive!

Automatic transmissions are hardly a delight in an XK either and converting to a manual gearbox is worth consideration. The parts needed from a manual car are the bellhousing, starter, propeller shaft, handbrake lever, slave cylinder, clutch master cylinder, tubing, linkages, pedal and reservoir, not to mention the clutch and flywheel, plus a new speedometer cable and rear engine mountings.

The conversion is carried out as follows. Once the engine and gearbox have been removed from the chassis, the clutch, flywheel, new bell housing and new engine mountings are fitted. A one-inch hole is then drilled in the bulkhead for the clutch pedal and the new handbrake lever fitted on the right-hand side of the gearbox tunnel instead of on the left as with the automatic cars. If the automatic car's handbrake lever is simply remounted on the right to clear the gear lever, it gets in the driver's (or passenger's) way depending on whether the car is right- or left-hand drive. Before returning the engine and new transmission to the car, remove the gear lever to give more clearance under the bulkhead. You can save the old automatic transmission tunnel cover by cutting a hole in it for the gear lever, remembering to cut another hole in the side of the tunnel to allow the manual gearbox's oil level to be checked. If the gearbox has an overdrive attached you can use the existing wires from the automatic transmission's speed hold as an overdrive switch. The reversing light switch wiring will have to be extended from under the instrument panel to the gearbox top and the automatic transmission's neutral safety starting switch removed

left Special equipment options for the
8:1 compression ratio cars of 1951.

right A Pycraft hardtop as fitted to a
120 roadster in 1952.

and the wires connected together to complete the starting circuit. Providing the
parts are available this desirable conversion is quite simple.

It is well worth while and quite simple to fit bucket seats to an XK, particularly
if it is intended for competition. Harper reckons that proper location for the driver
can be worth a second a lap!

Other equally desirable and quite simple conversions include fitting a limited
slip differential to the rear axle (essential for racers), converting the automatic choke
to manual operation (disconnect the terminal for the pressure switch and lead it back
to a dashboard switch and light, then earth that); and last, but probably most
important of all, fit a bonnet strap, preferably at the extreme bottom of the bonnet
lip to loop round the front apron.

For nearly thirty years the bonnets of XKs have been flying open for a variety
of reasons, with frequently horrifying results. A bonnet strap is one modification
that ought to be standard.

XIV

The Concours Cars

THE MEN who rebuild their XKs to concours-winning standards are a breed apart. Absolute perfection is their goal and they will spend years trying to achieve their aim. Even original and well-preserved cars have to be substantially dismantled and refinished if they are to compete with the best in the country, particularly in Britain, North America and Australia. This is because it is impossible to clean and re-paint components properly while they are still on the car. The engine, for instance, needs to come out and all its external parts must be taken off and 'given the treatment'. Aluminium castings must be polished to 'factory standards' (so that you can see your face in them) and all remaining parts, including the block, stripped and re-painted in the right colours. The right colours are, of course, the original ones, as points are awarded for this in the big concours competitions.

While the engine is out, the engine bay itself can be cleaned properly (even resprayed) and so can all the bulkhead components, throttle linkages, and so on. It is

Art Kinnear's magnificent 120 roadster, bonnet and boot open for inspection.

often more satisfactory to replace many of these fittings (such as electrical components, hoses and cables) because it is often well-nigh impossible to bring up the old ones to 'new' condition.

Likewise, it is virtually impossible to obtain a proper finish on an X K's front suspension without taking it all apart. The component parts can then be sand- or bead-blasted before repainting. Bead-blasting can be tremendously effective in making lots of other car parts look new, including fittings made of rubber, aluminium, or even wood. It is a 'must' for such things as roadster hood frames, which are a nightmare to strip if other methods of cleaning are envisaged. Alternatively, if there is no heavy rust or scale to be removed, you can take your components to a firm specializing in metal stripping; they can usually accommodate items as large as wings and doors in their dipping plant. It is virtually impossible to match their standards with hand tools alone. You can't get in all the nooks and crannies that these professional techniques treat so well.

It's the same with respraying. Leave it to the experts unless you have a great deal of time, patience and skill. You can save yourself money, however, and feel that you have been really involved in the car's preparation, by purchasing one of those cheap and simple electric spray guns, and then using it on small items such as suspension arms, radiators, brackets, heater units and so on. These little guns will give you a finish on these components which is practically identical to that on an X K when it left the factory so many years ago. It avoids non-original brush marks, you see.

By far the best education if you want to enter the exclusive concours world is to go to one of the bigger Jaguar club shows (for instance the X K Register's International X K Day in Britain, or a round of the Jaguar Clubs of North America concours championship series). Then crawl all over the top contenders (making sure not to leave sticky fingermarks or you'll be lynched!) and talk to the owners. There's nothing they like more than talking about their cars, they spend so many hours on preparation. And they are not people for keeping secrets; they'll tell you all about how they got their car to look so good, because it's really a matter of hard work and dedication, rather than expertise. It just helps to know how to go about things.

There's nothing better than competing in a concours, either, if you want to make it to the top. It's quite simple really. All you have to do to get a good, original, undamaged car to stand a chance of getting a highly-commended certificate, or something nice like that, is to get it really clean. First of all, the engine and underside should be degreased; then the entire underside scrubbed and hosed down; next polish all the metal work you can reach in the engine compartment, clean the hoses, and battery, paint the radiator, fan brackets and all the other little parts that ought to be painted but which are usually peeling; paint the underside (this is really good for the car), and exhaust system where necessary, clean the suspension thoroughly, and paint such items as shock absorbers.

On the outside of the body, touch up the stone chips, scratches and so on, then cut and polish the lot. Pay special attention to the wheels, cleaning them very thoroughly inside and out and touching up any damaged paintwork before treating them in the same way as the bodywork. Blacken the tyres if necessary, although not

XK Day finalists set the standard.

Centrepiece of the XK Day concours line-up: Ernie Foster's fabulous 120 drop-head.

Typical concours judging scene with these experts examining a 120 roadster fitted with the optional large 2-inch SU carburetters.

overmuch. Pay great attention to polishing the chromework—everybody does!— and remove and scrub all detachable fabrics. Clean the rest of the interior thoroughly, treating the seats with hide conditioner if necessary. Slightly faded upholstery is acceptable providing it has been well looked after. In any case, special dyes can be bought which will re-colour faded or rubbed areas without destroying the look of the leather; accessory firms sell these dyes by mail order. Polish any woodwork with furniture polish or strip and revarnish if its finish has been cracked by the sun; this means removing the wood, and treating it as if you were repainting an ordinary panel. Use several coats of varnish, each one being rubbed down in between. Then clean all the glass thoroughly—you would be amazed what a difference that alone can make!

Bob Baker, from Omaha, Nebraska, the JCNA's class II champion in 1977, started in this way. He bought a one-owner XK 120 roadster in exceptionally good condition in 1975. It had covered only 32,000 miles from new and was completely original and free from rust. But after two seasons on the JCNA concours circuit, it became apparent that a complete restoration would be necessary to win a place in the US national ratings. Bob told *Jaguar Journal*:

> 'With the help of my two closest friends, Jim Vakoc and Dave Kipling, this year's champ in class V, my 120 underwent what is generally termed as an uncompromising rebuild, with much regard and attention given to originality.
>
> 'Concours attended this year included among others Dallas, Texas, and Denver, Colorado (approximately 2500 round trip miles from Omaha for these two cities alone). Both were well within the 120's driving range with little or no difficulties encountered. This, to me, is where the true pleasure of the Jaguar lies—in the driving. . . .'

Other concours men do it the hard way and gain much satisfaction from restoring a wreck. One of the best cars in the British Isles belongs to Belfast dentist Ernie Foster. He found his XK 120 drop-head coupé UPK 762 in a farmyard:

'The Alsation dog that lived in it had eaten the upholstery and the damp had caused remarkable damage to the walnut dash and the carpets had rotted into holes. The floor was badly rotted and the sills non-existent. The doors almost fell off as the hinges were in the usual state for an unrestored XK. The engine was seized and the brakes disconnected. Still, it was an XK and it was love at first sight, so the princely sum of £115 was paid and the car was winched on to a trailer and brought home. It wasn't until I got it home that I discovered that it was even worse than I had thought. The rot which I thought only extended to floor level revealed itself in every part of the body as I probed with my screwdriver.

'However, my enthusiasm was undampened and the project was started. After a considerable amount of blood, sweat and tears and 800 man hours' work (each one chalked up on the wall of my garage), the car was presentable, but still required final trimming in Connelly hide. This was eventually completed after racing in my local club's January slalom, round a snow-covered course more suited to Minis.

'Since then the car has done many competitive events and still managed to take places in top concours such as those at XK Day in 1976 and 1977.'

Other concours cars have even more remarkable histories, such as the C type owned by Australian wine importer Ian Cummins. He spent five years rebuilding XKC037 to almost unbelievable standards. Like so many old racers, the car has quite a history. The original owners appear to have been Gerry Dunham and Nairobi Coca Cola bottler John Manussis. They raced the car extensively in Europe and East Africa in the early 1950s, eventually selling it to a colourful Australian, Dr John Boorman. He was a racing enthusiast of the old style. Fellow enthusiast Eric Wiseman remembered him in the *XK Bulletin* as

'. . . always being immaculate in full racing gear . . . when I first knew him, in the early 1950s, he had a very early XK 120, pale blue with disc wheels, spats and all. This went in favour of a British Racing Green XK 120 roadster with wire wheels. Dr Boorman, in true tradition, took off the windscreen and hood on delivery and, I remember, had trouble finding them when he eventually sold the 120. This car was highly tuned. The overheating troubles were beaten by grafting on oil and extra water coolers fabricated from bus parts. Unfortunately, from then on, he had trouble getting the motor warm enough.

'The 120 was immaculate. Dr Boorman had a bit of a thing about instruments and at the time I counted twenty-seven on his dashboard, including stop watches, Tapley meters, altimeters and outside air thermometers.

'There was great excitement when the C type was expected. It was supposed to be British Racing Green, but turned out to be some sort of mid-green. It had 2-inch SUs, but it was decided to change these for Webers. These were obtained from Italy at great cost, but without any word of instruction. Strong inquiries resulted in a handbook, in Italian. These instruments, three of them, were never understood by the mechanic, who put them on his Mark VII for a while, revelling in the extra performance until he found he was getting only about 10 mpg.

'The C type had a few adventures and demolished a few fences in the Cessnock, New South Wales, area where it was based. It must be pointed out that these diversions were no reflection on Dr Boorman's driving . . . people would insist on getting in the way.

'Then one night, a Sunday I think, while I and a few friends were standing around admiring our M Gs, as was our want, someone turned up and said there had been a mighty accident on the Nulkaba road. It was a Morris Minor, they said.

'What we found were the remains of two Ford Sedans and the C type, with its bonnet pushed on to where a Morris roof ought to be. The doctor was in hospital, head bandaged, giving minor medical treatment to a male nurse when we arrived. In fact, he said, he had achieved some sort of ambition. In the old days, he said, he had seen pictures of crashes during races when the drivers had been thrown out so violently their shoes could not keep pace with them. In this crash, his shoes had remained in the cockpit while he catapulted about fifty feet out of it. Looking at the fragile-appearing C type framework it was difficult to believe that it could have torn out the back axle of a Ford and severely bashed another of that ilk. But it had.

'As the owner of one of the Fords said in court, "It came round the corner at me like a great green wave."'

Cummins took up the story in the Australian *Jaguar Journal*:

'Frank Gardner, one of Australia's top racing drivers purchased the car in its damaged condition and with the aid of factory specifications from England completely rebuilt the car, campaigning it very successfully until 1959. Then Leaton Motor Racing in Sydney purchased the car for Frank Matich who also had success with it for twelve months or so.

'The next four years of the car's life are a bit vague as it passed through several private hands and deteriorated rapidly until March 1964 when John Kinsella purchased the car and rejuvenated it. The car passed on to Peter Lonergan of Surfer's Paradise and I purchased it from him in July 1969. By this time, even though the car was sporting a new coat of British Racing Green

right Before restoration: the front suspension of the Cummins C type.

left The Cummins C type hard on the tail of the great Australian Jaguar special, the Dalro.

Tom Hendrick's 120 roadster all glistening and gleaming: this magnificent machine was virtually unbeatable in US East Coast concours events between 1963 and 1971. Now more attention is paid to originality than chrome plating and underbonnet polishing, although this car was not a bad offender in this respect, reflecting more a love of ownership.

paint, mechanically it was becoming tired. I spent some time tidying up the whole car and replacing a few minor parts. In 1970 I ran the car in a couple of lap dashes and two vintage and historic races at Oran Park . . . I found the car very responsive and exhilarating to drive, unlike any other Jaguar I had driven.

'A month or so later I had the pleasure of co-driving John Goddard's D type Jaguar OKV 1 to Gundigai and back to Sydney, a round trip of 500 miles. It was during this memorable drive that I came to realise how tired the C type was, so a week later I embarked on a complete rebuild.'

This was incredibly thorough involving replacing practically every moving part, re-sleeving the engine back to 3.4 litres from the 3.8 to which it had been bored, dyno-tuning it out of the chassis to 223 bhp, stripping the chassis to the last nut and bolt, sandblasting, epoxy undercoating and spraying it like the coachwork. Many new parts were made, including a pinion for the steering gear, and the body was completely rebuilt with a new grille before being sprayed British Racing Green and retrimmed. Needless to say, the completed car was unveiled with wine and cheese, and Cummins then set to work on a more ambitious rebuild of a D type that had an even more adventurous history than that of his C type. At the time of writing he had just completed work on the monocoque of XKD510, the D type which was cut in half after hitting a lamp post in the 1963 Johore Grand Prix, was written off in a fatal crash when Tony Dennis accidentally changed from top to first gear at 110 mph while lapping Goodwood, and was reputed to have reached 200 mph in the Dakar Grand Prix with 17-inch wheels, ultra high gear and with Duncan Hamilton driving.

Not many concours cars have had a life like that; but there's not one successful XK that isn't living proof of man and woman's love affair with the motor car.

XV

The Jaguar Specials

ONE OF THE GREAT features of sports car racing in the 1950s was the spectacular performances of Jaguar-engined specials. It was quite feasible to try to improve on the performance of a C type or D type; these cars had been designed specifically for Le Mans, a circuit with a long straight and exceptionally good surface that made an old-fashioned rear axle no real handicap. It was when the works cars were exposed to the tight, bumpy circuits that abounded elsewhere that they came unstuck—literally! It was obvious that they needed a more sophisticated rear end. They were also rather heavy, having been built for endurance racing. The general feeling among the racing fraternity was that they had magnificent mechanicals but that the chassis offered plenty of scope for improvement. This theory was bolstered by the fact that the running gear was fairly easy to obtain and spares were plentiful; later the Jaguar factory openly encouraged the more professional special builders by supplying the equipment at reduced rates or on 'permanent loan'. The idea then was that Jaguar-powered specials beating the works Aston Martins was practically as good for publicity as running the recently disbanded works team.

By far the most successful of the special builders was Brian Lister. He had become interested in the sport in 1950, racing a Morgan 4/4 in East Anglian competitions; he progressed to a Cooper-MG and then a Tojeiro built near his works in Cambridge. The 'Toj' was really fast with its JAP dirt track motor cycle engine, if anything a shade too fast for Lister. He therefore offered it to a friend, Archie Scott Brown, who was already renowned for his exploits in an MG TD, despite being handicapped by a malformed hand and feet. Scott Brown made up for his physical handicaps by an extraordinary sense of balance and was soon dominating the smaller classes with Lister's Tojeiro–JAP.

Even then motor racing was an expensive business and Lister thought it best to capitalize on his investment by building a car under his own name. At least there would be a definite return on the investment in the form of publicity. In any case, mixing business with pleasure was attractive and he considered that he could make a very good racing sports car at the family's light engineering works. His father Horace and brother Raymond were persuaded to allow an investment of £1500, with the provision that if nothing worthwhile had been achieved in a couple of seasons, the project would be abandoned.

Lister's first chassis in the summer of 1953 set the pattern for all that followed: it was strong, simple and made from 3-inch diameter tubes. It was also wider than normal for that era, allowing the driver to set very low, between one chassis tube and the propeller shaft. This arrangement not only lowered the centre of gravity but reduced the frontal area, two factors which were always uppermost in Lister's mind. An ultra-low scuttle line emphasized this latter point. Armstrong coil spring–damper units provided the suspension medium front and rear, operating from fabricated uprights. Tubular wishbones were used at the front with a de Dion tube located by parallel radius arms and a central sliding block at the back. Steering was by the popular Morris Minor rack and pinion, with Alfin drum brakes all round. The first engine, the standard special builders' bored-out 1.5-litre MG XPAG, did not give enough power during initial tests at the Snetterton circuit in December 1953, followed by one or two races early in 1954, so Lister progressed to a highly-tuned Bristol unit midway through that year. The resultant combination of Lister, Bristol and Scott Brown dominated 2-litre club racing for the next eighteen months. Only the C type Jaguars and Aston Martins could beat it and several Lister Bristols were produced for other drivers.

One of the few 2-litre cars which could match its performance was the exotic Italian Maserati A6CGS, so the next step was to replace the Bristol engine (one of the tallest around) with the neat little Maserati unit. The frontal area was reduced, but all through 1956 the engine gave trouble.

Towards the end of that year hill climb exponent Norman Hillwood bought a Lister chassis and fitted it with a C type Jaguar engine and gearbox in place of the Bristol unit. The result was successful even on circuits despite its narrow wire wheels and drum brakes; it had plenty of power for an all-up weight of little more than 16 cwt. At the same time one of Lister's sponsors, Bryan Turle of Shellmex–BP, was demanding the same sort of car, powered by the more potent D type engine. In fact, Lister had probably been thinking along the same lines himself but had delayed acting for so long because he was more interested in getting Scott Brown into Formula Two at the time and the Maserati project seemed more logical on this line.

At any rate, Lister obtained a D type engine and gearbox in good time for the 1957 season and built up a similar chassis to that of Scott Brown's earlier car, beefed up only by the use of 14 swg tubing in place of 18 (16 swg was in short supply at the time) and reinforcement at places like the wishbone eyes. Braking was by Triumph TR 3 discs front and rear; Jaguar's triple-pad D type set-up was still too expensive at £750! The rest of the car was virtually the same as the 2-litre machine, with the exception of the 18-gallon fuel tank situated at the extreme rear with an 8-gallon dry sump oil tank. The exact location was chosen to ensure that as much weight as possible was concentrated on the rear wheels; in the event it worked out at 48 per cent over the front and 52 per cent at the rear. This meant that the Lister put down its power really well through the de Dion axle and ZF limited slip differential. Wheelspin was never a problem despite more than 250 bhp extracted from the D type engine by local tuner Don Moore's careful assembly.

Dunlop alloy wheels were fitted in the popular 16-inch by 5.5-inch size, with 600 section tyres at the front and 650 or 700 at the back. This first Lister–Jaguar

Lister–Jaguar number one, built by privateer Norman Hillwood, pictured in the hands of the present owner, Dr Philippe Renault in 1976.

had bolt-on wheels to save weight although later examples were invariably fitted with knock-off hubs to save time changing the wheels. Scott Brown simply dominated that season with the Lister–Jaguar, registered MVE 303, winning twelve out of fourteen races, being beaten only once by a works Aston Martin. Needless to say, customers were queueing up for Lister–Jaguars by then, the first 'production' example going to Dick Walsh at Torquay. It had a unique 'flat iron' body by Gomm of Woking and was registered HCH 736.

Lister produced about twenty of these cars during 1958, with 'knobbly' bodies. The coachwork made by Williams and Pritchard was designed to conform to, or defeat, the current Appendix C regulations for international racing. These regulations specified a rather tall windscreen which upset people like Brian Lister, to whom frontal area was of prime importance. He got round the regulations by having a scuttle lower than the bonnet line; thus the windscreen, being mounted on the scuttle, presented less frontal area than it would have done if the scuttle had been at bonnet height as was conventional at the time. The tail of this car was quite high, the same height as the windscreen, in fact. It housed a new, larger, 38-gallon fuel tank for long-distance racing, which sat partially over the rear axle to improve traction yet further; apparently the resultant raising of the car's centre of gravity was acceptable. The extra capacity was intended for long-distance racing, of course, and involved extra weight. Thus the chassis tubes were increased in diameter to four inches. Quick-change disc pads were also necessary for long-distance racing and Aston Martin had all Girling's units 'sewn up'. But, after 'suitable negotiations' by Briggs Cunningham, who had ordered three of the new chassis, these 12-inch all-round units were released, *Sports Cars Illustrated* reported. Knock-off hub caps were also fitted as standard. The magazine wrote:

> 'Throughout the body, the aluminium skin is riveted to a framework of half-inch 20-swg tubing which adds stiffness to the whole structure. This is specially the case around the engine compartment and in the nose section, which Williams and Pritchard have managed to make even lower than last year's.
>
> 'A Marston radiator, with an oil cooler in front of it, is canted steeply back to facilitate the escape of the warm air at the bottom of the car. Two ducts next to the radiator intake pipe air to the front brake discs.'

This system did not always work very well; Don Moore said later that holes had to be cut in the sides of Moss's car at the Silverstone Grand Prix meeting that year and numerous private owners have had similar problems since. But, on the whole, Lister cars were very tough and reliable, no doubt because they were of simple, uncomplicated design, and were produced by a firm with a heavy involvement in agricultural engineering.

Many of the 1958 cars were for export, particularly to the United States, and were designed to accommodate Chevrolet V8 engines. One of the Cunningham trio was a Lister–Chevrolet, built around an engine that the millionaire sportsman sent over for the purpose; the other Lister–Chevrolets left Cambridge devoid of engine and gearbox, which were to be fitted in America. These Lister–Chevrolets were fearsome machines and in later years many have been converted to Jaguar power, a much better combination. Many of the Lister–Jaguar chassis were sold without engines, too, so that the purchaser could fit his own; this was usually a 3.4-litre D type unit, although cars intended for international racing, where a 3-litre limit was in force, could be fitted with Jaguar's special 3-litre unit. The overall length of these cars was 13 ft 6 ins, six inches more than that of the original MVE 303. The wheelbase was 7 ft 6.75 ins, front track 4 ft 4 ins and rear track 4 ft 5.5 ins, three inches wider than the 1957 cars; the width was 5 ft 2.5 ins, and height 3 ft 3 ins, including the 12-inch deep windscreen. The price, including full D type running gear, and a Salisbury limited slip differential (the ZF was an extra) was a moderate £2750.

The only other variant produced during 1958 was the Monzanapolis car, virtually an open-wheeled version of the current sports car. The chief differences apart from the bodywork were beefed-up suspension to cope with the Italian track's bumpy surface and larger wheels, 17-inch at the front and 18-inch at the rear. Dunlop did not make the larger size in their popular alloy design, so wires had to be substituted at the back.

This gave the car rather a tail-up appearance, one that was not uncommon with Listers of that period. This was done on the 'knobbly'-bodied cars, apparently, because of problems with lift at the front end at speeds over 150 mph, a situation reported graphically in *Sports Cars Illustrated* by Bill Pollack, after he had driven down Riverside's straight in his Lister:

'Carroll Shelby, who had been standing on the course, said that it looked as though the front end was going to come completely off the ground. In fact, it was lifting a good eight to ten inches. This worried me because it cut down visibility from the car just at a point on the course when you wanted it—not to mention what it did to the steering. Later, I talked to Masten Gregory who had driven Listers in Europe. He claimed that they had had the same problem on the ultra-fast Avus circuit in Germany. The factory solution was to raise the car about two inches to spoil the airfoil. They also altered the shape of the front fenders to achieve the same effect.'

It was becoming obvious by the end of 1958 that the Lister would need more power and speed if it was to remain competitive in top sports car racing. The lift-off problem would no longer be accommodated by simply fitting bigger back tyres. So Brian Lister hired one of the best aerodynamicists, Frank Costin, from the de Havilland Aircraft Company. Costin had been chiefly responsible for the shape of the Mark 8 Lotus which had revolutionized sports car racing in 1954, and subsequently the highly efficient air penetration of the Vanwall Grand Prix car. He was also rather good at designing ultra-lightweight space-frame chassis which Lister hoped might make up for some of the power loss to rivals.

However, the 1959 Lister–Jaguar could not be completely redesigned in a few weeks, so the only real change for the new season was the bodywork and the substitution of Dunlop disc brakes. By Costin's standards the body was quite conventional, a logical development of the class-winning Le Mans Lotus car he had designed in 1957. It was a good deal more bulbous than the pared-to-the-bone 'knobbly' bodies, taking far more account of airflow. Most of the bulges and projections on the previous bodies were smoothed over and the cockpit and rear end redesigned to combat the lift problem without resorting to odd tyre sizes. A tonneau cover was essential to this moulded-screen–high-tail arrangement and was quite successful at keeping the front wheels on the ground without interfering with the existing weight distribution, which did such a good job at keeping the back end gripping well. However the screen had to be quite big to meet the international regulations and did nothing to aid visibility when inevitably it became smeared with rubber dust and oil during long-distance races. Small drivers also complained that the flowing body obscured their vision at vital points and made their handling less confident, although Lister went to a great deal of trouble to make the cockpit comfortable with good seats and lots of elbow room—unlike the 'knobbly'-bodied cars into which it was almost impossible to fit a passenger seat! Costin's calculations showed that this new body was good for 180 mph rather than 150, so Lister pressed ahead and it seemed that the new car did have the edge at high speed, although it was a bit awkward on tight, slow corners.

Meanwhile Costin pressed on with the new Lister chassis, a genuine space frame with every tube in compression or tension, and Carroll Shelby experimented with a 500 bhp Maserati V8 engine in one of the old chassis. The expense of all this development, aimed at winning Le Mans, was beginning to look frightening and Brian Lister, already depressed by the death of Archie Scott Brown, needed only to

learn of further fatalities to decide to call it a day. Later he told Doug Nye in *Auto-sport*:

The Costin-bodied Lister-Jaguar registered VPP 9, one of several cars claiming the works number, pictured in Australia.

> 'You had to live with motor racing to succeed in it and now I felt that I had other things to do to build up our original business. Racing was always a way of advertising our engineering skills and if we had not have been careful it could have become a profit absorber and destroyed the parent company it had been intended to promote.'

The spaceframe Lister was sold to Jim Diggory and performed well in club events until it eventually arrived at its destination, Le Mans, in 1963. By then its body had been extensively modified by Costin to the fixed-head coupé form more suitable for that event. Again it reflected Costin's thinking at the time in that the top, with its gull-wing doors, bore a close resemblance to one of his contemporary projects, the early Marcos. Sadly, the fixed-head Lister, in the hands of long-time Jaguar privateers, Peter Sargent and Peter Lumsden, quickly succumbed to minor misfortunes and that was the end of the Lister development story, although these historic machines have continued to dominate the events for which they were so well suited, the British club races.

Definitive Lister–Jaguar pictured in Cambridge in 1958.

Lister continued making parts such as wishbones for other special builders, particularly Paul Emery, who produced the Emeryson–Jaguar in the early 1960s, and for their old neighbours, Tojeiro. John Tojeiro's operation at Barkway, near Royston, had progressed from a shed in Little Gransden, near Cambridge, but still made Lister's look positively large! Nevertheless his Jaguar-engined specials (1956–59) were advanced for their days. The first Tojeiro–Jaguar, built for Essex farmer John Ogier, started life in a similar manner to the first Lister–Jaguar. It was simply an adaptation of an earlier 2-litre car, in this case powered by Lea Francis. As a result, the Tojeiro was smaller than the Lister–Jaguar with a wheelbase of 7 ft 3 ins and track of 4 ft 2 ins. Its design bore a close resemblance to a variety of other cars, both before and after it. The chassis, a multi-tubular spaceframe, was rather like Costin's Lotus in concept and similar to the last of the Lister–Jaguars. The suspension was basically the same as the Lister–Jaguar with sliding block location for the de Dion tube. The body bore a marked resemblance to that of a D type Jaguar without its fin. The Mark 1 version of this car, registered 7 GNO, was powered by a C type engine, possibly from the XK 120 sprinted at the time by Ogier, but a second car, again registered 7 GNO, had full D type running gear. It was this car which gave Bolster such a good time, although it lacked development in that its rear suspension was likely to go solid because of lack of travel for the de Dion tube, and the brakes could have done with a servo.

A third car was built to start the 1957 season alongside the second 7 GNO. It was nearer to Lister size with a wheelbase of 7 ft 6 ins and track of 4 ft 3.5 ins, plus a cleaned-up body. What is more, the car was even lighter at just over 14 cwt, yet it continued to put down its power very well because of Lister-like weight distribution. The handling was improved, too, by the substitution of a Watts linkage to locate the de Dion tube. This car, also registered 7 GNO, was easily distinguished from its predecessors by wire wheels in place of Dunlop alloys. Both these cars were subsequently written off by the start of the next season, so Tojeiro built yet another 7 GNO. The purchaser was David Murray of Ecurie Ecosse, who received a car substantially similar to the previous ones, except that it had a much prettier body. He also ordered another, with substantial reinforcement, long-range tanks and so on, for Le Mans 1959. This last Tojeiro–Jaguar bore an even more confusing registration number, RSF 301, which had been on an Ecurie Ecosse D type and their Lister, and was later to appear on Jim Clark's ex-Border Reivers Lister! Sadly, the best-known picture of this very pretty, heavyweight Tojeiro (it tipped the scales at around 17 cwt) is when Masten Gregory comprehensively wrecked it when the brakes failed at Goodwood in the 1959 TT race. The current 7 GNO was also damaged that year, at the Nurburgring, but was rebuilt in time to enjoy a good season in South Africa and was subsequently sold to David Lewis and his wife Vivienne for sprints in 1960. Mrs Lewis won her class with it at Brighton in 1961 but died in a crash while trying to repeat her victory in 1963. 'It was thought that she backed-off too abruptly on finishing her run', Nye reported in *Autosport*. However, the last of the 7 GNOs is currently being rebuilt, with the aid of parts from other wrecked Tojeiro–Jaguars.

These cars, and the Listers, were inspired by earlier efforts of Cooper and HWM to compete with Jaguar factory cars. HWM were first off the mark in 1951 through the efforts of a private owner, rather like Lister six years later. In fact, two distinct Jaguar specials came from Heath, Walton, Motors during the winter of 1951. The first car was based on an Alta Grand Prix machine which had been campaigned by one of the directors, George Abecassis. Hill climber Phil Scragg, from Macclesfield, had written off his potent XK 120 and hit upon the idea of installing its engine in the Abecassis car, redundant now that HWM were concentrating on producing their own racing cars.

Scragg felt happier, too, with the old Alta chassis as the new HWMs were

Jack Brabham in the Tojeiro–Jaguar leads David Piper's Lotus at Goodwood in 1957.

dual-purpose Formula Two sports cars and he felt that they were inadequate for the power of a hot XK engine. This Alta chassis was rebuilt with wheelbase shortened to 7 ft 10 ins and a ZF rear axle designed to cope with 300 bhp and HWM's rack and pinion developed from that used on the MGT series. The engine was prepared by well-known XK racer Hugh Howorth and a '1½-seater' body with cycle-type wings built by Leacrofts of Egham.

Leacrofts made a beautiful job of this body, although it was a shade on the heavy side by the standards of many of the spartan specials of the day. This car, fully road-equipped and registered RPG 418, had considerable success in hill climbs and sprints before Scragg moved on to more Jaguar-powered machinery in 1955. Even then this first HWM-Altar-Jaguar continued to score wins in club events, before being exported to Kenya and dominating circuit racing there from 1959 until 1964!

Meanwhile Moore, a motor trader from Finchley, was racing one of the dual-purpose HWMs, registered XMC 34, powered by an Alta engine. This unit was far from reliable and Moore resolved to do something about it for the 1952 season. The result was an XK 120 engine bored out to 3814 cc and a string of wins in 1952 for

the two-year-old all transverse leaf-sprung car. This cycle-winged vehicle used the
Armstrong Siddeley pre-selector box favoured by HWMs until 1953 when it was
replaced with a Jaguar Moss box. However, by 1954, privately-owned C types
were beating it, thanks to their better aerodynamics, and Moore sold the first really
successful Jaguar circuit special.

The ex-Osca Moore HWM–Jaguar
pictured at Shelsley Walsh in 1972.

In the meantime, HWM had started building their own Jaguar-powered
cars, particularly as their Alta units were becoming outclassed. The first works
HWM-Jaguar was based on an experimental single-seater that had been raced by
Abecassis in 1951. It had a C type gearbox like the Formula Two cars, so the Jaguar
engine was a natural substitute for its former Alta power unit. The front suspension
used a low-mounted transverse leaf spring as opposed to Moore's 1950-style high
spring and the 1952–53 Formula Two chassis, which used coil springs at the front.
The rear suspension was by torsion bars with a de Dion tube located by twin radius
rods either side and a central slide instead of the quarter elliptic de Dion axle used
on the 1952–53 Formula Two cars. The wheelbase was 7 ft 8 ins and Alfin drum
brakes were used all round, inboard at the back, as on the Moore car.

The all-enveloping two-seater body had been built for Scragg's car, although in the event he preferred his cycle-winged body for hill climbing. It was a preference he was to show repeatedly including an eventual cycle-winged adaptation of the Monzanapolis Lister. As with Scragg's other HWM-Alta body, it was beautifully finished with features such as the spare wheel mounted inside the wing where the passenger door might normally have been found.

The C type engine was one of the first to use triple Webers, and an American differential unit was fitted with quick-change spur gears to give a wide choice of rear axle ratios. It also allowed a very low propeller shaft line. This was the car registered HWM 1, tested by Bolster.

The unique suspension fitted to HWM 1 certainly worked well as Abecassis was to demonstrate in numerous events in 1953–55. Two other HWM–Jaguars were built in this period, VPA 9 and XPA 748, with coil spring front suspension, but neither seem to have had the edge on HWM 1, even when it was rebodied in steel to withstand the rigours of the Mille Miglia.

A new all-coil sprung car was built for 1955 with a much prettier body (reminiscent of a DB3S Aston Martin) and registered XPE 2. It was raced alongside the old faithful HWM 1 until 1956 when the original car was sold for hill climbing and re-registered YPG 3.

A new coil-sprung chassis, registered HWM 1, was built for the other man behind HWM, John Heath, who had done much to keep the British flag flying in early post-war Grands Prix, and who tragically died when the car overturned in the Mille Miglia. Soon after Abecassis quit racing and HWM built only two other cars of their own, SPC 982, on a Formula Two Alta base with D type engine and gearbox and cycle type wings for Scragg, and GPB 5, a futuristic fixed-head coupé with a much-modified 275 bhp C type engine for Abecassis to use on the road.

There is, however, a single-seater HWM-Jaguar that has been campaigned for years by its joint owners, Majors Lambton and Chichester. It was originally one of the 1952–53 Formula Two cars, fitted with an XK engine for Formula Libre racing in 1954. Later a supercharged Alta unit was substituted, but it returned to Jaguar power and has been storming hills with the odd circuit sortie thrown in ever since!

The other really professional Jaguar specials were made by the world-famous Cooper firm from Surbiton. They were historic machines in that they were the largest and last front-engined cars to be made by this company before they reverted to the rear-engined machines which later revolutionized motor racing.

Once again the Cooper–Jaguars owed their existence to the promptings of a privateer, Peter Whitehead, a wealthy farmer like Ogier. Whitehead also had interests in the textile trade, like Scragg. The request from Whitehead, who had always purchased the best cars money could buy, was logical: Cooper had one of the leading sports car chassis at the time (their MG and Bristol-engined cars were enjoying outstanding successes) and Jaguar engines were in a class of their own. Cooper, who had previously confined themselves to twin-tube sports car chassis and had even been copied by Tojeiro, thought they could go one better for Whitehead in 1954. He was one of their best customers, also running a Cooper-Alta Grand Prix car.

The first Cooper–Jaguar was a fascinating affair with a multi-tubular spaceframe which followed the proposed body contours closely. The idea was that such a chassis

The wide-angled D type engine pictured in the ex-Scragg hill climb HWM.

would save the weight of separate structures to support the body while retaining tremendous rigidity. In the event, it was fairly heavy at 17 cwt, as Cooper always built really strong cars! Even the cockpit was cross-braced, keeping the driver and passenger well apart! The all-independent suspension was by the traditional Cooper high-mounted transverse leaf springs, beefed up by double wishbones rather than lower wishbones only as on the smaller-engined cars. The body showed distinct teutonic influences with Porsche-like styling and exhaust pipes emitting high on the side in the manner of the current Mercedes Grand Prix cars. Jaguar showed considerable interest in this car, fitted with a special magnesium back axle casing, disc brakes and C type engine and gearbox. Its wheelbase was the same as a D type's at 7 ft 7 ins and track wider at 4 ft 4 ins. Three of these cars were built, UBH 292 enjoying considerable success in Whitehead's hands and PDH 22 and UUG 3 going to northern enthusiasts Bertie Bradnack and Jack Walton. However they were no faster than the rampaging HWM 1 and Cooper set about designing a Mark II version for 1955.

This much-improved model with full dry-sump D type power was obviously designed for long-distance racing with its 37-gallon fuel tank, more conventional body, and multi-drilled shackle plates to allow the rear suspension height to be adjusted to cope with rough roads. Whitehead had the first Mark II, Tommy

Sopwith the second (YPK 400), Michael Head, of C type fame, the third (HOT 95) and Bernie Ecclestone, later to become one of the leading lights behind today's Grand Prix circus, the fourth.

> 'Although the Cooper–Jaguar's independent suspension gave it considerably better road holding than the D type, particularly on bumpy surfaces, the car did have strong understeering tendencies which put it at a disadvantage, and it never looked like rivalling the Lister–Jaguars when they arrived.' (Paul Skilleter in *Jaguar Sports Cars*)

Nye reported in *Autosport* that Sopwith originally intended to use a Turbomeca gas turbine engine in his chassis through his family connection with Hawker Aircraft, but substituted an XK unit when the turbine took too long to develop. Sopwith was one of the leading lights of sports car racing at the time with his special-bodied Armstrong Siddeley-engined J2R Allard, called the Sphynx. This glorious old car continued to be campaigned, along with the odd HWM-Alta which was to receive an XK-engine on occasions. With a 3.8-litre XK engine, the Sphynx had more success in Brian Croot's hands in 1969–70.

Numerous other specials acquired Jaguar engines over the years, one of the most successful being the RGS Atalanta built near Ascot by garage owner Dick Shattock. Parts of this car dated back to a pre-war exotic, the Atalanta, built at Staines. The 'works' car, HBL 845, was based on a shortened Atalanta chassis with its ingenious independent trailing-arm horizontal-coil-spring rear suspension. Trailing arms were also used at the front with a cross-laminated Salter torsion bar running through the front transverse chassis cross-member, rather like the C type's rear suspension.

The wheelbase was 8 feet, rear Alfin drums were mounted inboard, and the first engine was a Lea Francis with Cotal electric gearbox. An alloy body with cycle type wings was fitted, then in 1953 a modified XK engine with C type head 'breathed upon' by Harry Weslake and twin 2-inch SU carburetters. Bolster gave the car, credited with around 250 bhp, a whirl in this form and extracted a 0–60 time of 8.2 seconds and a standing quarter mile of 15.2; the best time achieved for *Autosport* to that date. He found the 120 mph top speed disappointing, however, due to the 'vintage' body shape but liked the roadholding imparted by the novel suspension. Anti-roll bars and Michelin X tyres were fitted at around the same time and gave tremendous confidence in wet weather, Shattock reported later.

During 1954, he bought an all-enveloping HWM alloy body and made what is believed to have been Britain's first glass fibre sports car shell, using the HWM rear end, slightly modified, for both front and rear!

He fitted the first of these bodies to his RGS Atalanta and added fins to the back ('not so much for aerodynamics, just so you could tell which way it was pointing'), promptly increasing the top speed by 18 mph! He even beat Duncan Hamilton's D type in the wet and eventually sold about a hundred of his bodies for home-built specials, plus perhaps a dozen of his chassis. It was difficult to tell exactly how many chassis were sold. 'Some people used to buy a front unit, save up some more money and six months later buy a rear end', said Shattock, who recommended a wheelbase

Stan Jones rounds Jaguar Corner in his Cooper-Jaguar at Albert Park, Victoria.

of not more than 9 ft 6 ins. Such was the delightful state of British special building in the early 1950s.

American Jaguar specials at this era tended to be more amateurish. The Poguar of Tom Fox from Washington, who enjoyed considerable success in C-modified sports car racing in 1955–56 was a good example. The chassis was basically two angle girders with an 8 ft 4 ins wheelbase and 4 ft 6 ins track. It relied on Ford transverse leaf spring suspension like many of the hot rods of that time. The rear suspension used model A springs, a 1936 pick-up differential housing, a 1940 centre section and 1946 pick-up crown wheel and pinion. The Jaguar Moss box output shaft was machined to fit a Ford propeller shaft and the engine set back as far as possible in the chassis. This meant that the driver sat alongside the bell housing and the gear lever was extended forward by a remote control linkage. The steering gear was mostly Chevrolet from the mid 1940s. The 1951 XK unit was fitted with the Iskendarian cams beloved of hot rodders and three Carter sidedraught carburetters. Cooling was by courtesy of a Nash Ambassador radiator. The driver sat on the floorboards with his legs straight out to reduce the front area and a 'flat iron' glass fibre body was built as low as possible with a wing line reminiscent of the XK roadster which had donated its engine.

'I may put a new body on the car at a later date', Fox told *Sports Cars Illustrated*, 'one that's a bit more American. Still, since the car is half English and half American this might not be a bad compromise. It's a good car to drive with any kind of body. I go Poguar.'

Even the LGS special from Jersey which dominated the island's Bouley Bay hill climb in the 1950s was more advanced although construction had started in 1946. Frank Le Gallais built this mid-engined machine from a pair of 2.5-inch 19 swg tubes on each side with 6-inch cross members front and rear. Two more cross

Side by side, the Alta–Jaguar on the left and the Majors' HWM–Jaguar on the right.

members braced the chassis under the engine mountings. The wheelbase was 7 ft 10 ins, front track 4 ft 6 ins, rear 4 ft 5 ins, with Citroen-based torsion bar front suspension and swing axle rubber rear suspension built following consultation with Sir Alec Issigonis, the genius who was later to use this medium in the Mini. Steering was by rack and pinion and the whole 13-cwt car looked rather like a miniature Auto Union pre-war Grand Prix car without its rear cowling.

Le Gallais's first engine was a push-rod Jaguar Mark V unit, but he achieved his greatest successes after obtaining an XK 120 special equipment engine late in 1950. In this form the LGS proved to be the equal of top hill climb cars such as the ERAs (still acquitting themselves honourably in Grand Prix racing at the time) and far faster than a C type or Scragg's HWM–Jaguar.

Two of the other Jaguar-engined specials built by Gordon Parker were equally memorable. His Jaguara used a proprietory Buckler multi-tubular frame designed to take small Ford power units. The independent front suspension came from a Vauxhall Velox and the rack and pinion steering rack from a Morris Minor. The rear axle was standard XK 120 liberally located and suspended by coil springs. A 3.4-litre XK engine was fitted with supercharger, and the two-seater body was of the cycle-winged variety favoured at the time of construction (1952). The car was used for all manner of events, including circuit racing, with considerable success, although the prestigious fastest time of the day at the Brighton Speed Trials was always its main object.

The Jaguara never achieved this although it wiped up numerous other awards, and Parker built another, more fearsome, special in 1958. This was the HK Jaguar, a single-seater powered by a highly supercharged 3.4-litre XK engine. This relatively simple car was based on a two-channel tubular chassis with coil spring suspension all round and a de Dion tube at the back. It proved to be fantastically fast on a dry day but a monster in the wet! However, it achieved its object at Brighton in 1961 and later distinguished itself well in sprints and hill climbs in the hands of Anthony Charnock, alongside the Jaguara.

Needless to say, Australians have not been slow to build Jaguar specials over the years. Many XK 120s were supercharged, lightened, stripped, and rebodied in their search for speed, but 'the first true Jaguar special to emerge was the Austral-Union', Les Hughes reported in *Jaguar Driver*.

'This was an open-wheeled car which first surfaced on 28 December 1952, at Mount Druitt, New South Wales, in the hands of Larry Humphries, who had just built the car out of the wreckage of a road-going XK 120 which had been demolished earlier that year at Mount Druitt by its owner, Tom Duffy.

'The Austral-Union was a monoposto weighing a full 18 cwt with a de Dion rear suspension sprung by torsion bars, while the front was standard XK 120. Disc wheels, a standard 3.4 engine, and original brakes were used. It had a rather chequered career in its early life when it was rather unreliable and was nearly always eclipsed by another car called the Jack Robinson Special. The JRS was a far better car both in construction and preparation, and in the hands of Robinson, it built up quite a name for itself, and was undoubtedly the most successful Jaguar-powered car built in Australia.

'The Austral-Union re-emerged as a far better car in the late 1950s when it was completely rebuilt by Alwyn Rose and named the Dalro-Jaguar. It was a different vehicle in Rose's hands and had redeemed itself until 1961, when it was again badly smashed at Catalina Park, but rebuilt in only eleven weeks as the Mark II Dalro, and proved itself better still. As well as having its weight reduced to 13.5 cwt, it had a compression ratio of 13:1 and disc brakes were fitted along with many other modifications. This made it a much more competitive racer, but unfortunately it still was not a winner as the smaller rear-engined cars had been born, and outclassed the older front-engined Dalro. The JRS had also been made virtually obsolete by the smaller Coopers and others, but it had been a constant winner up until around 1960, still in Robinson's hands, and with very good preparation and constant modification had stayed competitive and more than earned its good name.'

Throughout the years there have been numerous XKs fitted with special professional coachwork, some of which have matched Lyons's immortal lines, and even first class amateur efforts by Col. Rixon Bucknall, who produced SS-like projectile based on an XK 140 chassis with triple carburetter 3.4 S type saloon power; a very well made XK 120 rebodied by engineer Bill Hodge to resemble the film

world's Chitty Chitty Bang Bang and an XK 120 with a hard top distinctly like that
of the 1961 E type Jaguar fixed-head coupé produced in Sydney in 1959 by John
Stranger. Pictures of these cars are worth thousands of words, while other Jaguar
specials, such as the Chevrolet-engined D types produced in the United States in
the late 1950s are best forgotten! But there was one Jaguar special produced in
Britain in 1969 which almost defies description—the ultimate mod sports car of
John 'Plastic' Pearson.

This amazing machine started life as an XK 120 drop-head coupé in 1954,
to be raced with a 3.8-litre Mark X engine and wide alloy wheels to great effect by
its owner and John Harper in 1969. Its transformation for 1970 made it exceptional.
Paul Skilleter told the story in *Motor*, in 1973:

'During the winter of 1969, the car was stripped to the chassis, moulds were
taken directly from the original body panels, and a complete glass-fibre replica
body eventually emerged. A new floor and transmission hump were fashioned
from aluminium, and the new glass fibre wings, doors, bonnet, bootlid and rear
section were installed on the chassis. The roll cage was retained but the hood
was cleverly replaced with an exact glass-fibre copy.

'When finished, the car looked just like it did the year before, except that if you viewed it against a strong light, it glowed!

'At this stage, little was done to the suspension. An XK handles pretty well, particularly on smooth motor racing circuits, and all that John did was to give the front wheels some negative camber, wind down the front torsion bars a little, and locate the rear axle with radius arms. The bottom end of the engine was left standard but it was given a big-valve E type head, prepared by John Middleton, which was set up with triple Webers using a Tecalemit Jackson fuel injection manifold. Braking was by XK 150 discs.

'First time out in 1970 was a disaster—John crashed the car heavily at Silverstone on the second lap of a very wet practice session. This uninspiring start to 1970 was to foreshadow a troublesome season; engine problems were rife, with five major failures, eventually tracked down to a rogue crankshaft. . . .' [With a new crankshaft the car soon became competitive.]

'The XK was considerably more modified in 1971, and made a correspondingly greater impression on the mod sports scene as a car of undoubted speed and character. Motor racing journalists called it things like "funny Jaguar special" and "red monster", but it won races and beat all the E types, which some people thought very funny. It is not on record what the E type drivers thought; or at least, it is, but I couldn't possibly repeat it here.

'Progress can be charted by lap times round Silverstone's club circuit. In "original" steel form in 1969 the XK circulated in 1 minute 8.2 seconds; in 1970, with plastic body, 1 minute 6 seconds; 1971, 1 minute 4.2 seconds; and finally, the best time for the 1972 season, 1 minute 2 seconds. Bringing the time down to 62 seconds was largely the result of suspension development and the car is now suspended front and rear by coil spring–damper units; being able to throw away the hefty front torsion bars and front of the rear leaf springs was helpful too! In fact, very substantial alterations have been made to the back end, the chassis having been semi-space framed in this area, outside the axle centres, to take the ex-Lola T142 spring–damper units which are mounted at 30 degrees to the vertical, and to provide mountings for additional locating arms for the 3.31 : 1 ratio axle. E type discs are used up front as well now.

'Engine reliability has certainly been found, emphasised by John's inadvertent, but habitual, use of well over 7000 rpm earlier this season, until he discovered that the rev counter was reading some 600 rpm slow. But no protest from the engine at all! The usual rev limit is 6500 rpm, with an at-the-wheels bhp figure of about 210, indicating at 290 or so at the flywheel, about the average for a racing E unit. The whole engine is set back 2.5 inches and is considerably lowered in the chassis.'

In fact, Pearson did not stop there with his car, modifying it still further with a rear-mounted radiator to improve the weight distribution and experimenting with supercharging before moving on to a Lotus Elan!

Nevertheless, this was the world's fastest racing Jaguar until the advent of the ill-fated 5.3 litre competition coupés: a very special XK that held lap records everywhere and is unlikely to be surpassed.

Jaguar XK Coachbuilding Supplement

below The four-seater 120 built in 1952 by Abbott of Farnham, now in New Zealand.

opposite above The Ghia Jaguar 120 exhibited at the Paris Motor Show in 1953.

opposite below Pininfarina's 120 of 1955, one of the few special fixed-heads that was as good looking as Jaguar's own effort.

Since the early 1950s, top coachbuilders, and one or two amateurs, have been trying to improve the classic lines of the Lyons XKs—with little success. Some of the best efforts with special bodies are included in this supplement of rare pictures.

An ultra-modern body fitted on a 120 chassis, showing strong GM Opel influences.

Brazilian special-bodied 120 fixed-head awaiting restoration.

The Oblin-bodied 120 awaiting rest-oration.

The Swiss special-bodied 120 owned by register member Fernand Eggen-schuider, with coupé top strongly reminiscent of an MGA.

An incredible combination of Morris Minor Traveller and 150 fixed-head have turned this English XK into a car for all the family, including the motoring dog.

John Goddard's 120 roadster, modified to his taste.

The ex-David Hobbs automatic 140 rebodied by Freddie Dixon in the 1960s, pictured at Prescott hill climb. Note the strong E type influences.

Ghia's Geneva Show 140 fixed-head of 1956.

The Boano 140 designed by Studebaker stylist Raymond Loewy in Paris in 1955.

A rare picture of the interior of a special-bodied XK, in this case the 1956 Ghia Geneva Show model.

opposite above Bertone's 150 fixed-head of 1958, showing strong Alfa Romeo influences.

opposite below Rear end of the 1958 Bertone 150.

XVI

Comparisons with Contemporary Rivals

THE XK 120 was almost unrivalled when it took the sports car world by storm in 1948; there was hardly anything to touch its performance in the next three years, and there never was anything to beat it for value. In the late 1940s, the only car with comparable performance was the Ferrari Barchetta 166, an Italian aristocrat produced in very small numbers almost exclusively for racing. This was a truly wonderful car with a price tag to match: around £4000 plus purchase tax if you could persuade Enzo Ferrari that you were worthy of such a steed. In fact, if you were that good and had that sort of money you might as well have got into a Jaguar works racer for half the price. Money aside, the Ferrari was a pretty good car. It was capable of reaching 60 mph from rest in little over 8 seconds, providing you could manage the all-or-nothing clutch. As ever, *Road and Track* put it rather well when testing one such car in 1952:

> 'The uninitiated novice does not simply seat himself in the Ferrari and make off with the greatest aplomb. And the expedient of revving the engine to near its maximum torque and then abruptly releasing the clutch, does not make for the best timed Ferrari runs over a measured distance. To be exact, this method of procedure avails little else than damage to the clutch, gearbox, or rear end. Proper Ferrari procedure is to release the clutch with the engine near its idle point—only depressing the accelerator after the drive train is completely coupled. For the sceptic's information, European road racing circuits are strewn with bits and pieces of Ferrari gears—left behind by over-zealous drivers.'

So that's what you got for four times the price of an alloy XK: a 123-mph thoroughbred with not a vestige of weather protection, which needed constant attention and even different carburetter jets if you ventured into town. Driving it through traffic was positively perilous. The XK might have got hot under the collar, but it was nothing near as bad as a Barchetta. The Italian car did not even have a fan! As old Enzo used to say: 'If the traffic is heavy and the engine is hot, you stop for an aperitif: and when the traffic is gone, you go. A Ferrari is for driving, not for standing still.'

The Frazer Nash High Speed model was nearly as stark as the Ferrari, with a

similar capacity, 2-litre engine, although only half the number of cylinders (six instead of twelve). It was, however, a good deal more practical than the Ferrari for road work, with a top speed in the region of 120 mph, providing it was fitted with the most highly-tuned of the Bristol engines. Like the Ferrari, it was produced only in small numbers and cost more than £3000 including tax, or double the price of an XK 120. Really, the XK was miles ahead of these rivals in terms of price, comfort and performance in the hands of the average driver.

Aston Martins were a different proposition. The Feltham firm's first XK rival, the DB1, was lovely to look at, but cost almost as much as the Frazer Nash and was slower. But the Aston that followed in 1950 was even more attractive, though it stayed in the £3000 price bracket.

This was the DB2 fixed-head coupé, capable of 116 mph, 20 mpg and 0–60 mph in 11.2 seconds, all with a high degree of comfort. This car was fitted with a 2.6-litre Lagonda engine of similar basic design to that of the XK: twin overhead camshafts and six cylinders in a line. Time would show that the Aston was not so durable as the XK, but it did have one big advantage. It held the road better.

> 'One of the chief impressions of the people who saw the racing at Le Mans was of the supreme steadiness and safety of the three Aston Martins. This feeling of absolute control is sensed immediately by the driver and very quickly imparted to the passenger, and the magic three-figure mark can be frequently attained in England with perfect safety and with no particular inconvenience to other road users.' (*The Motor Year Book*, 1951)

There were two fast sports cars in the same low price bracket as the XK 120, but both were rather primitive: the Allard J2 and the Healey Silverstone. Both were produced in small numbers; both had cycle-winged bodies and both were slower than the XK, although variants of the Allard could equal the Jaguar on the racetrack.

Basically, the Healey was a lightweight version of the Warwick firm's lovely touring cars, powered by a 2.5-litre Riley engine and good for 110 mph; like the Allard, it offered few creature comforts and could hit 60 mph from rest in around 12 seconds. Before the XK started to sell in large numbers, Allard did a roaring trade in America, exporting cars without engines, because of British import restric-

John Tojeiro's AC Ace-Bristol, with Ferrari Barchetta-like body.

tions. The Allard chassis was designed to take virtually any American V8, particularly the new 5.4-litre Cadillac unit, one of which the south London firm had obtained for development. These engines produced 150 bhp in standard form against the 115 bhp of the 4.3-litre Mercury unit fitted in Britain, with no extra weight penalty. Thus the American Cadillac Allards were often more than a match for the XK with similar power to propel only 17 or 18 cwt. But they were wild and primitive sports cars, with none of the beauty and practical appeal of the XK; in any case Allard only managed to produce 173 J2s between 1950 and 1952 when they became completely outmoded. Healey just managed to clear the 100 mark with the Silverstone before they moved up a bracket with the Nash Healey.

This was a complete contrast to the Silverstone even though it used a similar chassis! The 3.8-litre six-cylinder power unit came from an American Nash Ambassador complete with three-speed gearbox and automatic overdrive. The car weighed 21.5 cwt (around 3 cwt more than a Silverstone and that much less than an XK), but with 125 bhp under the bonnet was capable of 110 mph and a 0–60 mph time of 10 seconds. The body was designed by Farina in Italy and looked nearly as sleek as that of the Jaguar, but for no discernible reason the Nash-Healey was not a commercial success and production ended in 1953. A few examples were produced with Alvis engines for the home market.

Soon after the introduction of the Frazer-Nash High Speed model a slightly modified private entry finished third at Le Mans and became the basis of the Le Mans Replica; then in 1951, Frazer-Nash performed a feat never before accomplished by a British car: outright victory in the Targa Florio road race. The result was a pretty all-enveloping roadster, called the Targa Florio and another called the Mille Miglia, both in a quite different price bracket above that of the XK.

Meanwhile, there was no stopping Donald Healey at Warwick. He had seen

the lucrative market being opened up in America by the medium-priced XK and the cheap MG Midget. So he got together with Leonard Lord at Austins and produced the spectacularly simple, yet good-looking Austin-Healey 100. This car not only sold at £750 before tax, but was capable of more than 100 mph with a 0–60 time of 10.5 seconds! Needless to say the Americans loved it, but it was not as fast as an XK and not so comfortable, so it did not cut into the Coventry firm's sales.

It spelled doom, however, for that glorious old square-rigger, the MG TD. And when Triumph introduced the TR 2 with a similar performance to the Austin-Healey and at virtually the same price as the £550-basic MG, it was the final nail in the coffin for the Midget. Jaguar, nestling in the glory of Le Mans, and with a still-unmatched product, were unaffected. There seemed no limit to the market that British sports cars were carving for themselves. It even started to worry the American giants.

Sales of European sports cars were soaring in 1953 when Chevrolet rushed out their two-seater plastic-bodied Corvette. They had decided to use glass fibre because it was easy to work and cheap for low-volume products, such as sports cars. This all-new American sports car used the same basic layout as the Healey, particularly the Nash-Healey, and the Jaguar, MG and Triumph, although it looked like nothing else on earth.

However, it was a disappointing car and sales failed to take off. The body leaked, the instruments were styled virtually out of sight and you couldn't have a sporty manual gearbox. You had to have a GM slushbox auto instead. It would be twenty years before the public went for automatic sports cars in a big way. The first Corvette's performance was not all that bad, though. Its truck-like 4-litre engine was good enough to take it up to 60 mph in 11 seconds and 106 mph flat out. But it just did not match up to the European sports car standards of the mid 1950s and

left The Triumph TR 3.

right The early Chevrolet Corvette.

A dynamic duo of Porsches.

only two thirds of the 4000 Corvettes made by 1955 had been sold in the first two years. By American standards it was a flop.

Ford ran into similar problems with their two-seater Thunderbird, introduced in 1954; it was discontinued in 1958 when they had sold only 53,000.

Meanwhile, Mercedes had been recovering from the war. Their factories had been devastated, and their workers dispersed. The first priority was to earn some safe money, so they concentrated on high-quality saloons and industrial vehicles; but chief engineer Rudolph Uhlenhaut was hard at work on an exotic new car, the 300 SL gullwing coupé. This was the vehicle that gave Jaguar such a fright on the racetrack, but like all Mercedes it was rather expensive. Nevertheless its performance, 135 mph and 7.4 seconds from 0–60 mph were enough to carry the price tag of something like £4000 in Britain. It was a little bit better than the XK 120 or 140 fixed-head coupé in everything except handling, price and availability, besides being rather on the twitchy side.

In California, Porsche sales were starting to soar as the relatively cheap little 1500 Speedster showed its paces. The figures of 102 mph, 0–60 mph in 10.3 seconds and 20–27 mpg for just under $3000 made it a serious rival to the XK 140, then selling

The fastest of the Big Healeys, the 100S, chases a D type in 1957.

Chapman's lovely Lotus Elite of 1957.

at $3800, although, of course, the British car was superior in every department, particularly speed and handling. Porsche did have one model at the time which reached nearer to the XK's performance, the Carrera coupé (120 mph, 0–60 in 11.5 seconds), but that cost $6000. The prices here are quoted in dollars because hardly any of these cars reached Britain, such was the demand for them in California. That market was insatiable, with none of the European manufacturers being able to meet the demand, particularly Jaguar and Porsche.

Similar problems were faced by Alfa Romeo with their beautiful little Giulietta Spyder. It was cheaper than the XK at $3000 and handled a shade better; but it was a good deal slower at 100 mph and 0–60 in 14.8 seconds. Its Italian compatriots, the Ferraris and Maseratis, had by now exceeded the XK's performance, but not reliability, and they cost the earth.

At this time, 1955, the MG management at last persuaded BMC to let them compete with the Triumph and Austin-Healey and brought out an immediate best-seller, the MGA. This aerodynamic 1.5-litre two-seater sold for only £960, yet was capable of just on 100 mph with a 0–60 mph time of 15.6 seconds—much faster than the TF Midget it replaced. It might not have been as fast as the Triumph or the Austin-Healey, but it handled better, was really durable and bore the magic name of MG. Unlike the XK and other desirable sports cars, it was readily available, being produced by the biggest sports car factory in the world, at Abingdon, near Oxford.

The demand for Allards had been falling fast in the face of such an onslaught, and by the time they brought out their XK 140 powered Palm Beach it was too late. Their production cycle had been so disrupted that they couldn't meet the potential demand and stopped making production cars altogether after half a dozen of the Jaguar-engined examples.

But there was still hope for the small manufacturer. By 1956, AC at Thames Ditton had got into their stride with the Ace, a pretty, handbuilt two-seater based on a current Tojeiro racing sports car. It certainly looked good and handled beautifully, but with its rather old-fashioned 2-litre six-cylinder engine was capable of only 104 mph with a 0–60 time of 11.4 seconds, rather slower than the Ferrari Barchetta which it resembled. However, despite being handbuilt, the price was competitive at £1450 including tax, against the XK 140, which cost £200 more. Higher up the price scale, the first of the popular Porsche 1600 coupés were starting to reach Britain at £2000. Their top speed was 103 mph with a 0–60 mph time of 14.4 seconds and exceptional economy of 27–33 mpg because of their efficient aerodynamics. The Porsche, selling at virtually the same price as the XK 140 in America, was becoming even more popular there.

Late in 1956, the Austin-Healey acquired a six-cylinder engine of the same capacity as its 2.6-litre four-cylinder predecessor and became much more like a cheap Jaguar in concept, selling at £1150 including tax. The new engine was much smoother than the old 'four banger' although rather disappointing in that it gave no extra performance.

Meanwhile Triumph introduced the TR 3 with disc brakes in 1956; the first mass-produced car to offer such a system. Like most sports cars of the 1950s, including the XK 120 and 140, the TR 2 had suffered from inadequate drum braking. Triumph used discs on the front only to save money and to ensure that the handbrake worked properly.

Few handbrakes operating on rear discs have been really efficient as XK 150 owners were to testify after the model's introduction in 1957. It was just as well that Jaguar were working on the XK 150 design in 1956 as former Allard engineer Zora Arkus-Duntov had been hired to get to grips with the Corvette in America. This European-born development specialist immediately set about improving the Corvette's handling and standardizing V8 power to combat a pepped-up Thunderbird and all the foreign sports cars. He raised the Corvette's power to 210 bhp, and a manual gearbox was offered for the first time. The plastic giant promptly did 120 mph, 0–60 in 7.5 seconds and sales never looked back. Suddenly it was close to Jaguar standards of straightline performance.

The XK 150 was still in a class of its own though. The only real difference between its market domination and that of the XK 120 and 140 was that there were more sports cars for sale in the late 1950s, occupying little niches of their own. Aston Martin, for instance, had progressed to a two-plus-two configuration like the XK 150 fixed-head coupé, offering similar performance but better handling at a much higher price: 120 mph, 0–60 mph in 9.3 seconds for £3077 including tax in the case of the DB 2/4 Mark 3. Nevertheless this was 'cheap' when compared to its main German and Italian 3-litre rivals, which were right out of the Jaguar class, of course, and were little, if at all, faster.

One of the first Ferraris intended purely for roadwork, the 250 GT, cost three times as much as the XK 150 and twice as much as the Aston, but was capable of only 126 mph with a 0–60 time of 7.1 seconds although, admittedly, it did it all in great style. It was a softer, easier car to drive than the early offerings from Maranello. *Road and Track* said it all again when testing the 250 GT in 1960:

> 'It is a car designed for those who know, and appreciate, the difference and can afford to pay for it. A man or woman (the car is so easy to drive that it can be, and is, driven every day by women) who savours the sound, the feel, the stability

and performance of a car like this will consider the money it costs well spent. This is a car designed by enthusiasts for enthusiasts, and it shows.'

Really it was only cars like these which were in the same class as the XK 150. The Alfa Romeo 2000 Spyder cost a little more and had drum brakes like the Aston and Ferrari, but could hardly be criticized for these as they worked very well. However, close as it was to the XK 150 concept, it was appreciably slower at 111 mph with a 0–60 time of 14.2 seconds; the smaller Alfa Super Spyder performed as well as the 2000 on only 1290 cc and cost a couple of hundred pounds less than an XK, but looked like a Dinky-toy by comparison.

Mercedes' 2-litre offering, the 190 SL, was not a real sports car; it was much more of a de luxe tourer for the quasi-sporting. Like all Mercs, it cost a good deal

The lovely little Alfa Spyder.

Hollywood luxury liner: the Mercedes 190SL.

more than a Jaguar. Top speed was 106 mph with a 0–60 time of 13.5 seconds, hardly in the XK class. The 300 SL roadster had a similar performance to the XK 150 at more than double the price. It was a slightly watered-down version of the early gullwing coupé and apparently its handling was a good deal better.

Arkus-Duntov followed the example of Mercedes with the 300 SL by fitting fuel injection and a four-speed gearbox to the Corvette for the 1957 season. With 270 bhp, the Corvette was capable of 122 mph and 0–60 in 6.8 seconds. Repeated styling changes and some racing successes boosted sales to 6000 in the year. Chevrolet needed an exciting sports car to improve their churn-it-out image.

The staid old Daimler company certainly caused a stir when they introduced their extraordinary new Dart sports car in 1958. It was a sort of mini-Corvette with a Citroen fish-like nose for good air penetration, a huge luggage boot in its glass fibre body, and a brand new 2530 cc V8 engine based on the mighty Triumph twin motor cycle unit. It churned out 140 bhp and the 19 cwt car was good for 120 mph and 0–60 in 9 seconds; it could also stop quicker than a Corvette, thanks to its four-wheel disc brakes. Its handling, however, was dubious and its doors flew open when you drove over bumps; it was not a great success and was never a threat to the XK 150, although its performance, at a similar price, looked good on paper.

Corvettes were beginning to get bigger and heavier in 1958 as the stylists made them even tartier. The top engine was a 290 bhp V8, but it was not enough to impress the enthusiasts, who were shocked at the car's poor seats and styling. Some of the Corvette's designers really had no idea what sports car people wanted and sales failed to soar that year.

This pre-production photograph of the Daimler 2½-litre V8 emphasizes its vast luggage boot.

There was one new rival for the X K 150 in 1959, the D B 4 from Aston Martin. It was a real indicator of how the exotics were going in the 1960s. It had a completely new twin overhead cam 3.7-litre six-cylinder 'square' alloy block engine producing 263 bhp, with a four-speed gearbox and platform chassis. The whole lot was clothed in a luxurious alloy body and was capable of 140 mph and 0–60 in 9.3 seconds. It was everything the wealthy enthusiast wanted, providing he could wait for delivery at £4000 including tax. There were quite a few who could afford that, but opted for an X K 150 with much shorter delivery dates at less than half the price. As it happened, they were wise. The early D B 4s were most unreliable, with clutches and tyres lasting little more than 10,000 miles and the gearbox suffering mightily from the powerful new engine.

Meanwhile the Big Healey's performance was improved with a new cylinder head, to be followed by a 3-litre engine and disc brakes in 1959. This car, the 3000 Mark I, was capable of 116 mph with a 0–60 time of 10.8 seconds, all for around two-thirds the price of an X K 150. However, it was a much rougher and less sophisticated car (it had not even progressed beyond the sidescreen stage at that point) and sales went along happily hand-in-hand.

At the same time Arkus-Duntov was organizing things beautifully at General Motors. He steadily improved the Corvette, with even more power and an alloy head engine. Demand continued to rise with over 10,000 Corvettes sold in a year for the first time, more than the total production run of the X K 150 between 1957 and 1961.

There was not much new in 1960. Cars continued to pour off the production lines and there were rumours of great things to come. News struck the sports car world in March 1961: the sensational new Jaguar E type had arrived, and made the X K look old fashioned overnight. But before Jaguar produced that car there was practically nothing to touch an X K, and certainly nothing to beat it on all its scores.

XVII

Log Book Specifications

Part One: Colour Combinations

ONE OF THE BIGGEST headaches when restoring an XK is discovering the original colour combinations, especially now when originality is all the rage. It's no good proclaiming that your lovely white XK with a green interior is standard, for instance. No matter how good such a combination might look, Jaguar wouldn't have thought much of it. They fitted green interiors only to green or grey cars, unless it was to special order. They would even match a pair of underpants for that! How do you tell the original colour of your XK if it has been subjected to repeated, multi-coloured, resprays? Peering inside the top of the scuttle is often the answer. It's a pretty long-lasting part of the body and people don't often spray in there.

Index of colour combinations

From 1949 to December 1952:

Reference no.	Colour	Interior
1	Bronze	Biscuit
2	Bronze	Tan
3	Black	Biscuit
4	Black	Pigskin
5	Silver	Red
6	Silver	Light blue
7	Silver	Dark blue
8	Cream	Biscuit
9	Cream	Pigskin

From December 1952 to October 1954: *Colour references 1–9 above, plus*

10	Dove grey	Tan
11	Dove grey	Biscuit
12	British Racing Green	Tan
13	British Racing Green	Suede green
14	Old English White	Red
15	Old English White	Biscuit, Red
16	Old English White	Pale blue
17	Birch grey	Red

Reference no.	Colour	Interior
18	Birch grey	Biscuit, Red
19	Birch grey	Blue
20	Birch grey	Grey
21	Birch grey	Pale blue
22	Yellow	Black
23	Yellow	Pale blue
24	Red	Red
25	Red	Biscuit, Red
26	Pastel blue	Blue
27	Pastel blue	Light blue, Dark blue
28	Lavender grey	Red
29	Lavender grey	Suede green
30	Lavender grey	Pale blue
31	Suede green	Suede green
32	Black	Red
33	Black	Biscuit, Red
34	Black	Tan
35	Black	Grey
36	Battleship grey	Red
37	Battleship grey	Biscuit, Red
38	Battleship grey	Biscuit
39	Battleship grey	Grey
40	Pastel green	Suede green
41	Pastel green	Grey

From October 1954 to April 1956: *Colour references 10–41, plus*

42	Pearl grey	Red
43	Pearl grey	Blue
44	Pearl grey	Grey
45	Pacific blue	Blue
46	Pacific blue	Grey
47	Dove grey	Tan
48	Dove grey	Biscuit
49	Cream	Red
50	Cream	Biscuit, Red
51	Cream	Pale blue
52	Maroon	Red
53	Maroon	Biscuit

From April 1956 to January 1957: *Colour references 10–53, plus*

54	Arbour green	Tan
55	Arbour green	Suede green

From January 1957 to January 1961: *Colour references 10–55, plus*

56	Imperial maroon	Red
57	Imperial maroon	Biscuit

Reference no.	Colour	Interior
58	Claret	Red
59	Claret	Biscuit
60	Sherwood green	Tan
61	Sherwood green	Suede green
62	Cornish grey	Red
63	Cornish grey	Grey
64	Mist grey	Red
65	Mist grey	Blue
66	Mist grey	Grey
67	Indigo blue	Red
68	Indigo blue	Light blue
69	Cotswold blue	Light blue
70	Cotswold blue	Grey

Hood and tonneau covers were made from Black, French grey, Blue, Gunmetal, Fawn, and Sand coloured material and were generally fitted as follows:

Coachwork	Colour of material
Black	Black, fawn
Grey	French grey, Black, Blue, Fawn, Gunmetal
Green	Fawn, Black, Gunmetal, French grey
Blue	Blue, Black, French grey
Red	Black, Fawn, Sand
Cream, White, Silver, Bronze, Yellow	Fawn, Black, Blue

Part Two: Mechanical Specifications, Dimensions and Production Figures

Jaguar XK 120 Roadster

7631 built between July 1949 and September 1954, chassis numbers from 660001 (right-hand drive), and 670001 (left-hand drive).

Engine

Six-cylinder, CUBIC CAPACITY 3442 cc; BORE AND STROKE 83 mm × 106 mm; MAX. POWER 160 bhp at 5000 rpm (standard), 180 bhp at 5300 rpm (special equipment); MAX. TORQUE 195 lb/ft at 2500 rpm (standard) 203 lb/ft at 4000 rpm (special equipment); COMPRESSION RATIO 8:1 (7:1 or 9:1 optional); CYLINDER HEAD A type, C type optional from April 1953; CARBURETTERS two 1¾-inch SU, two 2-inch SU optional from April 1953; SPECIAL EQUIPMENT ENGINE optional from August 1951.

Chassis

WEIGHT (dry) with alloy body 25½ cwt, with steel body 26 cwt (alloy body discontinued after chassis 660058 and 670184); WHEELBASE 8 ft 6 ins; FRONT TRACK 4 ft 3 ins; REAR TRACK 4 ft 2 ins; LENGTH 14 ft 5 ins; WIDTH 5 ft 2 ins; HEIGHT 4 ft 4½ ins (with hood erect); TURNING CIRCLE 31 ft; FRONT SUSPENSION independent wishbone, torsion bar, anti-roll bar; REAR SUSPENSION live axle, semi-elliptical leaf springs; BRAKES Lockheed hydraulic drums all round, two leading shoe front, leading and trailing rear; GEARBOX four-speed (ratios) 1st–12.29, 2nd–7.22, 3rd–4.98, 4th–3.64 (ENV axle) 4th–3.54 (Salisbury axle fitted after chassis numbers 660935 and 671797). Rear axle (ENV) standard ratio 3.64:1, 3.27, 3.92, 4.30 alternatives, (Salisbury) standard ratio 3.54:1, 3.27, 3.77, 4.09 alternatives; STEERING Burman recirculating ball; SHOCK ABSORBERS Newton telescopic front, Girling PV7 rear; WHEELS 5K × 16 steel (later 5½K); 5K × 16 wire optional from March 1951; chrome wire optional from 1953; COLOUR references 1–41 (see Part One).

XK 120 roadster

Jaguar XK 120 Fixed-head Coupé

2678 built between March 1951 and September 1954, chassis numbers from 669001 (right-hand drive) and 679001 (left-hand drive), all with S prefix if special equipment models.

Engine
As roadster.

Chassis
As roadster except: WEIGHT (dry) 27 cwt, HEIGHT 4 ft 5½ ins, Salisbury axle fitted after chassis numbers 669003 and 679222.

XK 120 fixed-head.

Jaguar XK 120 Drop-head Coupé

1769 built between April 1953 and September 1954, chassis numbers from 667001 (right-hand drive) and 677001 (left-hand drive).

Engine
As roadster.

Chassis
As roadster except: WEIGHT (dry) 27½ cwt, HEIGHT 4 ft 5½ ins.

XK 120 drop-head.

Jaguar XK 140 Roadster

3347 built between October 1954 and February 1957, chassis numbers from 800001 (right-hand drive) and 810001 (left-hand drive), all with A prefix for standard 180 bhp model, S prefix for special equipment 210 bhp model.

Engine
Six-cylinder, CUBIC CAPACITY 3442 cc; BORE AND STROKE 83 mm × 106 mm; MAX. POWER 180 bhp at 5500 rpm (standard), 210 bhp at 5750 rpm (special equipment); MAX. TORQUE 210 lb/ft at 2500 rpm (standard), 213 lb/ft at 4000 rpm (special equip-

XK 140 roadster.

ment); COMPRESSION RATIO 8:1 (7:1 or 9:1 optional); CARBURETTERS two 1¾-inch SU, two 2-inch SU optional.

Chassis

WEIGHT (dry) 28 cwt; WHEELBASE 8 ft 6 ins; FRONT TRACK 4 ft 3½ ins, REAR TRACK 4 ft 3⅜ ins; LENGTH 14 ft 8 ins; WIDTH 5 ft 4½ ins; HEIGHT (with hood erect) 4 ft 4½ ins; TURNING CIRCLE 33 ft; FRONT SUSPENSION independent wishbone, torsion bar, anti-roll bar; REAR SUSPENSION live axle, semi-elliptic leaf springs; BRAKES Lockheed hydraulic drums all round, two leading shoe front, leading and trailing rear; GEARBOX four speed (ratios) 1st–11.95:1, 2nd–7.01:1; 3rd–4.83:1, 4th–3.54:1; REAR AXLE (standard) 3.54:1, 3.27, 3.77, 4.09 alternatives; 4.09 axle standard with over-drive option, ratios then 1st–12.4:1; 2nd–7.16:1; 3rd–4.95:1, 4th–4.09:1, overdrive 3.19:1; STEERING rack and pinion; SHOCK ABSORBERS Girling telescopic all round; WHEELS 5½K × 16 steel; COLOUR references 10–55.

Jaguar.XK 140 Fixed-head Coupé

XK 140 fixed-head.

2750 built between October 1954 and February 1957, chassis numbers from 804001 (right-hand drive) and 814001 (left-hand drive), all with A prefix for standard 180 bhp model, S prefix for special equipment 210 bhp model.

Engine
As roadster.

Chassis
As roadster except: WEIGHT (dry) 29 cwt; HEIGHT 4 ft 7 ins; automatic transmission optional from October 1956, using 3.54:1 axle ratio.

Jaguar XK 140 Drop-head Coupé

XK 140 drop-head.

2797 built between October 1954 and February 1957, chassis numbers from 807001 (right-hand drive) and 814001 (left-hand drive), all with A prefix for standard 180 bhp model, S prefix for special equipment 210 bhp model.

Engine
As roadster.

Chassis
As roadster except: WEIGHT (dry) 29.5 cwt; HEIGHT 4 ft 7 ins; automatic transmission optional from October 1956, using 3.54:1 axle ratio.

Jaguar XK 150 Roadster 3.4 litres

1297 built between March 1958 and October 1960, chassis numbers from 820001 (right-hand drive), 830001 (left-hand drive) in series with other models, but all 3.4-litre cars had prefix V.

Engine
Six-cylinder, CUBIC CAPACITY 3442 cc; BORE AND STROKE 83 mm × 106 mm; MAX. POWER 190 bhp at 5500 rpm (standard), 210 bhp at 5500 rpm (special equipment);

MAX. TORQUE 210 lb/ft at 2500 rpm (standard), 216 lb/ft at 3000 rpm (special equipment); COMPRESSION RATIO 8:1 (7:1 or 9:1 optional); CARBURETTERS two 1¾-inch SU, two 2-inch SU optional.

Chassis

WEIGHT (dry) 28¼ cwt; WHEELBASE 8 ft 6 ins; FRONT TRACK 4 ft 3¼ ins; REAR TRACK 4 ft 3¼ ins; LENGTH 14 ft 9 ins; WIDTH 5 ft 4½ ins; HEIGHT 4 ft 6 ins; TURNING CIRCLE 33 ft; FRONT SUSPENSION independent wishbone, torsion bar, anti-roll bar; REAR SUSPENSION, live axle, semi-elliptic leaf springs; BRAKES Dunlop discs, vacuum servo; GEARBOX ratios and alternatives as XK 140 roadster; STEERING rack and pinion; SHOCK ABSORBERS Girling telescopic all round; WHEELS 5½K × 16 steel; COLOUR references 10–70.

XK 150 roadster.

Jaguar XK 150 Roadster 3.8 litres

42 built between October 1959 and October 1960, chassis numbers from 820001 (right-hand drive), 830001 (left-hand drive) in series with other models, but all 3.8-litre cars had prefix VA.

Engine

Six-cylinder, CUBIC CAPACITY 3781 cc; BORE AND STROKE 87 mm × 106 mm; MAX. POWER 220 bhp at 5500 rpm; MAX. TORQUE 240 lb/ft at 3000 rpm; COMPRESSION RATIO 9:1 (8:1 optional); CARBURETTERS two 1¾-inch SUs.

Chassis
As 3.4-litre roadster.

Jaguar XK 150S 3.4-litre Roadster

888 built between March 1958 and October 1960, chassis numbers from 820001 (right-hand drive) and 830001 (left-hand drive) in series with other models, but all 3.4-litre S cars had prefix VS.

Engine
Six-cylinder, CUBIC CAPACITY 3442 cc; BORE AND STROKE 83 mm × 106 mm; MAX. POWER 250 bhp at 5500 rpm; MAX. TORQUE 240 lb/ft at 4500 rpm; COMPRESSION RATIO 9:1; CARBURETTERS three 2-inch SU.

Chassis
As XK 150 roadster.

Jaguar XK 150S 3.8-litre Roadster

36 built between October 1959 and October 1960, chassis numbers from 820001 (right-hand drive) and 830001 (left-hand drive) in series with other models, but all 3.8-litre S cars had prefix VAS.

Engine
Six-cylinder, CUBIC CAPACITY 3781 cc; BORE AND STROKE 87 mm × 106 mm; MAX.

POWER 265 bhp at 5500 rpm; MAX. TORQUE 260 lb/ft at 4000 rpm; COMPRESSION 9:1; CARBURETTERS three 2-inch SU.

Chassis
As XK 150 roadster.

Jaguar XK 150 3.4-litre Fixed-head Coupé

3445 made between May 1957 and October 1960, chassis numbers from 824001 (right-hand drive) and 834001 (left-hand drive) in series with other models, but all 3.4-litre cars had prefix V.

Engine
As 3.4-litre roadster.

Chassis
As 3.4-litre roadster except: WEIGHT (dry) 29 cwt; HEIGHT 4 ft 7 ins.

Jaguar XK 150 3.8-litre Fixed-head Coupé

656 made between October 1959 and October 1960, chassis numbers from 824001 (right-hand drive) and 834001 (left-hand drive) in series with other models, but all 3.8-litre cars had prefix VS.

Engine
As 3.8-litre roadster.

Chassis
As 3.4-litre fixed-head coupé.

Jaguar XK 150S 3.4-litre Fixed-head Coupé

199 made btween February 1959 and October 1960, chassis numbers from 824001 (right-hand drive) and 834001 (left-hand drive) in series with other models, but all 3.4-litre S cars had prefix VS.

Engine
As XK 150S 3.4-litre roadster.

Chassis
As 3.4-litre fixed-head coupé.

XK 150 fixed-head.

Jaguar XK 150S 3.8-litre Fixed-head Coupé

150 built between October 1959 and October 1960, chassis numbers from 824001 (right-hand drive) and 834001 (left-hand drive) in series with other models, but all 3.8-litre S cars had prefix VAS.

Engine
As XK 150S 3.8-litre roadster.

Chassis

As 3.4-litre fixed-head coupé.

Jaguar XK 150 3.4-litre Drop-head Coupé

XK 150 drop-head.

1903 built between May 1957 and October 1960, chassis numbers from 827001 (right-hand drive) and 837001 (left-hand drive) in series with other models, but all 3.4-litre cars had prefix V.

Engine

As 3.4 litre roadster.

Chassis

As 3.4-litre roadster, except WEIGHT (dry) 31½ cwt.

Jaguar XK 150 3.8-litre Drop-head Coupé

586 built between October 1959 and October 1960, chassis numbers from 827001 (right-hand drive) and 837001 (left-hand drive) in series with other models, but all 3.8-litre cars had prefix VA.

Engine

As 3.8-litre roadster.

Chassis

As 3.4-litre roadster, except WEIGHT (dry) 31½ cwt.

Jaguar XK 150S 3.4-litre Drop-head Coupé

104 built between February 1959 and October 1960, chassis numbers from 827001 (right-hand drive) and 837001 (left-hand drive) in series with other models, but all 3.4-litre S cars had prefix VS.

Engine

As XK 150S 3.4-litre roadster.

Chassis

As 3.4-litre roadster, except WEIGHT (dry) 31½ cwt.

Jaguar XK 150S 3.8-litre Drop-head Coupé

36 built between October 1959 and October 1960, chassis numbers from 827001 (right-hand drive) and 837001 (left-hand drive) in series with other models, but all 3.8-litre S cars had prefix VAS.

Engine

As XK 150S 3.8-litre roadster.

Chassis

As 3.4-litre roadster, except WEIGHT (dry) 31½ cwt.

XVIII

The Jaguar clubs

A SPORTS CAR like the Jaguar XK had to have a club for owners, and now there are more than two thousand of the cars listed by the XK Register, which is a club within the parent Jaguar Drivers' Club. The majority of the register's membership lives in the United Kingdom, but many keen owners abroad have joined to make it truly international.

The XK Register is now more than ten years old, having been formed in 1967 when it was possible to buy a very smart XK 120 roadster for as little as £125. Little did the founders know that within ten or twelve years the very best XKs would be fetching a hundred times as much! Whether this is a good or bad thing is still a subject for debate within the register, but everybody agrees that the standard of presentation and pride of ownership has increased in proportion over the years.

The register, started within the framework of the Jaguar Drivers' Club founded by XK owners in 1955, has since grown to more than five thousand members, making it one of the biggest one-make car clubs in the world. Beginning with a nucleus of nineteen keen members, the XK Register quickly grew to more than a thousand, interest being maintained largely by the monthly *XK Bulletin*, which appeared in 1968. This encouraged the interchange of ideas and spare parts, so vital for people running an obsolete car.

Activities promoted by the register are broadly divided into two categories, national and local. On the local level, area centres were established which meet once a month at a venue chosen by each centre; there are now more than twenty-five of these, covering most of the British Isles, and including Ireland. These centres organize such events as barbecues, manoeuverability tests and quizzes for their members, and send regular reports to the *XK Bulletin*.

On a national scale, the register is well known for its international XK Day, held annually and recognized, together with E type Day, as the largest gathering of Jaguars in the world. XK Day attracts all manner of Jaguar cars and enthusiasts from all over the world, with C types and D types adding even more glamour to the ranks of XKs.

Almost as popular is the register's Spares Day, which again is not restricted to XKs only. This is also an annual event and represents an ideal opportunity to find elusive parts from the thousands of items on sale, although the register's spares

secretary, Bill Lawrence, has been making great progress in obtaining or producing obsolete parts. In addition to spares day, the register is involved in a variety of national events, including the Jaguar Spring Rally at Beaulieu, Hampshire, which features top XKs vying for points in the concours d'élegance.

Duncan Hamilton arrives at the Jaguar Drivers' Club's Beaulieu spring meeting in a 120 drop-head.

Another practical advantage of XK Register membership is the insurance scheme, managed by the register's official brokers exclusively for members. This scheme caters for agreed-value insurance, and for the owner who uses his car only in the summer. It is arranged with a top established insurance company, and generally offers the XK owner good savings on premiums, plus the knowledge that there will be no arguments about the value of the car in the event of a claim.

The Jaguar Drivers' Club also organizes race meetings, sprints and hill climbs which usually feature special classes for XKs. Other Jaguar Drivers' Club registers cater for the Mark One and Two saloons, the Mark VII, VIII and IX range, SS cars up to Mark V, and the 'independent rear' saloons. All receive the club's professionally produced a monthly magazine, *Jaguar Driver*, while some publish their own newsletters like the XK Bulletin. Because of its relatively large membership, it is not expensive to join the Jaguar Drivers' Club and its registers, and further details can be obtained from the club's full-time staff at its offices in the Norfolk Hotel, Harrington Road, London SW7.

Overseas representatives are: *Australia* Ian Cummins, 77 Nelson Street, Annandale, N SW 2038; *Belgium* Jacques Gaudfroy, 30 Chemin des deux Maisons, Box 9, 1200 Brussels; *Brazil* W. G. Halberstadt, Rua Haddock Lobo, 281 Apt 0 122, Sao Paulo-Sp-01414; *Canada* Ian Newby, 6362 Chatham Street, West Vancouver, BC; *Denmark* Jens Roder, Lidevej 3A, 3060 Espergaerde, Denmark; *France* Dr Phillippe Renault, 39 Avenue de Laumiere, Paris 19; *Germany* Roger Dunn, Domane Mechtildshausen, 6200 Wiesbaden-Erbenheim; *Holland* E. B. Beket, Uilenstede K6 1183 A C Amstelveen; *Italy* Roberto Causo, Via Condotti 91, 00187 Roma; *New Zealand* Grant McMillan, 81 Pah Road, Auckland 3, New Zealand; *Norway* Dag Horne, Tekn A R V D L F E, Michelets vei 30, 1324 Lysaker; *South Africa* Norman Gilmour, PO Box 31437, Braamfontein 2017; *Switzerland* Aldo Vinzio, BP 34-1211, Genève 17; *United States* Tom Hendricks, 3601 John Carrol Drive, Olney MD 20832.

There are also a large number of clubs in North America, mostly run on an autonomous and mainly local basis, but recognized by the parent firm through British Leyland's New Jersey headquarters, which runs Jaguar Clubs of North America Incorporated. The J C N A publishes a quarterly magazine, *Jaguar Journal*, which is distributed to the membership of all affiliated clubs, while nearly all the individual clubs issue their own newsletters, too. One club, much bigger than the others, remains independent. This is the Eastern Jaguar Automobile Group of North America, run on a highly-efficient commercial basis with a membership stretching to Europe, Asia and Africa as well. The club, popularly called E J A G, caters for all Jaguar owners, and produces the magnificent monthly *E J A G News Magazine*. This publication includes articles on maintenance and restoration, descriptions of Jaguar events, product and book reviews, memoirs of Jaguar drivers, parts and service recommendations and advertising. The club also runs all manner of activities including shows—notably the Newport Jaguar Festival—technical sessions, museum tours, rallies and picnics from its headquarters, Box J, Carlisle, Massachusetts 01741.

Jaguar Clubs of North America has been in operation for more than twenty years and now lists more than forty clubs throughout North America and Canada, of which the Jaguar Drivers' Club of Northwest America in Washington and the Empire Division Jaguar Club (New York City) are particularly active. For complete club listings and other information write to the J C N A's secretary, Fred Horner, at 600 Willow Tree Road, Leonia, New Jersey 07605.

Australia and New Zealand are also great centres of Jaguar interest, with five clubs in Australia and one in New Zealand, organized on thoroughly British lines. The Jaguar Clubs of Australia produce their own first-class *Jaguar Journal* besides individual newsletters. Their club addresses are: the Jaguar Car Club of Victoria (secretary Dick Stevenson) Box 161, Ringwood, Victoria 3134; the Jaguar Drivers' Club of Australia (New South Wales), (secretary John Thomas), PO Box 2, Drummoyne, N S W 2047; the Jaguar Drivers' Club of Southern Australia (secretary Paul Evison), PO Box 30, Rundle Street, Adelaide SA 5001; the Classic Jaguar Club of Western Australia (secretary Peter Zoontyens), 3 Bowen Street, Langford WA 6155; the Jaguar Car Club of Tasmania (secretary Linda Butler), PO Box 131

opposite above A 140 roadster joins the 150s at Beaulieu.

opposite below The 150s on show at Beaulieu.

PO, North Hobart, Tasmania 7000; and the Jaguar Drivers' Club of Canberra (secretary Bob Lane), Box 400, Kingston, ACT 2604.

The numerous national Jaguar clubs throughout Europe and the rest of the world can be contacted through either the Jaguar Drivers' Club in London or the XK Register representatives, plus the ambitious Svenska Jaguar Klubben which has headquarters at Box 42092, 126 12 Stockholm 42, Sweden, and a most-impressive magazine, the *Jaguar bulletinen*.

It is at club level that the greatest amount of Jaguar enthusiasm is to be found and if you have an XK—or any sort of Jaguar—or fancy owning one you will find that your enjoyment of it will be greatly enhanced if you also belong to a club.

Index

Index of Illustrations

Picture Acknowledgements

The author is grateful to the following for permission to reproduce illustration material:

Associated Press, 91 top
Auckland Star, 157 top
Autocar, 48 bottom, 56, 57, 66, 169 right, 182 left, 198, 217

Bertone, 215

Caper, Paris, 213
Carrozzeria Pininfarina, Torino, 209 bottom
Cummins, Ian, 29, 154 top left and right, 188

Dawson, Ian, *CAR* magazine, 5, 31, 33, 35 top, 54

Ecclestone, Barry C., colour plate 19
Elmar Studios, Palmerston North, New Zealand, 155

Fraser, Ian, 98, 203

Halberstadt, William, 210 bottom
Hendricks, Tom, 189
Hingston, Harvey, Collection, 100

Holder, Tim, 2, 128, 132, 164, 167
Hughes, Les, 230 centre

International Publishing Corporation, 92

Jaguar cars, colour plates 1, 2, 6, 7; 8, 9, 11, 13 top, 13 bottom, 14, 16, 17, 19, 20 bottom, 26, 28, 30, 32, 41, 44, 47 bottom left and right, 52, 79, 80 top, 85, 87, 88, 90, 97, 99, 103, 105, 165, 169 left, 171, 229 top

Kalkreuter, H. E., 149 top, 154, 230 bottom
Kinnear, Art, Collection, 141 top, 183

Latham, A. R. E., 185 bottom
Leyland cars, 3, 4
Liljegren, Bernthe, 229 centre

Midland Car Restorations, 115–6, 134 top left
Miller, Karen, 141 centre
Motor, 18, 20 top, 48 top, 49, 51, 59, 61 top, 86, 91 bottom, 94 top, 219, 221, 231 top
Motor Trend, 139

Publicfoto, Milano, 80 bottom

Roder, Jens, Collection, colour plate 14

Sadd, Stuart, 175

Scatley, Fred, 109

Schendzielorz, Heinz, 129, top left, 147, 149 lower, 150, 152, 195, 229 bottom. 230 top

Skilleter, Paul, colour plates **cover, 3, 4, 5, 8, 9, 10, 11, 12, 13, 15, 16, 17, 18, 20, 21, 22, 23**; 6, 7 top, 7 bottom, 24, 35 bottom, 36, 38, 58, 61 bottom, 62, 69, 106, 107, 110, 113, 119, 126, 129 bottom, 134 top right, 134 bottom, 141 bottom, 145, 173, 180, 185 top, 186, 192, 199, 201, 204, 206, 212 top, 231 bottom, 235, 236

Stamp, Jack, Collection, 138

Temple Press, 23, 42, 70, 73, 76, 82, 102, 218, 220 bottom

Thompson and Taylor (Brooklands) Ltd, 223 top
Tod, C. N., 129 top right

Wheels magazine, 93
Woodiwiss, Trevor, Collection, 157 bottom